# FIVE SISTERS
## WOMEN AGAINST THE TSAR

# Suggested for further reading

Bergman, Jay. *Vera Zasulich*. Stanford University Press, Stanford, 1983.

Breshkovsky, Catherine. *Hidden Springs of the Russian Revolution*. Stanford, 1931.

Broido, Vera. *Apostles into Terrorists*. Viking Press, New York, 1977.

Brower, Daniel. *Training the Nihilists: Education and Radicalism in Tsarist Russia*. Cornell University Press, Ithaca, 1975.

Chernyshevsky, N. G. *What Is to be Done?* Ardis Press, Michigan, 1986.

Edmondson, Linda. *The Feminist Movement in Russia, 1900–1917*. Stanford University Press, Stanford, 1984.

Engel, Barbara. *Mothers and Daughters: Women of the Intelligentsia in Nineteenth Century Russia*. Cambridge University Press, New York, 1983.

Figner, Vera. *Memoirs of a Revolutionist*. International Publishers, New York, 1927.

Footman, David. *Red Prelude: The Life of the Russian Terrorist Zheliabov*. The Cresset Press, London, 1968.

Gleason, Abbott. *Young Russia: the Genesis of Russian Radicalism in the 1860s*. Viking, New York, 1980.

Kennan, George. *Siberia and the Exile System*. Praeger, New York, 1970.

Koblitz, Ann. *A Convergence of Lives. Sofia Kovalevskaia: Scientist, Writer, Revolutionary*. Birkhauser, Boston, 1983.

Kovalevskaia, Sofia. *A Russian Childhood*. Springer-Verlag, New York, 1978.

Stepniak-Kravchinskii, Sergei. *Underground Russia: Revolutionary Profiles and Sketches from Life*. London, 1883. *A Female Nihilist*. B. R. Tucker, Boston, 1886.

Kropotkin, Peter. *Members of a Revolutionist*. Grove Press, New York, 1970.

Lavrov, Peter. *Historical Letters*. University of California Press, Berkeley, 1967.

Leffler, Anna Carlotta. *Sonya Kovalevsky; Her Recollections of Childhood*. New York, 1895.

Meijer, J. M. *Knowledge and Revolution. The Russian Colony in Zurich 1870–1873*. Fernhill, New York, 1965.

Miller, Martin. *Kropotkin*. University of Chicago Press, Chicago, 1976.

Pomper, Philip. *Sergei Nechaev*. Rutgers University Press, New Brunswick, 1979.

Porter, Cathy. *Fathers and Daughters*. Virago Press, London, 1976.

Ransel, David, ed. *The Family in Imperial Russia*. University of Illinois Press, Urbana, 1978.

Stites, Richard. *The Women's Liberation Movement in Russia, Feminism, Nihilism and Bolshevism, 1860–1930*. Princeton University Press, Princeton, 1978.

Tishkin, G. A. *Zhenskii Vopros v Rossii v 50–60 gg. XIX v.* Leningrad, 1984.

Tuve, Jeannette. *The First Russian Women Physicians*. Oriental Research Partners, Newtonville, Massachusetts, 1984.

Venturi, Franco. *Roots of Revolution*. Grosset and Dunlap, New York, 1966.

Yarmolinsky, Avrahm. *Road to Revolution. A Century of Russian Radicalism*. Macmillan, New York, 1957.

# FIVE
# SISTERS

## WOMEN AGAINST THE TSAR

### The memoirs of five young anarchist women of the 1870's

*Edited and translated from the Russian by*
**Barbara Alpern Engel**
and
**Clifford N. Rosenthal**

*With a Foreword by*
**Alix Kates Schulman**

Boston
ALLEN & UNWIN
London      Sydney      Wellington

**Allen & Unwin, Inc.**
8 Winchester Place, Winchester, MA 01890, USA.

The U.S. Company of
**Unwin Hyman Ltd,**

P.O. Box 18, Park Lane, Hemel Hempstead, Herts HP2 4TE, UK
40 Museum Street, London WC1A 1LU, UK
37/39 Queen Elizabeth Street, London SE1 2QB, UK

Allen & Unwin Australia Pty Ltd,
8 Napier Street, North Sydney, NSW 2060, Australia

Allen & Unwin (New Zealand) Ltd, in association with the Port Nicholson
Press Ltd
60 Cambridge Terrace, Wellington, New Zealand

---

**Library of Congress Cataloging-in-Publication Data**

Five sisters.
Reprint. Originally published: New York: Knopf, 1975.
Translation from Russian.
Bibliography: p.
Includes index.
1. Radicalism — Soviet Union — History. 2. Women revolutionists —
Soviet Union — Biography. 3. Soviet Union — Politics and government —
1855–1881. 4. Alexander II, Emperor of Russia, 1818–1881 —
Assassination. I. Engel, Barbara Alpern. II. Rosenthal, Clifford N.
HN530.Z9R328   1987       322.4'2'0922       87–17584
ISBN 0–04–445034–6

---

**British Library Cataloguing in Publication Data**

Five sisters: women against the Tsar.
1. Revolutionists — Soviet Union I. Engel, Barbara Alpern II. Rosenthal,
Clifford N.
322.4'2'0922       DK62.9
ISBN 0–04–445034–6

---

Printed in Great Britain by
Billing & Son Ltd., London and Worcester

*To the women*

*fighting for freedom*

*throughout the world*

# CONTENTS

# ILLUSTRATIONS

# FOREWORD

Suddenly we have in English, rescued from the Siberia of dusty library shelves where for years they have languished untranslated in obscure collections, five new first-person eyewitness accounts of the first great wave of revolution in Russia. Five memoirs from the last century's tumultuous sixties and seventies and after, when the fires of revolution began to catch and spread, leading toward one act that seemed to some both a culmination and a new beginning: to kill the tsar. Five new accounts, each another window on that time—all by women. Vera Figner, Vera Zasulich, Praskovia Ivanovskaia, Olga Liubatovich, Elizaveta Kovalskaia: five heroes of the Revolution who lived to tell it, survivors of a much larger group of women, some famous in their time—now, somehow, almost lost to us.

Students of the Russian Revolution may be familiar with the two Veras, though there are no biographies of them in English. They may know of Vera Zasulich, who was hailed as a saint by the people of St. Petersburg for shooting the tyrannical Governor Trepov; but unless they know Russian, only now can they read her own report of what led her to it, what raced through her mind as she hit her mark. They may have heard of Vera Figner too, who helped make the bombs that finally killed the tsar, one of the last survivors among the assassins; may possibly have read an abridged version of her *Memoirs* published in translation here in 1927 and reissued in 1968. But who has heard of the others? With the lone exception of Figner's book, we have had in English until now only passing references in the writing of others—second-hand accounts, tantalizing hints, of the lives of these women, once so celebrated. (Liubatovich reports the arrest of a young male comrade for trying to enter a courtroom where some of the women were on trial. "He now confessed to me, his overriding desire had been to get a look at us, the 'Moscow Amazons,' who had grown up in baronial mansions, sampled all the charms of free intellectual work in the universities of Europe, and then, with such courageous simplicity, entered the filthy factories of Moscow as ordinary workers.") Even that great scholarly work on nineteenth-century revolutionary movements in Russia, Franco Venturi's *Roots of Revolution*, gives little more than passing notice to most of these women.

The five memoirs collected here, though still fragmentary, are treasures, allowing us an intimate glimpse into the lives and souls of a rare breed of woman, a group apart, living and acting in one of the most amazing moments in history. To read these lives is to be plunged into a world of intrigue and danger, of suffering and personal sacrifice, of courage and commitment. Each of the five is distinct, yet their lives (together with unwritten others) form a single story—separate strands of a single braid.

Who were they? Born mid-century, within five years of one another, they come from widely different provinces and stations: rich and poor, from Kharkov and Moscow and Tula province, one the illegitimate child of a landowner and his serf, one a village curate's daughter. But as soon as they leave home for boarding school, where the new populist ideas of social justice and equality move quietly among them, their destinies begin to overlap. "Boarding school resembled a monastery," writes Ivanovskaia. "Still the wave of new ideas of the sixties found their way to us, penetrating the stone walls of our cloister." At her school, Zasulich relates, "the seventeenth year of my life was filled with the most feverish activity. At last I took my fate in my own hands." One after another they are infected by the new ideas and the possibility of changing the world. They become restless. "What shall I do with my life?" agonizes the introspective Figner. To Zasulich "the specter of revolution appeared, making me equal to a boy. I too could dream of action. . . . Life beckoned to me, life in all its immensity."

Off they rush to embrace "life"—to St. Petersburg, where revolution is in the air, or to the university in Zurich where the heady intellectual currents of Europe touch them. They enroll in the first courses open to women, or they volunteer to teach classes to others. Some of them meet for the first time. Living intensely now, staying up all night to discuss the burning issues of the day, meeting in small groups to exchange ideas and devour the revolutionary literature, arguing, questioning, debating—those who are lucky enough to be in the right place at the right time become radicals and feminists and friends together. "In St. Petersburg," writes Kovalskaia, "women's meetings were so frequent we barely had time to get from one place to another." "Looking at them," wrote the Russian radical Dzhabiadori, upon meeting some of the Russian women students in Zurich, "one would have said that they were a family. And indeed, they were a family, not through blood but because they were comrades."*

Soon, however, women's meetings are not enough for them; soon it is not enough to talk and study among themselves; they must "go to the people" with their message; they must act. One by one, sometimes before they have even finished their studies, they make their irrevocable commitment to revolution. Aglow with dedication, they set out to follow their callings: one teaches literacy classes to workers in the city; another goes to the provinces to do propaganda, laboring among the peasants; one becomes a teacher, one a medic. With books and ideas they will "unite the people." "I made no distinctions between word and deed. . . . I believed in the power of words and the might of the human will," writes Figner.

But the books and leaflets they carry, the words they speak, are forbidden, and their most high-minded efforts are stifled by constant and ruthless police repression. It is only a matter

* Quoted in Franco Venturi, *Roots of Revolution*, Universal Library Ed., 1966, p. 525.

of time before the lines are drawn and these women are all
driven underground. They abandon their professions to become professional revolutionaries; from propaganda they turn
to political organizing. As part of an organized underground
they are doomed to lives spent dodging police, seeing comrades captured and killed, surviving mass trials, enduring
prison, banishment, exile, undertaking daring escapes or
flights abroad—always prepared to die at any moment, sus-
tained only by their unflagging revolutionary commitment.
"We made a strange distinction between our own fates and
the radiant prospects of the revolution," writes Figner. "About
ourselves we were always pessimistic: we would all perish,
they would persecute us, lock us up, send us into exile and
hard labor." With books and printing presses as illegal as
dynamite, with freedom of movement closely restricted, no
wonder they are "pessimistic."

Unable to conduct propaganda by word, the movement
turns increasingly to Propaganda by Deed—carefully selected
acts of terror—to spread their message. For many who feel
there is no alternative left them but terror, the ultimate deed
will be to kill the tsar. From page to page of these memoirs
the pressure mounts as the final act approaches. Even those
who, torn over means and ends, reject terror are nonetheless
affected by it: each act of violence sends the whole movement
into hiding. Though decades of prison and exile await them
all, they never question the value of their work. "How can you
count all the circles made by a stone when you toss it into
the water?" asks Kovalskaia.

In these memoirs the moods and actions vary, but the life
we glimpse is of a piece. For a moment we peer deep into the
Russian assassin's soul (how different the selfless Zasulich
seems from the lone, alienated assassins we know here, as
revealed, say, in Arthur Bremer's *Diary*). Through Ivanovskaia we learn of the harsh life in a clandestine printing collective: ". . . we were not to write or receive letters from
anyone, communicate with people outside the press, or attend
meetings, get-togethers, and the like, we were to live as if

there were nothing and no one around us, to reduce our existence to the life and work that went on within the walls of our apartment." Liubatovich reveals to us the painful factional fights whereby "yesterday's comrades began shunning each other like strangers." From Kovalskaia we learn the horrors of prison and the terrible suspense of attempts to escape. We hear the indomitable Figner describe each plot against the tsar, watch an aging Zasulich work quietly in exile.

Occasionally we even catch a glimpse of levity: a New Year's Eve party, a group tempting Fate by risking an evening at the theater, students' pranks. But such moments are rare. To speak of their private lives must be virtually taboo for these ascetic women; personal life itself seems to be a luxury. Though some of them are married and divorced, no romance appears in these pages; the "great cause of love" of which Zasulich writes is the Revolution itself. "It is a sin for revolutionaries to start a family. . . . Revolutionaries' lives are measured not in years, but in days and hours," declares Liubatovich, the only one of the five to bear a child. Originally radicalized in the atmosphere of feminism, all these women —lumped together by their contemporaries as the "Moscow Amazons" or the "women of our circle"—remain conscious of their special status; but it is appropriately Liubatovich who writes: "I understood . . . that I had to bear a double burden in life—the heavy burden of a human being and the burden of a woman as well.")

The collective portrait that emerges from these pages is of a woman different from all others we have known: more ascetic and idealistic in tone, humbler and tougher, than some of their male revolutionary counterparts whose memoirs we may have read; different too from the women of our own, more familiar radical movements, so often forced to choose between playing "helpmate" and remaining separatist. These women have ties of consciousness shared neither by the men of their time nor the women of ours. Looking at their pictures one feels they are a singular breed: soulful, serious Russian originals. Like everyone, of course, they were products of their time and place; but was there ever such a place as turbulent Russia before the Revolution?

"Write: you *must* write; your experience *must not* be lost," said Eleanora Duse to Figner. It is chilling to realize that, though all these women wrote of their lives, their experiences (like those of how many more?) might well have remained beyond our reach but for the diligent researches of Barbara Engel and Clifford Rosenthal.

ALIX KATES SHULMAN

# ACKNOWLEDGMENTS

Our thanks to Mrs. Suzanne Tumarkin,
for her invaluable aid in the translation
of the manuscript; and to Regina Ryan, our editor,
for her encouragement and well-founded suggestions.
All errors or shortcomings are, of course, our own.

BARBARA ALPERN ENGEL
CLIFFORD N. ROSENTHAL

To my wife, Elayne Grant Archer,
and my daughter, Dana Archer-Rosenthal

# INTRODUCTION

*The following will show what the women of our circle were. One night Kupreyanoff and I went to Varvara B., to whom we had to make an urgent communication. It was past midnight, but, seeing a light in her window, we went upstairs. She sat in her tiny room, at a table, copying a programme of our circle. We knew how resolute she was, and the idea came to us to make one of those stupid jokes which men think funny. "B," I said, "we came to fetch you: we are going to try a rather mad attempt to liberate our friends from the fortress." She asked not one question. She quietly laid down her pen, rose from the chair, and said only, "Let us go." She spoke in so simple, so unaffected a voice that I felt at once how foolishly I had acted, and told her the truth. She dropped back into her chair, and with tears in her eyes and in a despairing voice asked: "It was only a joke? Why do you make such jokes?" I fully realized then the cruelty of what I had done.*

—PETER KROPOTKIN,
*Memoirs of a Revolutionist*[1]

## I

In the 1870's, the Russian revolutionary movement reached mass proportions for the first time in its history. Revolutionary populism, dedicated to the liberation of the oppressed peasantry, attracted thousands of adherents, and arrest figures show that some fifteen percent were women. Women participated in every phase of the movement, from propaganda work among the peasantry, which predominated in the early part of the decade, to the stage of political "terrorism," which culminated in the assassination of Tsar Alexander II on March 1, 1881. Furthermore, women often assumed positions

[1] Horizon Press, New York, N.Y., 1968, p. 319.

of leadership. Of the five women whose memoirs are presented in this book, Olga Liubatovich, for example, belonged to the first group of revolutionary propagandists to take jobs as factory laborers; in 1878 Vera Zasulich initiated the terrorist phase with her attempt on the life of the governor of St. Petersburg, and in the period after March 1, 1881, Vera Figner became the recognized leader of the People's Will, the party that had carried out the assassination. The role played by women, which would have been extraordinary by the standards of any nineteenth-century movement, was all the more remarkable for the fact that Russian society was just beginning to emerge from feudalism. Legally, women remained subject to the absolute authority of their husbands or fathers; and as late as 1869, no education beyond the secondary school level was available to women anywhere in Russia.

In fact, it was by virtue of their oppression that women first became important to the radical movement in the late 1850's. Denouncing women's enslavement to the patriarchal family, male writers advocated love relationships in which women could retain their autonomy; they called for higher education and jobs to enable women to achieve economic independence. During the sixties, this initial formulation of the "woman question" was translated into action, as hundreds of young noblewomen left their homes in a quest for personal autonomy.

From the beginning, personal and political liberation were intimately connected—because, on the one hand, these women were pioneers, rebelling against the patriarchal relationships that oppressed all women; and on the other, because they soon perceived that fundamental social changes were necessary to produce significant improvement in women's position. It was for this reason that Nikolai Chernyshevskii's famous novel *What Is to Be Done?* proved so influential. It became a blueprint, providing practical solutions to the "woman question" from a revolutionary perspective: "fictitious"—that is, unconsummated—marriages contracted solely in order to extricate women from their parents' homes; separate rooms for couples who were living together in order to safeguard the emotional independence of both parties; and collective living and work situations to enable women to survive economically.

But it was education that was indispensable if women were to attain economic independence and intellectual equality with men, and it was, above all, the passion for education that motivated the women of the sixties and brought them together. During that decade, many women's groups, like Elizaveta Kovalskaia's in Kharkov, unsuccessfully petitioned for access to the universities of Russia. Until 1869, all that was available to women were boarding schools, the best of which provided little more than a superficial education; the pedagogical courses that opened in St. Petersburg in 1866; and a few courses to train midwives. Anything else women had to learn on their own. And so self-education circles—study groups—proliferated in the sixties.

Women also took an active part in efforts to extend elementary and political education to the working class. Vera Zasulich, for example, taught in the evening schools and Sunday schools established by radicals for workers in St. Petersburg. In Kharkov, Elizaveta Kovalskaia used her inheritance to set up an evening school for working women, where lectures were offered on feminism and socialism.

During the sixties women did not participate extensively, or on an equal footing with men, in other forms of radical activity. To be sure, men valued women as potential revolutionaries and often aided them in liberating themselves—by entering fictitious marriages, for example. But in Russia, where civil liberties were nonexistent and the government employed a large network of police spies, the small underground group—often dominated by one individual, invariably a man—had become the characteristic form of revolutionary organization. When women were involved at all, they played a peripheral or auxiliary role. Vera Zasulich, for example, was marginally associated with Sergei Nechaev, a revolutionary active in the student movement of the late 1860's. In his *Revolutionary Catechism*, written in collaboration with Mikhail Bakunin, Nechaev described the role of women in the revolutionary movement. One group, "the empty-headed, the sense-less, the heartless," must be exploited and made the slaves of men. A second group—women who were "eager, devoted, and capable" but not fully committed to the revolution—must be induced to reveal their sympathies, whereupon most would perish, while the rest would become true revolutionaries. Finally, there was a third group of women "who are truly ours" and must be considered "our most valuable jewel, whose help is absolutely indispensable." But even a "valuable jewel," such as Zasulich, was only a helper, excluded from leadership and decision-making.

For that matter, Nechaev demanded unquestioning obedience from the men in his small revolutionary organization, and when one of them, Ivan Ivanov, expressed certain doubts, Nechaev decided that he had to be killed. To four other members of the group, Nechaev asserted the existence of proof (which he never produced) that Ivanov was a traitor, and on November 21, 1869, they carried out the deed. Ivanov's body was soon discovered, and over a period of months the police arrested scores of radicals in connection with the case, although some had only the most tenuous relationship to Nechaev. Nechaev himself managed to escape abroad and elude the tsarist police for nearly three years. The revelations produced by his trial greatly influenced the shape of the movement of the seventies: in radical circles, the aversion to his dictatorial, dishonest methods was so strong that for years to come, any attempt to create a centralized, hierarchical organization met with great suspicion. The revolutionary groups of the early seventies were consciously egalitarian, basing themselves on the principle of honesty and mutual respect among comrades. Women were accepted as full-fledged members.

Higher educational institutions in particular proved important in shaping the women revolutionaries of the seventies. The establishment of the Alarchinskii courses in 1869 marked a turning point in the development of the women's movement in Russia: at last, the government had compromised with women's long-expressed desire for higher education to the extent of approving nondegree programs. From the beginning, the response was overwhelming, as hundreds of young women from all over Russia streamed into St. Petersburg. The Alarchinskii courses provided an invaluable opportunity for women to meet and develop their political and social views, while furthering their knowledge of science and mathematics. Feminist activity flourished. Elizaveta Kovalskaia describes the unending succession of meetings at which women students—men were excluded—discussed their position in the family and their role in society. Before long, the topics of study came to include other social questions as well, such as the situation of the working class and the peasantry. By 1871, these concerns had eclipsed feminism for many of the women. They concluded that Russia's most pressing need was a "social revolution"—one that would redistribute the land among the peasantry—and that they could best serve the cause by joining with men in mixed groups.

A similar evolution—from feminism to revolutionary populism—took place in Zurich. The establishment of the Alarchinskii courses had not satisfied women's desire for professional education, and so during the early seventies increasing numbers of Russian women went abroad. By 1873 there were over a hundred Russian women at school in Switzerland, studying medicine. At this time, Switzerland was also a haven for Russian radicals seeking freedom of expression. Political life was particularly intense in Zurich, and many Russian women students became engrossed in it: they attended meetings of the local section of the International Workingmen's Association, devoured the important works of European socialism, and helped set type for the radical émigré newspaper *Forward!* (*Vpered!*)—all the while pursuing their studies with a passion. In order to assimilate the new ideas they encountered, thirteen of these students, none of them over twenty years old, formed a study group, which they called the Fritsche circle after the boardinghouse in which most lived. The group included Olga Liubatovich and her younger sister Vera and the sisters Vera and Lydia Figner. By 1873, most of the circle had resolved to return to Russia to begin revolu-

tionary activity. They entered into negotiations with a group
of young male émigrés and in 1874 merged to form the Pan-
Russian Social Revolutionary Organization.

When they became radical populists, the Fritsche circle
abandoned feminism, as had the members of the women's
circles of St. Petersburg a few years earlier. In the seventies,
women and men alike regarded feminism as primarily concerned with women's struggle for individual autonomy; as
they saw it, such a struggle had no place in a radical movement operating under the harshest of political conditions, in
which loyalty to the group necessarily took precedence over
personal aspirations. Nonetheless, the importance of the feminist movement in shaping the women revolutionaries of the
seventies cannot be minimized. It gave them a sense of their
own capacity for action, along with the invaluable experience
of developing their political ideas independently of men; and
through it, they developed ties of sisterhood that they maintained in later mixed radical groups. Their own strengths enabled women to participate as equals in the populist movement.

## II

Russian populism[2] was an ideology of agrarian revolution.

On February 19, 1861, Tsar Alexander II had freed the peasants—the vast majority of the population—after centuries of
serfdom. But he had not given them the land they had so
long cultivated and which they felt to be rightfully theirs;
they had been obliged to redeem it from the government at
prices that sometimes far exceeded the actual market value.
The unsatisfactory nature of the Emancipation had provoked
violent but sporadic acts of resistance among the peasants,
and among the intelligentsia it had led to the emergence of
numerous small groups that believed in the necessity and

---

[2] The Russian word is *narodnichestvo*, derived from *narod*, "the people." The
populists were known as *narodniki*.

imminence of a revolution to bring about the redistribution of land. In 1866, Dmitrii Karakozov, a member of one such revolutionary group, paid with his life for an unsuccessful attempt to assassinate the tsar. When asked his motives by his captors, he replied: "Look at the freedom you gave the peasants!"

While the populists never developed a unified body of doctrine comparable to Marxism, they shared—at least until the late 1870's—a number of fundamental tenets. They believed that the peasantry was inherently socialist (as evidenced by their communal cultivation of the land) and that an agrarian revolution would thus make it possible for Russia to pass directly into socialism. But it was imperative that the revolution be carried out immediately, because capitalism, although still at an early stage in Russia, was already beginning to undermine the peasant commune (*obshchina*). A "political" revolution, aimed at replacing Russia's absolutist form of government with a constitutional regime would be of no benefit to the peasantry; only a "social" revolution, by and for the peasantry, would do.

But how were revolutionaries who sprang from the privileged classes to approach the peasantry, the people? On this question, Russian radicals tended to divide into partisans of Pyotr Lavrov and Mikhail Bakunin, the two writers most influential in making populism into a mass movement in the 1870's. Lavrov, in his *Historical Letters,* published in book form in 1870, argued that the culture of the educated classes had been bought with the sweat and blood of the toiling peasantry; that as a consequence, the privileged intelligentsia was morally indebted to the peasantry; and that the way to repay that debt was to put one's knowledge at the service of the people. Bakunin, on the other hand, argued that the revolutionary's duty was not to teach but to learn from and merge with the peasant masses. The peasantry was always ready for revolution—Bakunin pointed to the massive peasant rebellions led by Stenka Razin and Emilian Pugachev in the seventeenth and eighteenth centuries respectively—and needed only the spark to set it off. The revolutionary was to supply that spark and help unify local rebellions into one nationwide uprising.

Heated debates erupted between the respective adherents of Bakunin and Lavrov. But when the first mass movement "to the people" materialized in 1874, it was basically spontaneous and uncoordinated, and it accommodated both orientations easily. That summer, thousands of young people— primarily students—poured into the Russian countryside, singly and in small groups, to share the lives of the common people and spread socialist propaganda. They dressed themselves as peasants and sometimes learned trades such as cobbling in the hope that this would enable them to find work and establish contacts among the people. Some settled in one spot, but most engaged in "flying propaganda"—that is, they moved rapidly from village to village. The socialist ideas they preached sometimes took the form of parables phrased in the language of the common people, but often the propagandists merely paraphrased their own reading of Western European socialist works. The peasants' response varied: relatively few were sympathetic, the majority were bewildered, indifferent, or even hostile. In no case did the populists from the cities succeed in sparking a revolutionary uprising. But since freedom of speech did not exist in Russia and since the revolutionary propagandists usually acted openly, with little concern for their personal security, all but a few fell into the hands of the police. By the end of the year, four thousand people had been harassed, questioned, or imprisoned.

The members of the Pan-Russian Social Revolutionary Organization adopted a different approach when they returned to Russia early in 1875. Like all the populists of the early seventies, they believed that the peasantry had to be the main force of the revolution. But rather than organizing among the peasants themselves, they decided to conduct propaganda among factory workers, who were for the most part seasonal: when these workers returned home periodically to their native villages to help with the farm work, they would be able to spread socialist ideas more effectively than could outsiders from the cities. The organization, which included Olga Liubatovich and Vera Figner's sister Lydia, established contacts with workers in several cities, but within six months the entire membership had fallen into the hands of the police.

Thus, although it was far from defeated, by the end of 1875 the populist movement had suffered severe setbacks. A large proportion of the activists of the early seventies were imprisoned or under police surveillance. Nevertheless, there were still individuals making free-lance journeys into the countryside (as did Praskovia Ivanovskaia in the summer of 1876), and various groups developing new strategies for approaching the peasantry.

Land and Liberty, which became the most significant of these groups, began to take shape in 1876. According to its analysis, the first wave "to the people" in 1874 had been too haphazard and reckless and its propaganda too abstract. Although Land and Liberty did not establish an elaborate hierarchy, it was definitely a centralized organization, with a coordinating group in St. Petersburg that adhered strictly to conspiratorial practices—apartments and addresses known only to specific individuals, false identity papers, care in the use of written communications. The organization's program was based on what were perceived to be the existing desires and demands of the people: expropriation of all the land and its redistribution among the peasantry; the break-up of the Russian Empire in accordance with popular aspirations for local autonomy; and self-government through federations of peasant communes. Of course, these demands could be achieved only through violent revolution. But Land and Liberty adopted a cautious, long-range approach in spreading these ideas. Instead of "flying propaganda," more lasting bases—"colonies" or "settlements," as they were called— were established in the countryside; revolutionaries took jobs in these locations as paramedics (*feldshers*), nurses, schoolteachers, or clerks in the hope of gradually winning the trust of the local population. This became the dominant form of activity in the second phase of the movement "to the people" during 1877–78—not only for the members of Land and

Liberty, but also for people like Vera Figner and Elizaveta Kovalskaia, who chose not to join the new party.

Meanwhile, two mass trials helped to create widespread public sympathy for the revolutionary cause. The Trial of the Fifty, conducted in Moscow in March 1877, included most of the membership of the Pan-Russian Social Revolutionary Organization. The government was confidently expecting to discredit the revolutionaries as a band of cynical, dangerous criminals. Instead, spectators and reporters took away from the courtroom a picture of idealistic young people who, for the sake of a vision of social justice, had selflessly renounced their own privileged positions and shared the wretched lives of factory workers. The women defendants, in particular, made a strong impression: courtroom spectators repeatedly exclaimed, "They are saints!" One defendant, Sofia Bardina, concluded her statement to the court with a ringing challenge: "Persecute us—you have material strength for a while, gentlemen, but we have moral strength, the strength of ideas; and ideas, alas, you cannot pierce with bayonets!"

The Trial of the Hundred Ninety-three, which began in October of that same year, 1877, included a large number of the activists who had gone "to the people" in 1874. For their crime of preaching socialism to the peasants, they had suffered as much as four years of pretrial imprisonment under the harshest conditions; dozens were lost to illness, death (sometimes by suicide), or madness. At the trial, many of the accused expressed their contempt for the tribunal by refusing to present any defense, and when one man did attempt to describe the conditions in prison and make a political statement, he was repeatedly silenced by the judges and finally dragged from the courtroom. The government failed to prove the existence of a conspiracy (many of the defendants had never so much as laid eyes on each other); it managed only to discredit its own methods. The defendants, meanwhile, utilized the months-long trial to make acquaintances and build solidarity. When it ended, the majority were acquitted outright or released in consideration of their pretrial imprisonment. Prison had hardened them, embittered them, and strengthened their convictions. They resumed their political activity—many promptly joined Land and Liberty—with the determination to avoid the naïve errors that had made them easy targets for government repression years before.

The trial ended on January 23, 1878. Twenty-four hours later, the populist movement entered its "terrorist" stage.

Populist terrorism consisted of attempts to assassinate government officials. As its proponents pointed out, it was a highly selective form of revolutionary violence: whereas the government habitually employed arbitrary and excessive force against its subjects, the various assassination attempts of the so-called terrorists claimed only a handful of unintended victims other than bodyguards of the tsar. Terrorism was, simply, populism in its armed phase. It was in this phase of the revolutionary movement that the five women represented in this book played their historic roles.

On the morning of January 24, Vera Zasulich walked into the office of General Trepov in St. Petersburg and, in the presence of a roomful of witnesses, shot him to avenge his mistreatment of a political prisoner. Six days later, there was a gun battle when the police attempted to raid an underground press in Odessa; on February 23 there was an unsuccessful attempt on the life of an assistant prosecutor in Kiev; on May 25 a police official in Kiev was assassinated. Then, on August 4, 1878, Sergei Kravchinskii, one of the leading members of Land and Liberty, assassinated the head of the political police on the street in St. Petersburg and made a clean getaway. The government instituted special military tribunals to deal with such attacks and executed the participants when and if it caught them. But the campaign continued—armed resistance to the police in St. Petersburg in October and Kharkov in November; the assassination of the governor of Kharkov in February 1879; an attempt on the life of the head of the police in St. Petersburg in March 1879.

Until the fall of 1878, Land and Liberty, which had become the largest and strongest revolutionary organization, regarded this kind of activity as strictly subordinate to the task of organizing a revolution among the peasantry. It was a means to avenge fallen comrades, to strike fear into the hearts of government officials and deter them from further reprisals against the revolutionaries, and, by example, to stimulate popular resistance to the regime—"propaganda of the deed," as it was sometimes called. But by late 1878, government harassment and repression such as Vera Figner describes had made it virtually impossible for revolutionaries to conduct propaganda or even live among the peasantry—almost all of Land and Liberty's colonies had been abandoned—and a growing faction within the revolutionary movement was arguing that in fact it would *never* be possible to organize the peasantry in the absence of basic political liberties like freedom of speech, of the press, and of assembly. The emphasis was shifting from "social" revolution—that is, a revolution with the immediate aim of getting land for the peasantry— toward a conception of a "political" revolution that would compel the regime to make concessions by means of systematic attacks on high officials. Even the most stalwart defenders of traditional organizing among the peasantry had to admit that their approach seemed to have reached a dead end. But some strongly resisted the new "political" line on the grounds that attacks on officials would increase the repression and make organizing more difficult (not a very compelling argument under the circumstances, as Olga Liubatovich pointed out); and that if a constitutional regime dedicated to protecting political rights was achieved, it would benefit only the bourgeoisie and do nothing to improve the lot of the peasantry.

The conflict came to a head in March 1879, when Alexander Soloviev approached Land and Liberty with a plan to assassinate the tsar. Advocates of political revolution were sympathetic, partisans of peasant organizing vehemently opposed. They worked out a compromise, papering over the deepening rift: individual members could choose to aid Soloviev, but the party as a whole would provide no support. As it turned out, Soloviev made his attempt alone on April 2 and failed. However, the "politicals" did not abandon the idea of regicide. Over the next weeks, they organized their own secret group within Land and Liberty—it was called Liberty or Death—and they began to set up workshops to manufacture dynamite.

Neither faction in Land and Liberty relished the prospect of a formal split in the party, which would mean breaking old and strong bonds with comrades and, most likely, weakening the revolutionary movement. But there was an urgent need to resolve the conflict, one way or another, and so a party-wide conference was set for late June in the town of Voronezh. Anticipating an open rupture, the partisans of political struggle held a secret preliminary caucus in Lipetsk several days prior to the Voronezh meeting. They outlined a program calling for civil liberties and a national assembly elected on the basis of universal suffrage; unanimously endorsed the principle of regicide; and drew up statutes for a strictly centralized party. The expected split did not materialize at Voronezh. Another compromise was worked out, retaining the old program of Land and Liberty but sanctioning the continued assassination campaign, thus approving regicide in principle. Ultimately, however, regicide could not remain an abstract issue, nor one amenable to compromise. In August, after two months of fruitless intraparty negotiations (described by Liubatovich), the two factions agreed to go their separate ways.

This schism in Land and Liberty in the summer of 1879 was the most important such event in the history of the revolutionary populist movement. Two independent parties emerged: the advocates of regicide and political struggle established the People's Will, while their opponents rallied around Black Repartition.

Black Repartition,[3] the smaller of the two, maintained Land and Liberty's traditional emphasis on agrarian revolution: its name expressed the demand for the redistribution of all land among the peasants. The party was virtually stillborn; political conditions did not, in fact, permit peaceful organizing

---

[3] Interpretations of the group's name differ. Some believe that it refers to the tradition of land redistribution among the peasants of the "black lands."

activity among the peasantry. Black Repartition proved an important way station, however, for in 1883 its leaders established the first Russian Marxist group, Emancipation of Labor.

Vera Zasulich was among those leaders. On the basis of her attack on Trepov, she might have been expected to join the People's Will, which was carrying on the assassination campaign. But Zasulich never envisioned her action becoming a systematic policy, and in fact, as Olga Liubatovich writes, became extremely distressed by the series of assassination attempts that followed her own.

Black Repartition's program did provide for one form of terrorism: "economic terror," which consisted of attacks directed not at the central government, but at the enemies of the people at a local level—factory owners, landlords, and police officials or administrators. This was the stratagem that attracted Elizaveta Kovalskaia to the party. But it was one that Black Repartition proved unable and even unwilling to implement. A member of the party's central body rejected outright Kovalskaia's proposal to initiate economic terror in the south of Russia, whereupon she left the party and, with a comrade, formed a new organization, the Union of Russian Workers of the South. Perhaps more than any other revolutionary of the period, Kovalskaia was successful in linking a conception of armed struggle to a mass organization—within the space of six months, she organized about seven hundred workers into the Union.

The "political" faction of Land and Liberty, joined by veterans of other groups, formed the People's Will. The establishment of this party amounted to a major transformation of the populist movement, because of the explicit abandonment of peasant organizing in favor of political revolution. Moreover, with its discipline and strict centralization, the People's Will became the first party of professional revolutionaries in Russia's history. This transformation took a long time to consolidate—well over a year, Vera Figner estimated. Olga Liubatovich, a member of the party's Executive Committee from its formation, could not reconcile herself to the evolution she saw occurring during this period. To her mind, the People's Will was moving toward Jacobinism—that is, a revolution by a small group which would *decree* social transformations from above, rather than base itself on the will of the people. Furthermore, she felt that the party was endorsing a return to "Nechaevism"—that decisions were being taken without the full, equal participation of all members. Early in 1880, she left the party.

Praskovia Ivanovskaia and Vera Figner remained. Ivanovskaia served as a typesetter in the party's printing operation, and her memoirs provide an invaluable account of the daily routines and personal relationships of life underground. Figner was one of the leaders of the People's Will and took an active part in several assassination attempts, which she describes in this book.

The history of the People's Will is inseparable from its campaign to assassinate Tsar Alexander II. That campaign, begun in the fall of 1879, lasted far longer and exacted a far heavier toll than the party had anticipated: it took seven separate attempts over the space of a year and a half, drained all the party's energies away from organizing activity, and thus foreclosed any possibility of building a mass movement capable of maximizing the political impact of the assassination. Success came at last with a bomb-throwing attack on March 1, 1881. But it was followed almost immediately by a wave of arrests that threw the party on the defensive and prevented it from pressing its greatest triumph at a time when large segments of liberal society were sympathetic and even eager to aid it. By the middle of 1882, Vera Figner was the only member of the original leadership of the party still at liberty in Russia. With her capture in February 1883, the effective life of the People's Will came to an end.

## III

Earlier in this essay, we suggested some of the particular historical conditions that made it possible for women to play such an extraordinary part in the revolutionary movement of the seventies: above all, the fact that feminism had been a major concern of Russian radicalism for a number of years—that women had been able to develop their ideas, build sisterhood, and act politically *before* joining a mixed revolutionary movement; and that the populist movement, in turn, had been sensitized to the importance of egalitarian relations among comrades. These conditions alone, however, do not explain the reverence that the women of the seventies inspired both among their male comrades and among educated Russian society at large. The names contemporaries applied to them—"saints," "Moscow Amazons," "Russian Valkyries"—are all somehow inadequate: the first women revolutionaries in Russian history, they created their own mythology. They possessed a passionate and lucid moral vision which neither exile, imprisonment, nor imminent death could destroy. Sofia Perovskaia, the first woman in Russian history to be executed for a political crime, put it simply. "I have no regrets about my fate," she wrote to her mother on the eve of her death. "I shall meet it calmly, since I've long lived with the knowledge that it would come, sooner or later. And really, Mamma dear, my fate isn't all that dismal. I have lived according to my convictions; I could not have acted otherwise; and so I await the future with a clear conscience."

# NOTE ON SOURCES

The revolutionary populists left a rich memoir literature, probably the most important body of sources for the study of the movement. We have chosen writings that convey, we hope, the diversity both of populist activities and of the individual revolutionaries who carried them out.

All but one of the selections (the Liubatovich memoir) are composites which we have assembled from autobiographical fragments written and published at various times, particularly in the period immediately after the Revolution of 1905, when freedom of the press was greatly expanded, and during the 1920's, under the Soviet regime. In order to create coherent narratives that would not overwhelm the reader with names and incidents, we have eliminated much detail of interest to the specialist. In the interests of readability, we have avoided the use of ellipses to mark omissions; all ellipses appearing in the present text belong to the memoirists and indicate pauses. The sources of the original texts, as well as books of interest to the general reader, are cited in the bibliography.

Unless otherwise indicated, all dates are given in the Old Style.

# VERA
# FIGNER

*Figner appeared to be a super-revolutionary. A lot was said about her beauty, elegance, education, intelligence and ability to conduct herself properly in all social circles, aristocratic included. For us she was an ideal revolutionary, a woman with an iron will. After the fall of Perovskaia and Zheliabov [who had led the People's Will prior to their arrest], she was the only one everyone recognized as having unlimited revolutionary authority.[1]*

Vera Figner was born on June 25, 1852; she was the oldest of six children in a well-to-do gentry family. Her father was a forester, and her early years were spent in the backwoods, isolated from the world. At the age of eleven, Vera was sent off to a cloistered private school for girls of the gentry, which did little to enlarge her experience. She spent six years there, cut off from contact with anyone but her fellow students as she acquired the superficial education deemed appropriate for women of her station.

In 1869, she returned to her family's estate. "After being enclosed within the four walls of my boarding school," she wrote, "I was bursting with a joyful feeling of freedom. This excess of joy, this heightened emotional state demanded action. I found it unthinkable that I might live without making some mark upon the world."[2] Influenced by a liberal uncle, she came to see the disparity between her own privileged position and the destitution of the peasantry, and she resolved to work for their benefit. "Russian journalism and the women's movement, at its height in the early seventies, provided me with a ready

[1] I. I. Popov. *Minuvshee i perezhitoe* (Moscow, 1933), pp. 108–9.
[2] Vera Figner. *Zapechatlennyi trud* (Moscow, 1964), Vol. I, p. 100.

*solution for my philanthropic aspirations: I could become a doctor."[3] Since it was impossible for women to study medicine in Russia, she made up her mind to go to Switzerland, where universities had recently begun to admit women.*

*But her father forbade her to go: instead he took her to Kazan, expecting that the lively social season in that city would involve her in more "feminine" pursuits. As it happened, a young lawyer, Alexei Filippov, fell in love with her and asked her to marry him. Before she agreed, Figner persuaded him to abandon his job and travel abroad with her—once married, she would no longer need her father's permission to travel. In the spring of 1872, together with her husband and her sister Lydia, Vera Figner arrived in Zurich, where she was to receive the political education that led her to become a revolutionary.*

---

A dull, steady drizzle was falling. All I could see from the window of my small hotel room on Limmatquai were the tiled roofs of the houses, nestled close to each other. That rainy day, colorless, uninviting, and dreary, was my first in a foreign land, in an unfamiliar city.

Zurich! I had yearned to go for so long: over the last two years all my thoughts and desires had been centered on Zurich. There had been so much anxiety before leaving Russia. I hadn't planned to go until the fall, but in the spring the Russian papers had carried the news that Zurich University was introducing regulations that would make admission more difficult. We had made anxious inquiries of the rector and, receiving a reassuring reply—we could still enroll without taking exams—left our home province in a hurry.

It was a clear April day in 1872, a remarkable, invigorating day, abounding with sunlight and the scent of spring, when my sister and I set out from our native village of Nikiforovo, traveling briskly on a troika with bells ringing. From the administrative center of our district we had taken a steamship,

3 Ibid., p. 102.

then a train, to Switzerland. Now I was in Zurich, with its ancient, narrow streets, its miserable lake, unappealing in the rain, and that ugly view of the tiled roofs from my window.

On the second day, it cleared up, and we hastily set off to request permission to enroll in the university. We walked uphill all the way from the quay, the streets growing broader, gardens becoming more frequent, until at last we were standing in front of the large building of the Polytechnical Institute, which was part of the university. I ascended the broad staircase with a feeling close to reverence, as if I were about to enter a temple of science to be accepted as one of its votaries.

As it turned out, the rector admitted us as students without any formalities: he simply shook our hands, taking this as our promise to obey university rules. Having achieved our

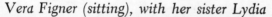

*Vera Figner (sitting), with her sister Lydia*

cherished goal, we practically ran back down the stairs. Now
our studies would begin. Nothing but studying and more
studying. "I won't go to the theater and I won't take walks"
—before leaving home I had thus assured my uncle. When he
pointed out that I would be tempted by the Zurich lake,
which was full of fish, I had insisted, "I won't even go fishing!" even though I loved to fish. "No! There'll be no fishing
or boating! There'll be nothing but lectures and textbooks!"

I was enormously enthusiastic—you could almost say
fanatical—about my future profession. For two whole years
I had been thinking about medicine and preparing myself
for the university—studying math, physics, German, and
Latin. Our earlier schooling hadn't prepared us women for
the university, but our desire to extract every bit of knowledge
from our narrow program was enormous. Our yearning to
travel abroad to study did not spring from faddishness or
frivolous vanity. We were still pioneers in the struggle for
women's higher education, and the journey abroad was not
easy for any of us: you needed real determination and un-
swerving will power to overcome material difficulties, the
prejudices of provincial society, parents' opposition to novelty
and their fear of letting their daughters travel to unknown,
far-off places. The young Russians living in Zurich in 1872
were of very high caliber, indeed.

I, too, had had to overcome material difficulties. Three or
four thousand rubles were needed to provide several years of
a modest student life for my husband and me. To economize,
I had buried myself in the backwoods, where it cost me nothing to live at my mother's estate. We set aside my husband's
entire salary for our intended trip, and I sold all the things I
had been given for my dowry. Relieved of all household goods
—both the necessary and the superfluous—carefree, young,
and happy, we were able at last to make our way to the source
of knowledge.

I was nineteen when I left, and my intellectual horizons
were still very narrow. In the two years I had been out of
school I had read few books or journal articles of a serious
nature, and I had come in contact with absolutely no one while

living in the countryside. My uncle was sympathetic to my aspirations to attend the university and become a doctor, the sort of doctor who would treat only the poor, the peasants, but aside from him, there was no one in our backwoods who could have opened up the world of ideas to me. This uncle had supplied me with some basic ideas about society—and that was the extent of my knowledge.

Early in the year, at a mineralogy lecture at the university, I found myself sitting next to a young woman with a whole bush of closely cut black curls. Her eyes were like coals in their narrow slits, and the brick-red blush on her homely round face gave her a distinctive expression, half provocative, half mocking. In fact, it was her nose that really appeared mocking, and it went with her sharply etched mouth.

"Are you in medical school?" I asked.

"No, I've enrolled at the Polytechnic Institute, in agronomy."

*Now, that's strange,* I thought. *What's agronomy? Why is she sitting next to me, then?* I thought people went abroad only to study medicine, and that every woman student could have but one goal—that she could resolve only to serve society, that is, "the poor." I understood service to society exclusively in the sense of ministering to "the poor," by which I meant the peasants. To me, medicine was the very best way to serve them.

"Why are you going into agronomy?" I asked my neighbor. "What good is it?"

"My family are landowners in Tver province," she replied. "I'll live in the village and use my knowledge in farming the land."

Until then, I'd only seen estates run by totally uneducated stewards, and by the so-called peasant "elders," who were also stewards, but were paid less and were even less competent. The only agricultural system I knew was the one that my father and grandfather had followed, as had generations

of peasants and landowners from time immemorial. I can't
say, then, that I understood the intentions of Sofia Bardina
any better after her reply.

On another occasion, Bardina informed me in class:
"There'll be a meeting of Russian women students today."

"Why?" I asked, rather afraid that it would take time
away from my studies.

"Someone suggested that we form a circle exclusively for
women, in order to learn how to speak logically. At meetings
with men," she continued, noting my bewildered look, "wom-
en usually keep quiet; we feel shy, and so we don't say anything. But maybe with practice we'll learn to develop our
thoughts logically, and then we won't be afraid to speak in
public. A women's circle would be a place where we could
learn."

"Well, that sounds really good! When will the meeting
be?"

"At eight, at the Palmenhof on Oberstrasse. Please come!"

That evening, after a meager student dinner, my sister
Lydia and I set off for the Palmenhof. There in the hall we
found a long dinner table, with a row of chairs alongside it.
Plainly dressed young women were waiting around; some
had broken into groups of two or three. There was a hum
of conversation, and somewhere a lively argument was going
on.

"Gentlemen [sic]! Kindly be seated!" announced a tall
blond woman with closely cropped hair—Doctor Emme's
wife. A bell was then rung energetically; people took their
seats, and the meeting began. Emme was chosen chairwoman,
and she gave the floor to the librarian whose idea it had been
to call the meeting. The librarian explained the goal of the
circle: to learn to speak logically. Then, as a means to this
end, she proposed that we read essays and hold debates.

We proceeded to discuss whether there was really a need
for such a circle, and if so, who should participate. No one
took issue with the circle's goal. On the other hand, passionate arguments arose as to whether the circle should be made
up exclusively of women. Many scoffed at this idea: they

found it ridiculous that women should be afraid in the presence of men, and thought that it would be both more natural and more expedient to form a self-education circle jointly with men, without fear of masculine competition. But these voices were drowned out in the majority decision to begin by organizing women students exclusively. We didn't work out a set of rules for the society, which was open to all women students. Once the general question had been resolved, we immediately got down to business, proposing that those who wished choose topics for the following meeting.

As it turned out, the first paper was prepared by the librarian. Strange as it may seem, her subject turned out to be the question of suicide, which couldn't have been further from our minds at that time.[4] She argued that every suicide, without exception, was the result of psychic disorder, and proclaimed that there could be no such thing as a perfectly normal suicide.

Although none of us knew anything about the question or had the faintest notion of psychiatry, the challenge—to us it seemed a challenge to comon sense—was taken up boldly. A passionate debate ensued; the chairwoman's hand got a real workout, shaking her bell to keep order. The meeting was chaotic; instead of debating in an orderly manner, everyone talked at once. It finally became clear that the majority opposed the one-sided views of the speaker, and we left for home, having exhausted ourselves over such questions as: What *is* a normal person? Is anyone really *normal*? Perhaps everyone's a little crazy, one way or another? Far into the night, loud voices resounded through the sleeping streets of Zurich: "Normal . . . abnormal . . . psychosis . . . where are the limits? . . . There are no limits!"

Varvara Alexandrova, a young, blond student who was a friend of my sister Lydia, gave the second paper. Its theme was the peasant rebellion of Stenka Razin. The paper itself was weak, but it set off a debate because it completely idealized Razin's personality—both as a mighty leader and as a de-

4 Later, of those present, Kaminskaia, Bardina, Zavadskaia, Khorzhevskaia, and Grebnitskaia took their own lives.—Figner.

structive hero in the Bakuninist sense. At this session, the question of science and civilization was raised. Were they really necessary for mankind? Did humanity need science to be happy? Did civilization yield any benefits, or—so long as the masses were enslaved and the upper classes enjoyed lives of luxury and refined culture—did it merely harm the people?

Rousseau and that incomparable apostle of destruction, Bakunin, were invoked by ardent disputants who took the side of those adversaries of civilization and culture. Others, upset by the violent attacks on all of humanity's gains, put up an energetic defense, as if our debates could actually bring about utter barbarism by somehow destroying civilization. My devotion to science was passionate, and I yearned to dedicate my life to it, so I, too, screamed with genuine frenzy about the value it could have and about how, in order to bring justice to this earth, we must not destroy civilization but instead disseminate it among all who were deprived. One passionate woman, half-Italian, half-Russian, annihilated civilization as befit her southern temperament. The meeting degenerated into chaos; everyone was flushed and impatient, and it became impossible to hear anything over the shouting. The Italian woman got a nosebleed, while the chairwoman reproachfully paraphrased Napoleon's speech to his armies in Egypt[5]: after ringing her bell furiously, she said with deep feeling, "Mesdames—all of Europe is watching you!" This reference to a Europe which was allegedly observing Russian women students in Zurich attentively sounded so funny that everyone roared with laughter, and all the ardor of the disputing sides was extinguished immediately. The meeting ended but the agitation did not subside, and in the fresh air of the streets everyone resumed arguing the merits of civilization and science.

Ridiculous as it may seem, that was the circle's last discussion. It was as if all our passion and eagerness to learn to speak logically had been absorbed in that debate about civili-

[5] "Forty centuries observe us from the height of these pyramids."—Figner.

zation. Perhaps we realized that our cause was hopeless. In any event, after all that disorderly and overheated verbiage, the opposition to excluding men grew very powerful. There was one more meeting, where the question of admitting the stronger sex arose again. The defenders of the original decision had toned down somewhat and lost strength. We argued for a while, talked a bit longer, and dispersed without reaching any decisions. It became apparent that the women's circle was falling to pieces; in contrast to its former verbosity, it expired silently, to the regret of no one with the possible exception of its initiator, and was not resurrected. However, during its brief existence it had served a purpose by bringing the young Russian women of Zurich together and giving them a chance to meet and size each other up. The arguments revealed various tendencies and temperaments, making it easier for people with similar views to get together. And indeed, several new circles were soon formed in the Russian colony.

*Among these was the Fritsche circle, a radical study group composed of thirteen women, aged sixteen to nineteen, most of whom were enrolled in the medical faculty. This group played a crucial role in Figner's political development.*

From my first days in Zurich, I had been confronted by a whole series of questions, the existence of which I had never even suspected and which began to shake the views I had acquired—unconsciously in childhood, actively after I left school. I was assailed by doubts and had to deal with them. Because of the moral issues that those questions raised, I eventually became a socialist and a revolutionary.

Just as I had been accustomed to viewing nature itself as something immutable, thinking about neither the past nor the future of the universe, up to this point I had accepted the existing social system and form of government without question, without examining their origins or the possibility of changing them. I knew, of course, that the world was divided into the rich and the poor—how could I have failed to see that?—but I hadn't the faintest idea of the social injustice

that this division engendered. I knew that society was divided
into estates—the gentry, the petty bourgeoisie, the peasantry
—but I had no conception of class distinctions. The expressions "capital," "proletariat," and "social parasitism" were
not in my vocabulary.

There is poverty in the world; there is ignorance and dis-
ease. People who are educated and—like me—born to well-
to-do families ought to share my natural desire to assist the
poor. Under the influence of my mother and my uncle, as
well as of the journal articles I'd read, I made up a social
program for myself before leaving for Zurich: some day I was
going to help peasants in Russia buy horses, or build new huts
after their old ones had burnt down; as a doctor I hoped to
cure people suffering from tuberculosis and typhoid, to perform operations and give advice on medicine and hygiene;
and as a *zemstvo*[6] activist I planned to set up schools, spread
literacy, and provide grain elevators to help the peasants save
money. As far as over-all political structures were concerned, I
either failed to think of them at all, or, to the extent that I
did, considered the form of government in Switzerland or the
United States to be ideal. But I never asked myself how such
a system could be established in Russia—the question never
even occurred to me. My uncle had once told me confidently,
referring to John Stuart Mill, "Every nation gets the government it deserves." Since his words carried great weight with
me, I took this as an axiom and it set my mind to rest. I
could think of no exceptions to this rule—which was correct
in a certain sense—and no one around me had anything else
to say at the time. But if the rule was true, then Russia possessed the very government that it deserved; when Russia became a different country, it would receive a government
resembling that of Switzerland or North America. And this
would all work out somehow by itself.

Then I went to Zurich, and the "foundation" I had built

6 The *zemstvo* was an organ for self-government in rural areas. Established in
1864, it had representatives from private landowners, peasant communities,
and qualified urban dwellers. Its work was primarily in the realm of education and medical care.

up by the age of nineteen began to be undermined from all sides. Like a bolt from the blue it hit me that I, who was virtually fresh from school and inspired by the finest aspirations toward science and goodness, I, at the age of nineteen, was already an exploiter, and my mother and my uncle and all of my relatives were all greedy, mercenary exploiters: they belonged to a privileged minority, under whose oppression the masses, the proletariat, were born, suffered, and died. At first I failed to understand—I refused to understand—that all of us were really like that. I did become confused and morally troubled, but then I began to deny everything; I argued against and refused to accept the villainous role ascribed to me and everyone close to me.

I was obsessed by doubts and contradictions, but I was ashamed to ask anyone for explanations, afraid of appearing stupid and ignorant. Everyone else who had arrived in Zurich before me seemed so learned and intelligent. They didn't doubt: they affirmed. Bardina, my classmate from the mineralogy lectures, seemed to me the only person who would not laugh at me and could lead me out of my difficulties, and so I began to speak to her frankly.

"My father was a forester, and then a peace mediator,"[7] I said. "How could he be an exploiter? Whom did he exploit?"

And with calm certainty Bardina would point out that peasants and workers paid various taxes to the treasury, taxes that went to pay the salaries of all government bureaucrats, including those of my father and my uncle. The people worked hard to pay those taxes out of their meager earnings; they went without necessities to send their hard-earned kopecks to the state treasury. Forced in addition to pay indirect taxes on salt and other necessary items, the people bore the burden of almost the entire budget.[8] They lived in poverty, on bread and *kvass*[9] and worked from morning till night, wearing bark

---

[7] Peace mediators—*mirovye posredniki*—were members of the gentry who helped to implement the edict of February 19, 1861, freeing the serfs. They mediated land disputes between landlords and peasants.
[8] In Russia the gentry were exempt from direct taxes.
[9] A sort of beer, made from fermented rye.

shoes and lighting their huts with splinters of wood. And this was the case everywhere: if you were a minister or a professor, a forester or a judge, a peace mediator or a *zemstvo* doctor, you lived at the people's expense, in luxury or at least in comfort. You engaged in easy, pleasant, and respectable intellectual pursuits, while the people, who fed everyone and paid for everything, bent their backs, went hungry, and lived in perpetual need and ignorance.

"But you can't do without teachers, doctors, or judges!" I would argue.

"Of course not," Bardina agreed. "But the remuneration for labor must be fair: a judge works less than a miner or a peasant, but he earns a hundred times as much as they do. The man who expends the greatest energy on his job, or performs the most difficult or unappealing tasks, should be paid the most. But now everything's just the reverse: the more a man works, the less he earns. Our whole social structure is built upon this injustice, and it's the source of everything that's evil in contemporary society. Those who benefit from such a system are exploiters and parasites, because they take what should belong to others; they live at the expense of others, stealing poor men's last morsels."

Thus, before my eyes stood, on the one hand, millions of human beings condemned to endless labor, to poverty and everything that went with it—sickness, ignorance, and crime —while on the other there was a small handful of people enjoying all the good things of life because others were laboring for them.

These ideas unexpectedly threw everything I had believed about people and life into a completely new light. My ideas and my feelings were at odds. Could a small group of people at the top be responsible for the horrors of the London slums, the shameful oppression of the factory workers, the sufferings of the laborers in industry and in workshops everywhere, as described by Flerovskii and Engels? If not for this small group, everything would be different! And I, Vera Figner, was one of those people on top; like them, I was responsible for all the misery of the vast majority.

It was difficult for me to digest such a notion—and still more difficult to accept it. All the more so because there was only one way out: if it was all true, then I would have to renounce my position, for it would be unthinkable to recognize that you are the cause of others' suffering and still retain your privileges and enjoy your advantages. But that would mean that I would have to descend into that very poverty, filth, and degradation that was the lot of the oppressed majority. It was terrible to draw such a conclusion, terrible to have to make up my mind!

I wouldn't give up. "But a person who puts money in the bank and gets interest on it—he certainly can't be living at another's expense, you can't call him an exploiter?" I asked.

Bardina demonstrated calmly and methodically that even the bank, that peaceful refuge, was a device to wring sweat from the workers, and that interest was also criminal income.

I borrowed from the library a book of statistics that every young man and woman was reading at the time. It contained cold, dry figures which demonstrated that, with only minor deviations, an inevitable number of thefts, murders, and suicides were committed year after year in every country. People lived their lives, thinking that they exercised free will, that they could choose freely whether or not to steal, whether or not to murder. But the statistics demonstrated that whatever the desires of any particular individual, out of every ten thousand people, so many people steal, kill someone, or take their own lives. Why was this fatal repetition of exactly the same figures inevitable? It must mean that there are more fundamental, more profound motivations than individual will. There could be only one answer: social conditions are such that, despite individual inclinations, temperaments, or desires, they inevitably produce crime. Hunger and deprivation of all kinds—these are the true causes of all theft and violence against human beings. Personal influences and judicial punishments are helpless against such a reality.

"Individual efforts are useless against the power of the social structure," Bardina would tell me as we paced the corridor of the upper floor of the Russian House in Zurich. "Consequently, we should direct all our resources not toward ameliorating the plight of isolated individuals, nor toward doctoring individual cases, but rather toward the struggle to subvert the social institutions that are the source of all evil. We must struggle against man's exploitation of man, against private property, against inheritance rights. All of these must be abolished," she said.

The books I was reading by Proudhon, Louis Blanc, and Bakunin told me the same thing.

It was easy enough to say, "Abolish inheritance rights," but I must confess I was sorry to part with them. I fully admit the selfishness of this feeling: I didn't want to find myself suddenly empty-handed. My father had bought some land when it was very cheap—ten or eleven rubles per *desiatina* [2.7 acres]—right after the peasants were emancipated. This land had gotten much more valuable, and in time I would inherit a part of it. How could I rebel against inheritance rights? I had a desire, a powerful instinct, to own property, even if only in the future; I certainly didn't want to stay poor. But logic led me inexorably to the conclusion that the money my father had once spent for land had been blood money. There was no avoiding it; still, I would need a great deal of time before I could rid myself of the desire to hold on to what I considered mine, or reconcile it with the new idea that labor—physical labor—is the basis of everything, that it creates all material wealth.

When people of our circle spoke of the nation's wealth, they rarely referred to the contributions of intellectual labor; the issue was discussed exclusively from the point of view of its disproportionately high compensation in comparison to that of onerous physical labor. Intellectual labor was also condemned because of its origins: it was possible only because certain conditions allowed some groups in society to liberate themselves from the burden of physical labor by shifting it to others, thus gaining the leisure to cultivate science and art. And so we placed the highest social value on physical labor, concluding that it alone was moral and pure. Laborers alone exploit *no one*—quite the contrary, everyone exploits *them*, thus committing an enormous social injustice.

But how would it be possible to do away with private property, or to abolish the rights of inheritance, when everyone wanted to keep what he had? Everyone would defend his property, and those who feasted at life's table would never *voluntarily* agree to relinquish their privileges!

Both the program of the International Workingmen's Association and socialist writings in general declared that the only way to subvert the existing order was social revolution. These two words embraced *everything*; they were complete and convincing unto themselves, without any further details. Social revolution would turn everything upside-down. The people would rise up (and we were sure that the army would at this point desert to their side) and *proclaim* the abolition of private property and inheritance rights. The land, the factories, and the mills would be declared public property. After the social revolution, everyone would have to perform physical labor. Everyone would have to labor six to eight hours per day; in their spare time, they would be able to do intellectual work or simply to enjoy themselves. Their needs would be satisfied by the product of their labor—which would be at the disposal of society as a whole. No one would need inheritance rights, because children would be raised and educated at the expense of society and not their parents. Society would also care for the sick, the elderly, and the crippled.

All of this seemed clear, simple, and easy. I was captivated by the picture of Fourier's phalansteries.[10] The formula "from each according to his abilities, to each according to his needs" seemed a miraculous solution to all the complicated questions about organizing production and consumption. In the mills and factories, laborers would continue their business—the business of production—naturally, without even the slightest disruption of routine; they would then bring the products of

---

[10] Phalansteries, as described by the socialist Charles Fourier (1772–1837), were communes in which men and women would be equal and social life would be governed by the "laws" of human nature.

their labor to public stores. Meanwhile, the peasants, having made the gentry's land communal property, would till the fields as before, bringing the grain to public warehouses. Then, factory and agricultural labor cooperatives would begin to exchange their products, evaluating them according to the amount of labor expended on them. All these labor cooperatives would form a free federation of free communes—the ideal of Bakuninist anarchism.

Only people who had lived in comfort before the revolution would find life difficult after it. It would be hard on those who had worked only with their heads and were not at all accustomed to physical labor. But here, too, Fourier was helpful, pointing out that even children could perform many of the easier tasks and could be useful to society. And since work would be required from each *according to his ability*, those who were weak would be assigned the easiest kinds of work.

Everything we read about seemed easily implemented and highly practical. To us, the word "utopia" did not exist: there were simply various "plans" for social revolution. Nobody raised objections: you could say that we were unanimous in our enthusiasms. Those who were less entranced—or not entranced at all—kept their distance, introducing no dissonance to the reigning harmony. We believed that all these new ideas of democracy and economic equality were, logically speaking, totally invulnerable, and that those who questioned them did so only out of egotism or cowardice.

If these ideas had not been subject to persecution in Russia, then it might have been possible to examine disagreements or doubts about them on their merits. However, those who defended and preached the ideas were indeed being persecuted, while all those who valued their own personal well-being were unable to accept them, for reasons of self-preservation—because to accept them meant to put them into practice. Those who were reluctant to forgo their privileged position, who could not find the strength to renounce it for the good of the people, would cry, "It can't be done! You're all daydreamers!"

"You go talk with the people a bit; you'll be the first to be strung up if there's a revolution!" I was told by Mrs. Shcherbatov, the wife of a justice of the peace, who seemed both old and out-of-touch to us twenty-year-olds.

*Well,* I thought, listening to her, *aren't you afraid that the peasants will hang you!*

In the circles I frequented most, the idea of social revolution played an enormous role. It was one of the ideas to which we'd grown accustomed, and, apparently, no one doubted that the revolution would come soon. There was no real reason for such confidence, but everyone was convinced nevertheless that the time was at hand. We looked hopefully to the Russian people. There had been great popular explosions in the past. In fact, from the outset, the entire history of serfdom had been the history of popular protest. In the most recent past, peasant riots had occurred sporadically throughout the first half of the nineteenth century. And hadn't the tsar himself said, before he emancipated the serfs, "It is better to free the serfs from above, than to wait for them to free themselves from below." In fact, the peasants had not been satisfied by the Emancipation; it had proved to be only a new form of slavery. Still dissatisfied, the people were waiting for a new emancipation, one that would give them all the land this time.

Bakunin proclaimed—and this was the predominant opinion in our circles—that their very position made workers and peasants socialists and revolutionaries. With this optimistic view, it was easy for us to face the future. "But if the people are ready, how come they're not revolting?" someone would always ask. The answer was that the people were divided; they were disorganized and weighed down by police oppression, which crushed every initiative. Therefore, it was the intelligentsia's role to bring its knowledge to the people, to organize them and to help them unite for rebellion.

Despite our absolute certainty of the masses' revolutionary mood and readiness to act, despite our belief in the proximity of a social revolution and in its ultimate victory over the entire existing order, we made a strange distinction between our own

fates and the radiant prospects of the revolution. About ourselves, we were always pessimistic: we would all perish; they
would persecute us, lock us up, send us into exile and hard
labor (we didn't even think about capital punishment then!).
I don't know how the others felt, but for me that contrast between a radiant future for the people and our own sad fate was
extremely influential when I was considering how to apply my
socialist beliefs in practice. That contrast was always an emotional undercurrent in the stream of ideas that flowed freely in
Zurich.

If not for the persecution, I'm not at all certain that I would
have become a socialist at that time.


Spring vacation of 1873 came as a welcome break. Lay-
ing aside our histology and physiology textbooks, eight of us
women students got on a train and left Zurich to spend a few
weeks in different surroundings. For some reason, we had
chosen Neuchâtel—which wasn't especially picturesque—for
our vacation: perhaps we were drawn there because it was the
home of an eminent member of the International, James
Guillaume, whom the Fritsche group had met at a congress
of anarchists in St. Imier.

When we reached Neuchâtel our first goal was to appease
the voracious appetites we had developed on the trip. We
entered a restaurant, which was completely empty, and settled ourselves around a table as if we were at home. The soup
was served, then a second course arrived—but what in the
world was it? The whole dish was just a mass of little white
backs, with pairs of tiny white legs attached! Were they some
sort of bird, we wondered? Was it possible they were baby
chicks? "Something's suspicious," the younger Liubatovich
grumbled. "Could they really have exterminated so many
chicks?" Kaminskaia grieved.

"Auntie," we whispered, "ask the proprietor what kind of
dish this is. We won't eat it until we find out."

Several of the Fritsche had nicknames. We called Bardina
"Auntie" on account of her reliability and diplomatic talents.

Vera, the younger Liubatovich, was called "Wolfie" because of her morose stare and her habit of swearing "by the devil" and "by the bourgeoisie." For her insatiable appetite, Olga, the older Liubatovich, was jokingly called "Shark," and Dora Aptekman was nicknamed "Hussar" because of her masculine appearance.

Bardina placed her pince-nez on her pointy nose and posed the question.

"Those are frogs' legs, Madame!" the proprietor answered.

Of course no one would touch them, and our host removed the dish, amazed that we would scorn such a delicacy.

After we satisfied our hunger, and indulged in a good laugh over the frogs' legs, we set off together to explore the area, escorted by a pack of street urchins who shouted, "That's not a woman, it's a man!" at the sight of our "Hussar."

We wound up in Liutri, a village three or four kilometers from the city, on the shores of a lake. It was an unprepossessing hamlet, and the lake was one of the least appealing we had seen in Switzerland: its shores lacked mountains, the finest ornaments of a Swiss landscape, and the water had neither the blue nor the green hue characteristic of the country's lakes. But however undistinguished the village, it did have a boarding school for young ladies, who at the moment were off on vacation. We rang the bell and were greeted by a person resembling a class woman[11] in our own Russian girls' schools: an old maid, wearing glasses, with the stern expression of a schoolteacher. This was Mlle. Auguste, the woman who ran the school.

None of us was over twenty-one, and many of us had short hair and so appeared even younger—indeed, we could have been taken for a bunch of those very schoolgirls who were in Mlle. Auguste's charge. She surveyed us critically, asked who we were, and inquired about our plans; then she went inside to confer with her mother, a good-natured old woman who had charge of the household. Mlle. Auguste returned with an

---

[11] Class women (*klassnye damy*) were monitors, responsible for the behavior and study habits of the students, whom they accompanied to all their classes.

affirmative reply, and for a moderate price we installed ourselves in that tranquil refuge for young spirits. The dormitory
—we got two rooms with eight beds—was at our disposal, we
ate in the dining room, where they fed us quite meagerly, and
if we liked, we could spend the entire day in the garden. The
dormitory was crowded, but that didn't bother us: it was fun
to lie in bed in the morning and at night, chattering, joking,
and teasing each other. Sometimes the barbs would be aimed
at Auntie, sometimes at Wolfie, but most often at Hussar, in
whom we discovered some ludicrous eccentricities.

"Hussar! What time is it?" someone would shout from
beneath the covers. Hussar would remain silent, although she
was awake and was nearest to the clock.

"Hussar!" Wolfie would snarl. "Let's have an answer!"

Not a word from Hussar. We redoubled our shouts—in
vain!

At last, like the hissing of an old wall clock, our answer
came through the friendly laughter of the entire group: "You
know I don't talk in the morning!"

And we never found out what time it was.

Liutri was only a stone's throw from Neuchâtel, where Guillaume was leading a section of the International. How could
we miss the chance to attend a meeting, listen to Guillaume
and the debates among the workers, and finally walk out to
the strains of the revolutionary Carmagnole?[12] And so, one
ill-fated evening, while I stayed home with another girl, my
friends set out for Neuchâtel. The evening ended up in a
scandal that rocked all of Liutri: Russian opinions came into
conflict with Swiss customs.

Of course, the meeting of the section didn't start before
eight or eight thirty at night, after the working day had ended
and supper was over. It lasted until eleven, and then my
friends had to travel three or four kilometers to get back to
Liutri. By that time our little village was lost in darkness; in

[12] The Carmagnole was a song and dance popularized by the French revolutionaries of 1789.

fact, citizens went to bed early all over Switzerland. The lights were out in our boarding school as well. The village bell had rung ten—the fateful hour when all decent Swiss folk were in their beds—but our ladies still weren't home! It got to be ten forty-five, then eleven . . . Mlle. Auguste, alarmed, came to our room and demanded an explanation. It was indecent for young ladies to roam the streets at night, she cried; our friends were compromising not only themselves, but also the school that was sheltering them. After such a scandal, who would want to send their daughter to her school? It was twelve o'clock—midnight!—and the ladies she'd welcomed into her home still hadn't returned!

To top it all off, a storm had gathered and the rain started pouring down. Mlle. Auguste's mother was so upset she couldn't sleep, and the half-empty house, with frightened people constantly running over to the windows, seemed to us charged with electricity. All the complaints and cries of the well-meaning Swiss pedagogues were borne by the two of us who had stayed, and we began to get nervous ourselves: perhaps something really had happened to the tardy travelers?! We waited and waited.

Finally they arrived, excited and soaked to the skin. A torrent of reproaches fell on their frivolous heads, and none of Auntie's diplomatic talents, which had always saved us at difficult moments, could help us through this delicate situation. As I recall, we were asked to leave that quiet refuge as soon as possible, but in any case we had only planned a brief stay in Liutri, and as it happened, the incident was soon forgotten.

But see what the force of conviction can do: Aptekman, the Hussar, began to propagandize Mlle. Auguste, who quickly became attached to the Russian girl and was converted to socialism. The bugbear of nihilism,[13] which had reared its head when the young students returned home after midnight was banished, and thereafter Mlle. Auguste was ready to do anything—even break the law—for Aptekman.

[13] Russian nihilists were known for their rejection of traditional mores and values.

In 1873, at the close of the spring semester, the Russian newspaper *Government Herald* published a directive concerning the women students in Zurich. Hypocritically bemoaning the passion of young people for revolutionary and communist ideas (it was no accident that a reference to our debate on Stenka Razin and the Paris Commune was inserted), the Russian government forbade women students to remain in Zurich any longer. If they proved obstinate, the government threatened to bar them from licensing examinations in Russia. This directive depressed us all. After our great efforts, it deprived us of the goal that had brought us to Zurich. We had wasted our energy—our knowledge would never be applied in practice. Our plans to work for the good of society had been destroyed. And, as if that were not enough, the government had even resorted to filthy slander: the directive declared, for all the world to hear, that under the guise of studying science, the women students were practicing free love and using their medical knowledge to destroy the fruits of that love. That accusation we found the most offensive of all. We were hurt and angry at being driven from Zurich, forced to scatter and to abandon our university studies, but that, at least, did not impugn our honor.

After we had considered the practical side of the matter and had read the text of the government decree more carefully, we found an easy way of circumventing the threat: the circular referred only to Zurich, saying nothing about other universities abroad. In the future, only those who remained in Zurich would lose their rights. In fact, those who wanted to continue studying abroad took the obvious solution, moving to other cities.

But we, the younger, more radical women, could not remain silent about the accusation of immorality; we wanted to protest that slander, and protest publicly, in the newspapers. Once again a meeting was called solely for women. This time we were not meeting to learn to speak logically, but to cry out: "Don't slander us!"

The meeting in the Russian House was crowded. Everyone came, even women who usually stayed away out of prudence, or because they were too busy. Disagreements and conflicts of interest were immediately apparent: we first- and second-year students energetically defended the idea of a protest, while the party of "complacent bourgeois liberals"—women who were closer to finishing their program—tried to prove how inadvisable, dangerous, and futile such a step would be. After passionate debates, they finally declared that if we printed a protest, they would sign and publish a counterprotest. We were outraged, both by their moral stance and by the fact that our public statement would not be effective unless everyone signed it.

The meeting broke up late that night, after stormy, bitter debates. Not only would we have to endure public insult without a murmur, we had been beaten down by our own comrades.

The government's directive destroyed the student community in Zurich, thwarting our plans and scattering us all in different directions. But before we left Zurich, the Fritsche group drew up a modest program with a set of regulations to formalize our little association, which hitherto had rested solely on unspoken agreement. In a general way, this document formulated the socialist goals of the organization and the means to be used to bring them about. As I recall, these few paragraphs were an exact copy of the organizational principles of the Swiss section of the International: pallid and nondescript, they totally ignored Russia's political and economic conditions.

But could anyone really have expected us to understand our native land? We were all young, fresh from boarding school, when we went abroad and settled in a free country—an environment totally alien to Russia—as if it were our natural element. Everything we saw, heard, or learned about Western European conditions and attitudes we interpreted as being totally applicable to Russian life—to the Russian village, to the Russian factory, to the Volga peasant and the worker of Ivanovo-Voznesensk. The initial program, naïve and unsophisticated, which the Fritsche group drew up and adopted in Zurich, inevitably reflected our total estrangement from everything native, everything Russian.

Once we had a charter, the next step was necessarily practical activity. The most pressing question thus became the form of activity the Fritsche group should adopt when they returned to Russia.

Our circle in Zurich had arrived at the conviction that it was necessary to assume a position identical to that of the people in order to earn their trust and conduct propaganda among them successfully. You had to "take to plain living"— to engage in physical labor, to drink, eat, and dress as the people did, renouncing all the habits and needs of the cultured classes. This was the only way to become close to the people and get a response to propaganda; furthermore, only manual labor was pure and holy, only by surrendering yourself to it completely could you avoid being an exploiter. Consequently, from both the ideological and practical perspectives, you had to leave the university, which led to a doctor's diploma, renounce your privileged position, and go to work in a factory or mill in Russia.

Most of the Fritsche resolved to do precisely that. Student concerns became extraneous to them, and by 1874—within a year after they left Zurich—they had set off for Russia.

I was a renegade on this issue of manual labor. But before I could make up my mind and tell my comrades that I wouldn't join them in Russia, that I would stay at the university, I went through a period of emotional turmoil.

Was it really necessary, I asked myself, to become a factory worker, no matter what? Did I really have to renounce the position, the tastes and habits of a member of the intelligentsia? But on the other hand, could I in all honesty refuse to simplify my life completely, to don peasant dress and felt boots like a peasant, or to cover my head with a kerchief and pick through foul-smelling rags in a paper factory? Would it be honest of me to hold a position as a doctor, even if I were also conducting socialist propaganda? Finally, would it be honest of me to continue studying medicine while the women around me—also of the educated class—were abandoning their scientific studies and descending to the depths of our society for the sake of a great ideal?

I could see clearly all the beauty of my friends' consistency and sincerity, and I knew they would be doing the very best sort of work. It tormented me that I couldn't bring myself to do it, too, that I didn't want to become a worker. For so many years I had longed to go to the university; I had been studying so long, and the idea of being a doctor had become so much a part of me. Now, even after my plans for engaging in cultural activity in the *zemstvo* had been replaced by the goals of a socialist propagandist, I still wanted the trappings of a doctor's life. A worker's life was horrible, inconceivable to me! The very idea made my blood run cold. But I lacked the courage to declare outright, "I don't want to." I was ashamed to admit it, and so I said, "I can't."

I found reasons, of course: "I'm not strong enough," I said. "Why, I asked, "must everyone enter the factories? Socialists can do other things, too, even in less 'democratic' positions. A *zemstvo* doctor might seem like just another master, remote from the people—but what about a paramedic [*feldsher*]? I'm studying and I'll continue to study in order to acquire knowledge, not a diploma. Once I know enough, I won't have to become a doctor, I can serve as a paramedic in a *zemstvo*—it will still be necessary for me to bring as much knowledge as possible to the village."

The Fritsche circle was tolerant of the individual opinions of its members. It is true that many of them held the most extreme views and—as if showing off for each other—we all chose as our heroes the most irreconcilable leaders of the great French Revolution. Some were enthralled by Robespierre, while others would settle for no less than Marat, the "friend of the people" who demanded millions of heads. Nevertheless, the original decree neither compelled us to pursue a particular kind of activity nor told us when to begin, and after the rest of the Fritsche group resolved to return to Russia and begin practical work, Aptekman and I, remaining behind to complete our studies, never heard a word of reproach or saw any sign of disapproval. However, as soon as the others left Switzerland, we two were completely cut off. We heard nothing about their talks and subsequent merger with a men's circle from the Caucasus, nothing about their contact with the editors of the *Worker*.[14] I found out about all this only after I had left for Russia myself.

The inclusion of the masculine element proved very beneficial to the Fritsche: the organization's plans for action became more practical. The men were also partly responsible for the fact that the regulations of the combined organization, after being reworked in Russia, became the first ones to be based on the principles of discipline and solidarity.

The revised plan of the "Moscow Organization,"[15] as it came to be called, was this: two or three members would take turns staying in the city, to act as an administrative center for the general affairs of the organization. Everyone else was to go off to the various industrial centers—Moscow, Kiev, Odessa, Tula, Ivanovo-Voznesensk, and Orekhovo-Zuevo— where, along with some workers from Moscow who had been propagandized by earlier activists, they would enter factories and mills.[16] There were no plans to go to the villages: it was difficult for women to get positions as workers there. Besides, the circle's primary goal was clearly defined as conducting propaganda among industrial workers. When they abandoned the factories twice or three times a year for field work or to return home to their families in the villages for the holidays,[17] they would in turn influence the people—the peasantry—

---

[14] The *Worker* was published by a group of Bakuninists in Geneva; it was the first attempt to found a working-class organ in the Russian language. It lasted a year, ceasing publication when the Pan-Russian Social Revolutionary Organization collapsed in Russia.

[15] Or the Pan-Russian Social Revolutionary Organization, as it called itself.

[16] Except for the men who were already workers before they were recruited, only the women in the organization actually undertook factory work.

[17] Factory workers in Russia were usually seasonal.

through oral and written propaganda. After propaganda had prepared the soil, there were to be local uprisings, which would then merge into a nationwide insurrection.

However, nothing went as planned. Everything fell apart in the very first stage.

In Moscow, Prince Tsitsianov and Vera Liubatovich served as the administration, while Bardina, Kaminskaia, and, for a while, my sister Lydia, took up factory work. Olga Liubatovich went to Tula and Alexandra Khorzhevskaia to Odessa; Anna Toporkova, Varvara Alexandrova, my sister Lydia, and two male workers were sent to Ivanovo-Voznesensk. But all these beginnings were quickly aborted. Lydia Figner and later Bardina and Kaminskaia had to slip away from the factories. It proved impossible for elegant young "ladies" dressed up as peasant girls not to attract attention in the miserable surroundings of a factory. Everything they did set them apart: their small, tender hands were unaccustomed to working, and ten or twelve hours of labor in an unsanitary workshop— Kaminskaia, for example, had to work with filthy rags in a paper factory—exhausted them beyond endurance. They couldn't even conduct propaganda, because the consciousness of their female co-workers was too low, and so, disguised in their worker's clothing, defying custom as well as the outright prohibition of the factory administration, they went to the barracks of the male workers to try to get them interested in books. They offered the material to everyone, but since very few workers were literate, they eventually resorted to reading aloud. The sight of a solitary young woman, reading in the filthy, ill-lit, stinking barracks to a circle of those workers who hadn't yet tumbled into bed, was extraordinary to behold. Since the women would permit no "fooling around," the workers couldn't figure out why they were there.

Factory routine frequently got them into trouble. For instance, when they left the factory on holidays, the "ladies" had to carry their revolutionary publications along in their knapsacks. They couldn't leave them in trunks in the barracks, where they might be found during a search or even by some accident; but on the other hand, workers' knapsacks had to be searched whenever they left the factory. Thus, as my sister was leaving the Gubner factory where she worked until she went to Ivanovo-Voznesensk, the factory guard tried to detain her and she barely managed to escape.

By 1875 the Moscow group was in jail. Nikolai Vasiliev, a worker, was captured on March 29, and Daria, the woman he lived with, led the police to the group's apartment, where everyone was immediately arrested. Subsequently, between May and September 1875, the organization's members in Ivanovo-Voznesensk, Tula, and Kiev, and the "administrators" who had remained in Moscow were all arrested.

At Ivanovo-Voznesensk the entire group was arrested shortly after they had begun their work at the factory. They had rented a small apartment, the kind usually occupied by laborers, and everyone lived together there as a work collective. It's unclear whether the police saw something suspicious about this, or whether they had somehow intercepted a letter that put them on the organization's trail; in any case, the police appeared unexpectedly and captured everyone. They found revolutionary literature in the apartment, and in order to shield her comrades, my sister Lydia immediately declared that all of it belonged to her. She was initially sentenced to five years at hard labor for this; but since all her comrades were living in Ivanovo-Voznesensk on false identity papers, they were given comparable sentences, too.

In Tula, the girlfriend of a local worker, assuming that he was cheating on her, made a denunciation to the police and led them to the apartment of Olga Liubatovich, with whom her lover was in contact. This was roughly similar to what had happened in Moscow.

After that, the "administration" of the Moscow Organization came crashing down. Prince Tsitsianov and Vera Liubatovich lived in an apartment where—just like everyone else in those days—they took no conspiratorial precautions whatsoever. Their apartment held a cache of revolutionary literature and a fully equipped "passport bureau": identity papers were cleansed with a solution that filled the rooms with a suffocating odor of chlorine, and false residency permits were concocted on the desk, in which stamps, ink, and an extensive correspondence were stored. Many people visited this place for one reason or another; the organization's sizable funds were kept there to be distributed according to need. The Subbotina sisters, who were members, had generously contributed this money, placing the whole of their large fortune at the disposal of the organization.[18] When the police raided the apartment, Prince Tsitsianov engaged in armed resistance—the first such action in the history of the revolutionary movement of the seventies.

At almost exactly the same time, Khorzhevskaia and Zhdanovich were arrested in the south, at a railway station where they were waiting to pick up a consignment of literature. They were caught with a complete text of the organization's program and statutes, and later it was all produced as evidence against them in court.

Of course, the members of the organization had established ties with various people, and the police zealously pursued all leads. Occasionally, they stumbled on the trail of people who actually had been involved in the Moscow Organization's work; in other instances, however, they contrived to tie in people who were not implicated at all. That's how the "Trial of the Fifty" came about. It included eleven of the women who had studied in Zurich; a twelfth, Kaminskaia, was not brought to trial, ostensibly because she became mentally disturbed during her preliminary detention. There was a rumor that the quiet melancholia from which she suffered would not have saved her from trial if her father hadn't given the police 5,000 rubles. After her comrades were sentenced, Kaminskaia's thwarted desire to share their fate led her to poison herself by swallowing matches.

By the fall of 1875 I was in my seventh semester of medical school in Bern. Since there were only nine semesters

---

[18] When he was arrested in Tsitsianov's apartment, Kardashev was caught with 10,000 rubles, which he had been given for one assignment—an indication of how much money the organization possessed.—Figner.

in the program, I was to start work on my dissertation within a year. But my life had reached a critical juncture.

Mark Natanson came to Europe that November, seeking to bring back to Russia the revolutionaries who had migrated west. He spent time in London and Paris, and when he got to Switzerland, he sought out Aptekman and me to tell us about the wretched state of the socialist cause in Russia. The Moscow Organization, including the original Fritsche group, had been destroyed, he told us; all of its members had been arrested and no one was left to continue their work. Nevertheless, wherever they had been active, they had established connections, and these had to be maintained. And so, in the name of the revolutionary cause and for the sake of comradely solidarity, he was inviting us to leave the university and come to the aid of our perishing comrades. These comrades, behind prison walls, were calling out to us, he said, to become their reinforcements in the emptying ranks of propagandists and agitators.[19]

Natanson's proposal took me totally by surprise. I had received no letters from my friends since they left; it had never even occurred to me that I might in general be needed in Russia, or that they in particular might need me. I had been moving toward my goal calmly and confidently, intending to begin my practical activity only after I'd finished my studies. Natanson's invitation came as a real catastrophe.

Once again I was forced to ask: What should I do with my life?

For the third time since I'd left the provinces and forsaken the peaceful country fields, I was plunged into painful introspection, faced with the sort of choices that decide the direction of one's life.

I had first been tormented by hesitation and doubt when I was passing from the secure camp of liberalism and complacent philanthropy to the uneasy sphere of revolution and

---

[19] When she returned to Russia, Figner discovered that this was untrue, that her comrades had never asked Natanson to convey a message to her, nor to request her to return to Russia.

socialism. I suffered torments for a second time when my sister and our friends were leaving for Russia. And now, after all that had finally passed and I had regained sufficient confidence to devote myself to what I was doing, now, for a third time, I was confronted with those disturbing moral questions, questions that demanded immediate answers. My soul was divided, my feelings were at war.

The Fritsche group had themselves demonstrated all the difficulties facing a woman of the intelligentsia who tried to become a laborer. Their experience showed how brief such unaccustomed activity would be—activity that put you in an illegal position from the very start, since you had to use false identity papers. The results of their noble attempt to become ordinary laborers did not encourage others to choose that method of approaching the people; henceforth, moderately "democratic" positions, such as I had chosen—that of a paramedic—were seen as providing opportunities for enduring work.

But if I was going to serve as a paramedic in a *zemstvo*, why did I need a doctor's diploma? If I had no intention of becoming a doctor, why did I have to finish school? All I needed was enough knowledge to carry out my duties and help the people—and I had that much already: surely three and one-half years of study were sufficient time for that. If I wasn't seeking the piece of paper that would publicly attest to my knowledge, why shouldn't I leave the university at once and rush to the aid of the revolution and my friends who were serving it?

And . . . suddenly I realized that the diploma, that piece of paper of which I'd been so scornful, was in fact precious to me: it enticed me and bound me. It would signify official recognition of my knowledge, evidence that I'd finished what I'd started, achieved the single, absolutely fixed goal I had pursued for so many years with such energy, constancy, and self-discipline. How could I retreat now, how could I abandon the program without finishing? I was ashamed to abandon it —ashamed in my own eyes and in relation to others. What would be the reaction of all the people who knew about my efforts, which had no precedent in our provincial backwoods? What about the friends and relatives who had sympathized with me, encouraged me, and sent me off to Zurich with their best wishes for my success in a pursuit that was still so new to women?

Yet, on the other hand, there was the revolutionary cause, which, I was told, also needed my energies! Locked in cells, bound hand and foot, my friends were calling out to me for help! Now that they had communicated their needs to me, could I ignore them and give preference to my pride, my vanity, and—alas!—my ambition? I had never admired these qualities in others and had tried never to let them rule me either, but now I realized how strong my vanity and ambition really were! Would I actually succumb to them? My self-esteem, my faith in myself demanded that I answer "No!" Nevertheless, it was painful; I regretted having to leave the university, regretted that I, Vera Figner, would never have the right to sign my name "Doctor of Medicine and Surgery."

I asked myself, did they really need me in Russia—for the revolutionary cause in general, and to maintain the contacts of the Moscow Organization in particular? This was the first time I'd met Natanson; I had never heard anything about him before, and he brought no letters of introduction—all he told me was that Varvara Shatilova, a relative of the Subbotina sisters, was the only one left in Moscow after the arrest of my friends, and despite her best efforts, she couldn't cope with all the problems facing her. The people she had managed to enlist to do some work had also been quickly arrested, and there was no one to replace them.

Rationally, I knew that either Aptekman or I ought to check things out personally to make sure that we were really needed in Moscow. Only one of us would have to leave Bern to do this, and if temperament counted for anything, Aptekman ought to be the one: she was calm and judicious, and would make a thorough examination of the existing conditions. If she found that the two of us weren't really needed, she would return and keep me from going. On the other hand, if I left the university to go to Russia, it could safely be predicted that I would never return.

But Aptekman remained silent; I could see that she didn't want to go.

Why couldn't I say to her: "There's no need for both of us to leave right now. You're cautious and level-headed—you go first and then write me to come, if it's necessary. If I go first myself, I'll never come back"?

But I couldn't say it. I was incapable of asking another person to do something I wouldn't do myself.

And so, with these feelings, I approached Aptekman and said: "You stay! I'll go alone and write whether it's worthwhile for you to come, too." That's how I made the decision that determined the course of my life.

The spiritual crisis I underwent in order to make this decision was my last. My personality had been formed and tempered during those years of struggle with myself. After the decision was made, my mind was finally at rest, and I vacillated no longer; I set to work without a backward glance. Social concerns had gained ascendance over personal ones for good. It was the victory of a principle that had been imprinted long ago on my thirteen-year-old-mind, when I read in the Bible "Leave thy father and thy mother and follow me. . . ."

I left the university without earning my diploma; I abandoned Switzerland, where I had found a new world of generous, all-embracing ideas, and, still feeling the effects of my recent emotional turmoil, set off for Russia. I was twenty-three years old.

On my way to my homeland, I stopped off at Geneva. There was a little café there, the Café Gressot, that was famous among the Russian colony, and whenever I was in Geneva, I visited this refuge for émigrés. During this final trip, I met three strangers among the usual guests there: Ivan Debagorii-Mokrievich, Gabel, and a young man whom everyone called the "Landlord." We were introduced, and they must have taken a fancy to me, because they invited me over to their place. We made our way to a squalid little garret. The place was a mess. They were evidently very poor: two cots served as beds for Gabel and Mokrievich, while the Landlord, who was younger, lined up three or four chairs to sleep on, using a few newspapers for his mattress and blanket; some sort of bundle—probably illegal literature—served as his pillow.

After we'd managed to make ourselves comfortable in this garret, my new friends began to propagandize me. All they knew about me was that I was a student, and so, to pull their leg, I pretended to be a total ignoramus. They talked to me about Russia and about revolutionary activity there—about how the people needed us to instill revolutionary passion, not theoretical propaganda; about how the people were on the verge of a general explosion, and how the intelligentsia had to be the spark that set it off. Ivan Mokrievich did most of the talking, and he spoke beautifully—with energy and enthusiasm. With his words he painted for me an inspiring scene on the immense canvas of Russia—a scene like the ones that had excited me in books I had read describing revolutions.

There would be a national uprising; the din of the tocsin would fill the villages and resound through the fields. Led by a mighty chieftain—another, modern-day Emilian Pugachev or Stenka Razin—a horde of peasants armed with scythes would abandon their homes, families, and fields and go into battle, to conquer or to die. I could see banners streaming, hear the people's army tramping. The people still trusted the tsar and regarded him as their benefactor, but this faith would become a powerful weapon in the hands of a popular revolutionary leader from the ranks of the intelligentsia; he would proclaim that he belonged to the tsar's family. And beside this glorious leader there would stand a beautiful woman, her hair flowing loose, a banner in her hand. . . . The people would capture arsenals and arm themselves, and the guns of revolution would begin to roar. The troops—who were the sons of peasants—would join the insurgents; the regular army would be smashed, the government overthrown. The landlords' country estates would be in flames, while the peasants took possession of the land. Smoking ruins would cover the earth that for so many centuries had been irrigated with the blood and sweat of the people, and a new, just social order would be born from the ruins, as the phoenix arises from the ashes.

All night long I listened to my hosts develop this theme. The beauty of their words, their revolutionary ardor and enthusiasm appealed to me. They all tried to persuade me to leave the university and, along with them, devote myself to the revolutionary cause in Russia. They mustered all possible arguments against my university education and any further stay abroad, fervently summoning me to return home with them. I listened.

Gabel began to expound the basic principles for a revolutionary organization: its members should be united by the strongest bonds of friendship and devotion, should share all joys and sorrows—particularly sorrows! In their attempt to demonstrate the indissoluble bonds of comradeship uniting the three of them, they told me about a recent incident.

In December, Geneva celebrates a three-day holiday called Escalade. During this time, any man can go up and kiss any woman he meets on the street. The young Russian émigrés were overjoyed at this opportunity and started kissing all the attractive women who crossed their path. The cause of the incident was this: Ivan Mokrievich rushed to kiss a beautiful Englishwoman who was walking beside a healthy young Englishman. Seeing his companion in the embrace of a stranger, the Englishman began to beat Mokrievich over the head with his walking stick. Mokrievich's companions saw their comrade in distress and rushed to demonstrate their solidarity by attacking the Englishman. The police intervened and took Mokrievich off to the police station. But hadn't Gabel and the Landlord vowed to share with their comrade sorrow as well as joy—and for as long as they lived? This was a golden opportunity to demonstrate their fidelity to their oath. Gabel and the Landlord demanded that they, too, be brought to the station and put in the lockup—which was, in fact, done. The misfortunes and torments of prison confinement were not, however, prolonged: all three were released the following morning.

Gabel related this episode in utter seriousness. I was appropriately attentive.

The conversation continued through the night; my hosts kept talking, trying to win me over, while I maintained the role of a politically naïve student. There was no time for sleep—it was already growing light. At that point, I took out my gold watch to check the time. The Landlord extended his hand, and, playing with the gold chain, said, "Give me your watch!"—probably to measure my attachment to material objects.

Both the watch and its chain were family heirlooms, the only ones I had taken with me when I left for Zurich. At the time, I had thought, *I'll sell them only when I'm in dire need.* Now, as the Landlord said "Give it to me," I was struck again by the poverty surrounding us; these émigrés hadn't even a centime. I took off my watch at once, and placed it in the Landlord's hand. The following day they sold it for next to nothing—a pitiful forty francs.

Now it was completely light, and the cafés were open. The four of us decided to go to the Gressot to have our morning coffee. But before we left the room I revealed my innocent hoax, laughing a little to myself because my new acquaintances had taken me for a novice, and had spent an entire night trying to convert me to their faith. With some ardor, I announced that I belonged to an organization whose members had been arrested in Moscow, and that I had already left the university, packed my things, and would be leaving for Russia in a few days.

I then asked when they themselves planned to return to Russia.

"We can't leave," Mokrievich said. "We'd really like to, but we have no money." He told me that he had originally left Russia for Herzegovina with his comrades to take part in the rebellion against the Turks. As it turned out, they made virtually no contribution to the rebellion: they were only a

burden to the mountain-dwelling Herzegovinians in their difficult military maneuvers. It reached such a point that the
mountaineers had to carry the Landlord around on their
backs, since the Russian volunteers weren't used to local conditions.

"And now," Mokrievich continued, "we're stuck here, and
we've almost lost hope. Since we've had no money, we've
been living on Gressot's credit and are terribly indebted to
him; and then there's the money we'd need for the three of
us to get back to Russia."

"How much would you need to pay off your debts and get
to Russia?" I inquired.

"Not less than six hundred rubles," Mokrievich replied.

"Well then, I'll get it!" I exclaimed. "And I'll send it as
soon as I get to Russia." I found it unbearable to think that
such outstanding revolutionaries, eloquent and bold, were
vegetating idly abroad on account of a mere six hundred
rubles. They were needed in Russia; there they would move
mountains to carry out their plans.

I never ceased worrying about getting them home. When I
arrived in Petersburg, I immediately began seeking the required money. I appealed to one wealthy acquaintance, enthusiastically relating the story of my meeting with the three
socialists who were uselessly stuck in Geneva, and the story
made no less of an impression on her than the meeting itself
had on me. I received the necessary sum at once.

My mother was just about to go abroad with two of my sisters—Evgenia, who had just finished school, and Olga, who
was still a little girl. I gave the money for Mokrievich to my
mother, but I was afraid that she'd be searched at the border,
and I didn't want to make her anxious, so I entrusted Olga
with the letter to Mokrievich, after impressing on her the
tremendous importance of the little note I had rolled up like
a scroll. Gripping it tightly in her hands, the eleven-year-old
girl jumped for joy at having been entrusted with such important business. Then, hitching up her shoulders in a way
that made me laugh, she yelled: "If they try to question me,
I'll say: 'Leave me alone! I'm a minor!' "

The note, meanwhile, contained only a few affectionate words.

The meeting with the three émigrés had really affected me: the night I spent in their company has stayed with me, partly because our encounter was so brief. Everything I had read about revolution in action—all the beauty and the pathos—I heard that night in animated and impassioned speeches. I found Mokrievich particularly interesting: he seemed remarkable, an implacable rebel. He had dressed Russian reality, that slovenly Cinderella, in the gold-brocaded finery of Cinderella the princess. . . . I was in ecstasy: his words took possession of my mind. Actually, at the time I made no distinctions between word and deed: I believed that whoever spoke with such energy and force would also have the strength to translate their words into action. I believed in the power of words and the might of the human will.

I was no prophet, however; I couldn't foresee that although Gabel would wind up in Siberia, in administrative exile, Mokrievich would start giving music lessons in Kiev, and eventually become a peaceful constitutionalist. And the Landlord, that proprietor of imaginary Spanish courts and castles, became an actual landlord after his lengthy stay abroad.

When Figner arrived in Russia, she found that there was nothing she could do to help her comrades of the Moscow Organization. She got her license as a paramedic (concealing her studies in Zurich, which were politically suspect), obtained a divorce from her husband, and set out to establish herself among the peasantry. Henceforward, her life was totally bound up with the revolutionary movement.

In the following pages, drawn from Figner's statement at her trial in 1884, she describes the stages in her political development.

When I returned to Russia and found that the movement had already suffered defeat, I underwent an initial crisis, but before long I was able to find a good number of people whose ideas were similar to my own, and whom I liked and trusted; together, we worked to develop what came to be known as the populist program. I then left for the countryside.

As the court knows, the goal defined by the populist program was the transfer of all lands to the peasant collective—a goal that was, of course, against the law. However, the revolutionaries who went to live among the people were to begin by playing a different kind of role: we were to engage in what is known in all other countries as "cultural activity."[20] I, for example, became a paramedical worker in a *zemstvo*. Thus, although I went to the countryside as a committed revolutionary, my behavior would never have been subject to persecution anywhere but in Russia—indeed, elsewhere I would have been considered a rather useful member of society.

In short order, I found that a whole league had formed against me. It was headed by the marshal of the gentry[21] and the district police officer, and included, among others, the village policeman and the clerk. They spread all sorts of false rumors: that I had no identity card, that my diploma was false, and so forth. When peasants were unwilling to make an unprofitable deal with the landlord, it was said that Figner was to blame; when the district assembly lowered the clerk's salary, it was alleged that the paramedic was responsible. Inquiries about me were made in public and in private; the district police officer came by to see me; some peasants were arrested and my name was raised when they were questioned; there were two denunciations to the governor, and only the fact that the chairman of the *zemstvo* administration interceded on my behalf spared me further trouble. I lived in an atmosphere of suspicion. People began to be afraid of me: peasants made detours through back yards when they visited my house. Finally, I was forced to ask myself: What can I do under these circumstances?

I'll tell you frankly: when I settled in the countryside, I was

---

[20] See the discussion of Land and Liberty in the Introduction, pp. xxvii–xxxi.

[21] The highest official elected by the gentry.

old enough to avoid making crude mistakes with people simply out of tactlessness, old enough to be more tolerant of the views of others. My goal was to explore the terrain, to learn what the peasant himself was thinking and what it was he wanted. The authorities had no evidence against me: they were just incapable of imagining that a person with some education would settle in the countryside unless she had the most dreadful aims. What I was actually being persecuted for was my spirit, my attitudes.

Thus, even physical proximity to the people had become an impossibility for me; not only was I unable to accomplish anything, I couldn't even have the most ordinary kind of contact with them. I began to wonder: *Perhaps I'm making mistakes that could be avoided if I move to another place and try again?* But as I reflected upon my own experience and gathered information about that of other people, I became completely convinced that the problem wasn't my personality, or the conditions of my particular village—the problem was the absence of political freedom in Russia. Hitherto, I had been concerned strictly for the peasantry and its economic oppression; but now, for the first time, I was experiencing for myself the drawbacks of Russia's form of government.

I had two options at this time: I could either take a step backward—go abroad and become a doctor, but a doctor for rich people, and not for peasants; or—and this was my preference—I could use my strength and energy to break through the obstacle that had dashed my hopes. Somewhat earlier, Land and Liberty had invited me to join up and work among the intelligentsia. I hadn't accepted at that time, because I'd already decided to work among the peasantry, and when I made decisions, I stuck to them. Now, out of bitter necessity and not through any lack of serious consideration, I was finally relinquishing my original views and embarking on another path. When I was ready to leave the countryside, I announced to Land and Liberty that I considered myself free of any obligations and wanted to join the party. I was invited to the Voronezh Congress [June 1879].

At this time, various people were beginning to suggest that

the element of political struggle had to play a role in the tasks of the revolutionary movement. Two factions, drawn in different directions, had emerged in Land and Liberty. Although the party didn't split at the Voronezh Congress, everyone's position became more or less clear: some people said that we had to continue working as before—i.e., that we must live in the countryside and organize peasant uprisings in particular localities; others asserted that we should live in the cities and direct our activities against the central government itself.

Shortly thereafter, when the party finally broke up, I was invited to become an agent of the Executive Committee of the People's Will. I agreed. My past experience had convinced me that the only way to change the existing order was by force. If any group in our society had shown me a path other than violence, perhaps I would have followed it; at the very least, I would have tried it out. But, as you know, we don't have a free press in our country, and so ideas cannot be spread by the written word. I saw no signs of protest— neither in the *zemstvos*, nor in the courts, nor in any of the other organized groups of our society; nor was literature producing changes in our social life. And so I concluded that violence was the only solution. I could not follow the peaceful path.

Once I had accepted this proposition, I remained committed to it until the end. I had always demanded that a person—myself as well others—be consistent, that she harmonize word and deed. Thus, once I had accepted violence in theory, I felt a moral obligation to participate directly in the violent actions undertaken by the organization I had joined. In fact, the organization preferred to use me for other purposes, for propaganda among the intelligentsia, but I desired and demanded another role for myself. I knew I would be judged, both in court and by public opinion, according to whether I had participated directly in acts of violence. That is why I did the things I did. My deeds—deeds that some people might call "bloodthirsty" and might regard as terrible and incomprehensible, deeds that, if they were simply enumerated, might seem callous to the court—were prompted by motives that, to me in any event, have an honorable basis.

The destruction of the absolutist form of government was the most vital aspect of our program, the part that had the greatest importance to me. I really didn't care whether the regime was replaced by a republic or a constitutional monarchy: the crucial thing was that conditions be created under which people could develop their capacities and apply them to the benefit of society. It seems to me that under our present system, such conditions do not exist.

After the congress in Voronezh, I went underground, going through all the metamorphoses involved in that process, such as adopting a pseudonym. I settled in Kviatkovskii's apartment in Lesnoi for a while, but after the division in the party was finalized, we moved to the city. Under the name of Likhareva, I lived with Kviatkovskii in the apartment where he was arrested that November.

After completing its theoretical and organizational work, the Committee announced to the members its decision to organize attempts on the tsar's life at three different points as he was en route to the capital from the Crimea. Designated individuals were instructed to go to Moscow, Kharkov, and Odessa, respectively. Although all the attempts were to involve blowing up railroad track with dynamite prepared in advance, each team of agents was left free to determine precisely where and how it would act. The various plans they devised were to go to the Committee for confirmation. Agents could choose assistants from among the local people. Each agent was to be kept in the dark about the personnel and methods used at the other points.

In addition to all these operations, the Committee was preparing an explosion at the Winter Palace in St. Petersburg. None of us agents[22] were privy to this secret.

I was not among those assigned to carry out the assassination. However, the prospect of bearing only moral responsibility for an act that I had endorsed, of having no material role

---

[22] Members of the Executive Committee referred to themselves as agents in order to conceal their importance from the police.

in a crime that threatened my confederates with the gravest punishment, was intolerable to me, and so I made every effort to get the organization to give me a role in implementing the plan. After being reprimanded for seeking personal satisfaction instead of placing my resources at the disposal of the organization, to use as it thought best, I was sent to Odessa, where a woman was needed.

Early in September I left for Odessa with the supply of dynamite needed for the operation there. Nikolai Kibalchich[23] and I found a suitable apartment within a few days, and moved in as the Ivanitskiis. Soon Kolodkevich and Frolenko arrived; Tatiana Lebedeva followed. All meetings and conferences were held in our apartment; the dynamite was stored there, the gun cotton dried there, the fuses prepared, induction apparatus tested—in short, all our work was carried out there, under the direction of Kibalchich, but with the aid—sometimes the very vital aid—of others, myself included.

We decided that the best plan would be for one of our people to get a job as a railroad watchman and lay the mine from out of his cabin. I volunteered my services in obtaining the job. I went as an anonymous petitioner to see Baron Ungern Sternberg, an influential person in the administration of the Southwestern Railroad, and asked him to place a man I knew, representing this request as an act of philanthropy.[24] Sternberg couldn't help me, but he wrote a note to the engineer who was actually in charge of the post. I noticed that the reception given me by the baron was not the sort usually accorded to society people, and so I hastened to correct the mistakes I had made in my outfit before my next interview. I appeared in velvet, dressed as befitted a lady petitioner. This time, my reception was courteous in the extreme, and they asked me to send "my man" over the very next day. I went home and made up a passport for Frolenko in the name of Semyon Alexandrov, the name I had given to his future superiors. The next day, he went to the admin-

---

[23] See the selection by Praskovia Ivanovskaia, p. 114.
[24] This was a common practice at the time.

istrator of the railroad division and was assigned to a place eleven to thirteen kilometers from Odessa, near Gniliakov.

Frolenko was given his own cabin, and he brought Tatiana Lebedeva there as his "wife." We transferred the dynamite to him so that he could plant it under the tracks, but then Grigorii Goldenberg arrived unexpectedly and demanded that we send some of the explosives back to Moscow, since they didn't have enough there and the Moscow-Kursk railroad was the line that the tsar was most likely to use. We had to submit.[25]

A second operation was established in the vicinity of Kharkov. Here a group of seven spent weeks channeling under the tracks. By the time the two trains carrying the imperial party approached, the dynamite was in place, but it failed to explode when the detonating circuit was closed—apparently there had been a technical error. A day later, as the trains approached Moscow, a third attempt was carried out. The People's Will had purchased a small house adjacent to the railroad and had dug a tunnel from its cellar. The tsar's trains reached the ambush at about 10 p.m. on November 19. Sofia Perovskaia, who lay waiting in the bushes alongside the railroad tracks, allowed the first train to go by, assuming that it was testing the way; she gave the signal as the second train passed, and the resulting explosion derailed and destroyed it. As it turned out, the tsar had been traveling on the first train after all, and so he escaped unharmed. A fourth attempt took place in the tsar's residence itself. In September 1879, Stepan Khalturin, a skilled carpenter and member of the People's Will, had gotten a job on a renovation project in the Winter Palace. Along with the other workmen, he started living in the basement of the Palace. Despite the tight security surrounding the tsar, over a period of months Khalturin gradually smuggled in

[25] Goldenberg left Odessa for Moscow, but at Elizavetgrad he was arrested and proceeded to betray the party. Nevertheless, the party carried out the bombing on November 19 as planned.—Figner.

a substantial quantity of dynamite, which he stored among his personal belongings. He was able to determine the tsar's routine, and at dinnertime on the evening of February 5, when none of the other workmen were around, Khalturin lit a slow fuse and left the Palace. Moments later, the explosion resounded. A first-floor room was destroyed, and a number of soldiers were killed or wounded, but the royal dining room on the second floor was only slightly damaged.

Figner remained in Odessa after the operation there was abandoned.

Frolenko and Lebedeva soon gave up the cabin near Gniliakov, then left Odessa altogether. Kibalchich left the city in mid-December, Kolodkevich in January. The remainder of the more influential people went with them, and the party's work was turned over to me and a few little-known local people who proved so unsuitable that I had to get rid of them later on. But in any case, after Kibalchich's departure I rapidly established an extensive circle of acquaintances among all classes of society—professors and generals, landlords and students, doctors, civil servants, workers, and seamstresses. I advanced revolutionary ideas and defended the methods of the People's Will wherever possible, but my favorite sphere was the youth, among whom feeling was so strong and enthusiasm so sincere. Unfortunately, I knew few students personally, and those I did know were generally pessimistic about the rest, resolutely refusing to believe that there were good people among them.

In March or April 1880, Nikolai Sablin and Sofia Perovskaia arrived in Odessa. They announced to me that they'd been sent by the Executive Committee to prepare mines in Odessa, in the event that the tsar passed through the city en route to the Crimea. Meanwhile, I had been busy preparing another terrorist action—the assassination of Paniutin, right-hand man of the governor-general. Everything was practically ready, but Perovskaia's arrival with the Committee's instructions forced me to abandon this project.

Sablin and Perovskaia had come with a plan for the attempt: they were to choose the street most likely to be used by the sovereign in getting from the station to the steamship pier; to rent a store on this street and carry on a business as man and wife; and from this store, lay a mine under the pavement of the street.[26]

We found a shop on Italianskaia Street and began work immediately. We had to hurry; the sovereign was expected in May, and it was already April. Moreover, we could work only at night, since the shaft had to be laid from the store itself, rather than the attached living quarters, and of course customers were around during the day. Instead of digging, we proposed to use a drill. The work turned out to be very difficult: the ground was clay, and it choked the drill, which required enormous physical effort and even then advanced exceedingly slowly. At long last, we found ourselves beneath the paving stones: the drill bit moved upward and emerged into the light of day.

Shortly thereafter, Grigorii Isaev lost three fingers in an explosion caused by careless handling of mercury fulminate. He bore it like a stoic, but we were terribly upset—he should have stayed in the hospital.[27] After this incident, everything that we had been keeping at Isaev's—the dynamite, mercury fulminate, wire, and so forth—was brought over to my house, since we were afraid that the roar of the explosion in his apartment might have aroused the curiosity of all his neighbors.

So we had one less worker. I offered to bring some local people I knew into the operation, but everyone was opposed to this. We decided to stop using the drill temporarily, make a tunnel a few yards long, and then resume drilling. It was

26 In short, this was the very project that was later carried out on Malaia Sadovaia Street in St. Petersburg.—Figner. [That is, the successful attempt of March 1, 1881.]

27 Anna Iakimova, who was present during the explosion, acted promptly. She bound Isaev's hand, cleaned up the blood and pieces of flesh, and brought him to a *zemstvo* hospital. She even managed to be present during the operation, for fear he would talk under the anesthetic. [See also the Ivanovskaia selection, pp. 121–2.]

imperative to remove all the dirt as soon as possible, in the event that the houses along the tsar's route were checked. We got rid of some of it, and the rest was brought over to my apartment in baskets, packages, and bundles. After sending the maid off on errands, I would empty them in a place I'd found there.

But meanwhile, rumors of the tsar's trip died down, and the Committee instructed us to stop our preparations. We proposed taking advantage of the work we had done to blow up Count Totleben: at the time, we envisioned destroying the entire institution of governors-general[28] by systematically exterminating its individual representatives, but the Committee turned us down. It did give us permission, however, to make an attempt on the count's life by some other method, and so Sablin, I, and a few people I enlisted began following the governor-general around. We intended to use some kind of projectile, and if we had had the devices Isaev and Kibalchich invented somewhat later, the count certainly would have lost his life.[29] But all we had was dynamite and some unperfected fuses: any projectile we made would have been of awkward size and might not have been accurate. Even so, we would have carried out our plans if Count Totleben hadn't been transferred out of Odessa. After he left, all our preparations had to be liquidated. First we covered the tunnel with the earth we had extracted. I helped with this work, which wasn't very difficult: at night I would drag sacks of dirt from the living quarters and lower them into the basement, where the men trampled down the loose earth. We closed up the shop on Italianskaia Street. When everything was in order, Sablin and Perovskaia left. Isaev and Iakimova followed.

Through them I transmitted a request to the Committee, asking that they recall me from Odessa and designate a person to whom I could transfer local party business and contacts. However, I left for St. Petersburg—it was July, I think—

[28] In the spring of 1879, the government attempted to subdue the revolutionary movement by establishing six special regional commands, each headed by a governor-general who was given far-reaching powers over civilian life.

[29] These bombs were used for the first time on March 1, 1881.

without a successor's having arrived. I was greeted with a reprimand for my absence without leave, which had destroyed the possibility of effecting a personal transfer of contacts to the new agent.

*In February 1880, in response to the bombing of the Winter Palace, Alexander II had created the Supreme Administrative Commission, headed by General Loris-Melikov. Until then, repression had been relatively indiscriminate; the most timid criticism of the regime could bring harsh penalties, and as a result much of liberal society had become sympathetic to the revolutionaries. Melikov's regime—the "dictatorship of the heart," as it became known—made repression more selective and rational, focusing its full force on known revolutionaries and on them alone, while offering limited concessions to the liberals: a greater voice in public life at the local level, less stringent censorship, and certain positive measures in the area of education.*

*The People's Will did not accept Loris-Melikov's policies as evidence of the regime's commitment to fundamental reform. However, as indiscriminate police repression was curtailed, the possibilities for propaganda and organizing increased significantly, and the party moved to take advantage of them.*

The period from the fall of 1880 through the beginning of 1881 was one of intensified propaganda and organizational work for the People's Will. The absence of police harassment and gendarme searches during this period made work among the students and factory workers a lot easier: in St. Petersburg itself, propaganda, agitation, and organizing were being conducted on a massive  scale. Everyone was animated and hopeful. The depression that had appeared as a result of the failures of the early 1870's and the ensuing reaction was gone without a trace. The demand for regicide still resounded loudly, because the policies of Count Loris-Melikov deceived no one: the essence of the government's attitude toward society, the people, and the party hadn't changed a bit—the count had merely substituted milder forms of repression for crude, harsh ones. And so the Executive Committee devised another assassination: a shop would be rented on one of the streets in St. Petersburg most frequently used by the tsar, and from there, a mine would be laid for an explosion. I proposed to the Committee that my friend and comrade Iurii Bogdanovich serve as the store's proprietor, and he was accepted for this role [Anna Iakimova posed as his wife]. Meanwhile, the Committee's technicians were working to perfect explosive projectiles: these were to play an auxiliary role in land-mining operations, which had hitherto proved inadequate.

As for me, I didn't know the location of the shop, or Bogdanovich's alias—"Kobozev"—until the end of February, when I had to make up duplicate identity papers for him. My role during this period was propaganda and organizing. I participated as an agent of the Committee in two organizational groups that operated in two different spheres; I also went with Zheliabov from time to time to speak to military men—his special area of involvement. In addition, the Committee designated me secretary for foreign communications in the fall of 1880. The bombings of 1879 and 1880 had stimulated tremendous interest among all strata of Western European society, and in view of the importance that European public opinion could have for the party, the Committee decided to publicize our goals and aspirations abroad and acquaint Europe with the Russian government's domestic policy. I sent party reports, biographies and photographs of revolutionaries who'd been executed or imprisoned, revolutionary publications, and Russian journals and newspapers to Lev Hartman;[30] later, after March 1, I sent him a copy of the Executive Committee's letter to Alexander III[31] and a drawing showing the inside of the Kobozev store, done by Kobozev—that is, Bogdanovich—himself.

In January 1881 the Executive Committee suggested that

[30] Hartman, a participant in the November 19 train bombing in Moscow, was forced to flee abroad because the police were on his trail.
[31] In mid-March 1881, the Executive Committee set forth its political demands in a letter to Alexander III, son and successor of Alexander II.

Isaev and I establish an apartment exclusively for its members. We found a place, and lived there together as the Kokhanovskiis. During February, a series of important meetings were held on alternate days at this apartment. The Executive Committee had called together its agents in the provinces, Moscow, and St. Petersburg and asked them for detailed accounts of the state of party affairs in all localities and spheres of activity. These, in turn, were summarized in one general account and presented by the Committee to the assembly of agents, who were invited to express their opinions on certain internal organizational questions, as well as on the party's over-all policy. In particular, the Committee wanted to know whether the agents considered the party organization sufficiently strong and extensive, and the public mood sufficiently favorable, for the question of insurrection to be placed on the agenda immediately—that is, should all subsequent party work be aimed at fomenting an insurrection in the immediate future, and should the central group devote itself to elaborating a serious, detailed plan for that insurrection? By a huge majority, the agents responded that a practical formulation of the question of an insurrection was indeed warranted. At the conclusion of the meetings, the agents were dispersed by the Committee to begin work pending new, detailed instructions.

Several months earlier, in November 1880, Alexander Mikhailov had been arrested. This was an irreparable loss, one we remembered whenever misfortune struck us. Mikhailov had guarded party security from within: he was the organization's all-seeing eye, the guardian of the discipline so essential to the revolutionary cause. Now, around the time of the February meetings, we lost the one remaining person most valuable to the organization, the external guardian of its security: Alexander Kletochnikov, who had made his way into the government's Third Section,[32] and, for the past two years, had helped to ward off the government's attacks against the party by warning us in advance.

By this time, the tunnel in the Kobozev store had been com-

[32] The political police.

pleted. One Sunday in mid-February, the tsar passed by the Kobozev shop on Malaia Sadovaia on one of his weekly visits to the riding hall. There was general dismay in the party that we had missed this opportunity because the mine wasn't ready yet: we might have to wait a whole month before he passed by again. The Committee ordered that all work both on the mine and on the projectiles be completed by March 1. By that date our agents had been familiarized with the plans: there would be an underground explosion as the ruler was passing, and in case the explosion didn't coincide with the tsar's passage, or proved too weak to achieve its intended goal, people stationed on opposite sides of the street would throw explosive shells. We also knew that the personnel involved in the attack had already been chosen. Beginning March 1, we were to expect the attempt on each and every Sunday.

I don't remember the twenty-seventh of February at all, but the twenty-eighth is clear in my memory—I think because Andrei Zheliabov was arrested on the evening of the twenty-seventh, and on the morning of the twenty-eighth, Sukhanov brought us the news at our apartment.

On the twenty-eighth, the Committee sent Isaev to the Kobozev store in order to lay the mine. That same day, we learned that not one of the projectiles was ready yet; furthermore, the people responsible for the apartment where all the technical operations were to be carried out had announced the evening before that they thought their apartment was being watched. At the same time, a rumor was spreading through the city that the police believed they were on the trail of an extraordinary discovery in the very precinct where the Kobozev store was located. Some young people had conveyed to us a conversation overheard between the concierge of the Kobozev apartment house and the police concerning a search in the building; then Bogdanovich-Kobozev himself stopped by our place to tell us that the shop had been inspected by an alleged health commission that was obviously acting under instructions from the police. Although Kobozev told us the inspectors had turned up nothing—indeed, they had fully legalized him

—his story left us thunderstruck. It was clear that our mission —conceived long ago and brought nearly to conclusion through all the difficulties and dangers, the mission that was to climax the struggle that had bound our hands for two years—was hanging by a thread and might be thwarted on the eve of its execution.

We could have borne anything but that! It wasn't that we were worried about the personal safety of individual members of our organization—the party's entire past, our whole future, was at stake on the eve of March 1. There was no nervous system that could have tolerated such intense strain for long. Thus, when Sofia Perovskaia asked the Executive Committee how to proceed if the tsar did not go down Malaia Sadova on March 1, whether in that situation we should act with only the shells, the Committee responded, "Act in any case," and drew up a contingency plan. Sukhanov alone expressed some reservations, because the shells had never been used in action.

The Committee's decision was made on February 28. I was informed that three people would arrive at our apartment at 5 p.m.—Sukhanov, Kibalchich, and Grachevskii—and work on the shells all night.

During the early evening, agents stopped in at the apartment continually, some with news, others with routine requests, but this hindered the work, and so around eight o'clock they all dispersed. Five people were left in the apartment, including Perovskaia and myself. I persuaded the exhausted Perovskaia to lie down in order to marshal her strength for the following day; then I began helping the workers wherever an inexperienced hand could be of use—pouring metal with Kibalchich or, along with Sukhanov, trimming the tin kerosene cans I'd bought to serve as molds for the shells. I left them at 2 a.m., when my services were no longer needed. When Perovskaia and I got up five hours later, the men were still working. Two shells were all finished, and Perovskaia took them away; Sukhanov left shortly thereafter. I helped Kibalchich and Grachevskii fill the other two cans with detonating jelly, and Kibalchich took those away. And so, at 8 a.m. on the morning of March 1, four shells were ready, after fifteen hours of work by three people.

The Committee had instructed me to remain at my apartment until 2 a.m. on March 1, in order to receive the Kobozevs, who were supposed to abandon the store—he an hour before the sovereign passed, she after a signal that the sovereign had appeared on Nevskii Prospect. A third person was to activate the electric current; should he survive the explosion produced by his own hand, he was to leave the store, pretending to be an outsider. But the Kobozevs never showed up at my place. Instead, Isaev appeared, with the news that His Majesty hadn't passed by the store, and that he had proceeded home after finishing at the riding hall. I left the apartment, thinking that, for some unforeseen reason, the attempt hadn't been carried out. I totally forgot that the Kobozevs hadn't been notified of the Committee's final decision: to use bombs at a particular point on his return trip.

Everything was peaceful as I walked through the streets. But half an hour after I reached the apartment of some friends, a man appeared with the news that two crashes like

*The assassination of Tsar Alexander II*

cannon shots had rung out, that people were saying the sovereign had been killed, and that the oath was already being administered to the heir. I rushed outside. The streets were in turmoil: people were talking about the sovereign, about wounds, death, blood.

On March 3, Kibalchich came to our apartment with the news that Gesia Gelfman's apartment had been discovered, that she'd been arrested and Sablin had shot himself. Within two weeks, we lost Perovskaia, who was arrested on the street. Kibalchich and Frolenko were the next to go. Because of these heavy losses, the Committee proposed that most of us leave St. Petersburg, myself included. I wanted to remain, however, and so I argued with the Committee until it gave me permission. Unfortunately, my stay turned out to be a brief one.

On April 1, Isaev failed to come home. He was arrested on the street, like several other agents who'd been caught during March. To avoid worry and misunderstandings, we had previously agreed that the people responsible for the party's apartments were not to spend the night away from home without prior arrangement; consequently, by 12 midnight of April 1 I was certain that Isaev had been arrested.

For various reasons, our apartment had gradually become a warehouse for all sort of things: type and other printing equipment, all the utensils and a large supply of dynamite from the chemistry lab, half of our passport department, party literature, and so forth. Such resources could not be allowed to fall into the hands of the police: I decided to save everything and leave the apartment absolutely empty. During the afternoon of April 4, Sukhanov appeared, and with his usual efficiency, removed everything of value from the apartment in the space of two hours. He insisted that I leave the house immediately, but I saw no need to go before morning; I was sure Isaev wouldn't give the police our address. I stayed till morning, then, finding a suitable pretext to get rid of the woman who came to clean, I left, locking up the ravaged apartment. I've heard that the authorities arrived before the samovar I used to make tea that morning had cooled.

*Vera Figner before her arrest, 1883*

In the period after March 1, 1881, Vera Figner became the acting leader of the People's Will. She tried to restore the party to its former strength, securing funds, recruiting new members, and working to expand its organization among military units. But most of the other experienced leaders were in jail, and the party had been infiltrated by the police; on February 10, 1883, Figner was arrested.

In September 1884, at the Trial of the "Fourteen"—members of the People's Will who continued to be active after the assassination of the tsar—"Vera Figner alone succeeded in getting herself heard out. Both the judges and the public listened with uncommon attention, and the chairman of the tribunal did not stop her once," recalled a co-defendant, A. A. Spandoni.[33] She received the death penalty, but her sentence was subsequently com-

[33] A. A. Spandoni. "Stranitsa iz vospominanii." *Byloe*, No. 5. May, 1906.

*Vera Figner after her release from prison, 1906*

muted to life imprisonment. She spent the next two decades in the Shlisselburg fortress.

After the revolution of 1917 Vera Figner wrote extensively of her experiences as a revolutionary. She died in the Soviet Union in 1943.

# VERA
# ZASULICH

In July 1877, General Trepov, the governor of St. Petersburg, ordered the flogging of a political prisoner, Alexei Bogoliubov, for failing to remove his cap in Trepov's presence. Public outrage against this assault on human dignity was widespread. A revolutionary group in the South organized a squad of six men to assassinate Trepov. But it was Vera Zasulich, acting independently, who carried out the retribution. So as to avoid jeopardizing her comrades, she waited until the Trial of the 193 had ended; then on January 24, 1878, she went to Trepov's offices and shot him in full view of a roomful of petitioners. Henceforth, revolutionaries would meet violence with violence.

Vera Zasulich was born into an impoverished gentry family in 1849, the youngest of three daughters, all of whom subsequently became involved in radical politics. When Vera was three, her father died, leaving a small estate. Her mother proved unable to raise the children on her meager income, so she sent Vera to live with wealthy relatives, the Mikulich family of Biakolovo.

When Zasulich finished school at seventeen, she went to St. Petersburg and found a job as a clerk. The radical movement of the sixties was at its height, and Zasulich became involved almost immediately, joining a bookbinding collective and teaching literacy classes for workers. She soon got to know one of the most important leaders of the student movement, Sergei Nechaev. It was Zasulich's connection to Nechaev that led to her arrest in 1869, then four years of imprisonment and exile.

By the time she completed her term of exile, Zasulich had become a committed revolutionary. She joined the Kievan

Insurgents, a militant Bakuninist group in the south of Russia. Over the next few years she went "to the people" and worked in an underground press. Even before her shooting of Trepov made her a heroine both in Russia and abroad, Zasulich was greatly respected by everyone who knew her. Of her comrades in the Kievan Insurgents, only Zasulich had substantial revolutionary experience, and only she had endured prison and exile. As a friend later recalled, "Because of her intellectual development, and particularly because she was so well read, Vera Zasulich was more advanced than the other members of our circle. . . . Anyone could see that she was a remarkable young woman. You were struck by her behavior, particularly by the extraordinary sincerity and unaffectedness of her relations with others."[1]

Her memoirs begin with her childhood in the village of Biakolovo, under the care of her governess, Mimina.

---

Mimina had been educated in an orphanage, at the turn of the nineteenth century. She had probably been placed there right after her birth; in any event, she never had any family. She lived her entire life in other people's homes, raising other people's children. I was the first child to be completely in her charge; in Biakolovo, at least, I existed especially for her. She had been living at Biakolovo for ten or twelve years before I was born, and she had raised my aunts and my uncle. When their father died (their mother had died earlier), my eldest aunt was twenty, the youngest fourteen, and my uncle was sixteen.

Mimina had to remain at Biakolovo. Decorum required her presence—and she in turn demanded a child in the house as a condition for staying. She had finished raising Lulo, the youngest aunt, and she couldn't be left with nothing to do. That's how I wound up at Biakolovo.

She must have taken me in hand eagerly.

---

[1] Lev Deich. "Iuzhnye buntari," *Golos Minuvshago*, Vol. 9, p. 54.

I can recall my early childhood, but I can't remember when I learned to read and write Russian and French. I've been told that she contrived to teach me all that—and some poetry and prayers besides—when I was three years old.

Birching was not the custom at Biakolovo; I never heard of anyone being beaten there. Besides, they say I was very sweet and amusing then, and only got spoiled later. So when Mimina "beat" me—and then it was only lightly—it must have been simply to "improve" me. I don't remember feeling any pain, but I do remember that the operation had to take place on a bench in the bathhouse. First they would lay me down on that bench, then I would try with all my might to drag myself to the edge and roll underneath it; then they'd lay me on the bench again, and so it would go, endlessly.

When one of my aunts got married and had her own children, there was no longer any need for Mimina, or for me either. That was probably when I got spoiled.

Perhaps Mimina loved me in her own way—but it was a painful sort of love. When she was alone with me she was forever talking about something. She spoke mainly in French, and about serious, unpleasant, and sometimes frightening things. If I tried to get away from her, she made me return to my seat. She was fulfilling her duty when she talked to me: my duty was to listen and make use of her exhortations while she was still alive. I disregarded whatever bored me, but the things that frightened me stuck in my memory. "You'll be sorry when I die. You'll want to run away and see Mimochka then. You'll come to the cemetery: there'll be a little stream, two or three birches, and you'll weep real tears. That'll be a beautiful moment. I don't need any others. You'll come, see a crack in the ground, and look into it, and something horrible and revolting will look back at you from under the ground. You'll see a skull with bared teeth, but you won't see Mimochka anymore."

In her own way, she was well-educated for that time. Sometimes she'd recite verses for me instead of giving lectures: "A coffin stands where feasts were held. . . . Wraiths howl there above the graves." I had never even seen a grave, but I knew that they were long and terrible; I imagined crimson, disembodied wraiths hovering above them, crying "Ooooo" with gaping mouths. Among my terrors I also included an ode, "God," which Mimina declaimed so frequently that involuntarily I had learned it by heart by the time I was six. At night, if I hadn't managed to fall asleep before Mimina began to snore, that weird God, "Endless space—faceless in the Holy Trinity," would stick in my mind and, together with a skull, the wraiths, and other terrors, it would run through my brain against my will and keep me from falling asleep.

Mimina knew French poetry in a similar vein: "Oh, to him who opens all the heavens like a book." Later, I discovered that this had been written by Voltaire. I had already learned about atheists and Voltaireans from her, and I doubt she knew he had written it.

She was probably going through a difficult period at this time. From a comparatively honorable position—I still remember when food would be offered to her before everyone else at meals—she must have felt that her position was gradually being degraded to that of a hanger-on, even beneath a governess.

She was about sixty, with weak eyes, and she was so short and fat that she was almost spherical in shape. It was too late for her to find a new position, and there was no one but me she could discuss this with. She would be a hanger-on until she died. . . . She probably did some thinking about death, but not for very long. She lived another thirty-five years and was still alive at the end of the 1880's.

The fact that Mimina didn't want me to love my aunts was probably another expression of her love. Time and again she would say to me vehemently, "We don't belong here. No one will take pity on us." I remember vividly that it was just such speeches that grieved me most. I did not want to reconcile myself to being an outsider. I can even remember waging an unyielding battle against one boy, the son of a Cossack. He would stick his head out of the anteroom and whisper urgently. If one of the adults happened to turn around, the head quickly disappeared, only to re-emerge again. You couldn't hear anything, but it was obvious that he was whispering "Verochka Zasulich"; I would whisper back resentfully, in rhyme: "It's not true—Mikulich, Mikulich!"[2]

But the older I grew, the more I became convinced that I was indeed an alien: I didn't belong. No one ever held me, kissed me, or sat me on his knee; no one called me pet names. The servants abused me.

I must have been about eleven when a copy of the Gospels first appeared at Biakolovo. It was a newish book, without a binding; its pages hadn't even been cut. There had probably been earlier editions, but in Slavonic, and no one ever read them. Now every day during Lent I had to read aloud a chapter or a page. All my aunts, Mimina, the children, and even the nurses would listen.

Until then I had paid no attention to the content of religion; I hadn't even thought about it. I had occasionally enjoyed the practice of it, but mainly it bored me. Mimina taught me a few short prayers when I was three, and then added some slightly longer ones. It was my job to rattle them off in front of the icon twice a day, as quickly as possible. Before I was seven (my first confession) I learned the Credo and a brief sacred history in the form of questions and answers. I also knew how to cross myself, say a prayer and, once I'd finished, bow to the ground and run away. I didn't understand what I was saying, but I didn't care. During holidays we would often celebrate vespers and matins. This was quite boring, and it was impossible to amuse yourself: you were watched to see that you stood quietly and crossed yourself from time to time. Usually, I waited impatiently for the reading of the Gospel. In the first place, it meant the service was almost over, and secondly, it was fun. We children had to go up to the priest,

2 Mikulich was the name of Vera Zasulich's foster family.

the youngest first, me at the end. He covered us all with his stole, which rested on my head because I was the tallest.

"Good shepherd, Ye gave Thy soul for Thy sheep, but the hireling of God would not"—and I would see a long-legged hireling running along the floor, going somewhere in the darkness. But I never really cared what the point of it was. While I was standing there with my head covered, the questions: "What's going on? How did the shepherd 'give his soul' and where did the hireling run?" would pass through my mind. But as soon as the all-night service was over, my interest would end, too. I never asked the "big people" anything, since it always wound up with them scolding me. Mimina would have responded at great length, delighted to be questioned, but in the end she would have turned out to be the good shepherd, and I the sheep—and then only if I was lucky. At other times, I would have been the hireling who was always ready to flee when someone taught him or wished him well.

It was a joy to attend Mass. The church was five kilometers away, and we were taken rarely, and only in the summertime. I was also taken visiting at a neighboring landowner's place where there were children, and for walks in the forest. But the visits and the walks took place after dinner, while we went to church in the morning. Everything looked different then: there was a different sun and another sky, and I walked around in a fancy dress and a straw hat. There were icons in the corners of the church and stained glass windows which turned the incense smoke such pretty colors when the light fell on it, while spots of blue, yellow, and green strangely transformed the old women's scarves. Before I could even get bored there, they had already started to sing the final hymn. And of course, Christmas and Easter were the happiest times of the year. But somehow God and religion never took on real meaning for me.

I repeated, "I have a cross, I have a cross," on my own, when I was frightened in the dark. A housemaid who was also frightened taught me that one, assuring me that it helped— Mimina's prayers were of no use for this. There were other times when I rushed to pray, but those times I used my own words. This happened when I felt I was being accused or scolded unjustly; upset, in tears, shaking all over, I would stand in the empty room in front of the icon and whisper and whisper, sobbing all the while.

I don't remember expecting to get anything out of it or thinking that God would somehow take my part. I was simply protesting my innocence, almost reproachfully, to the "all-knowing": "But you know the truth, don't you? Did I ever do it?"

I remember I was caught once. One of my aunts followed me—probably she had found something to add to her lecture —and found me whispering in front of the icon. If I had told her what I was whispering, I think it would have made a favorable impression. But of course I wouldn't confess; when asked what I was whispering, I replied, "Nothing." It goes without saying that I received an additional lecture: "Don't you dare whisper your nonsense in front of the icon—you should turn to God only with prayers."

At first I didn't like to read the Gospels aloud. I would have read them on my own—at that time I read everything I could lay my hands on—but out loud, in front of grownups. . . . After a while, however, the content of the book began to intrigue me. I saw immediately that Christ was completely different from Mimina's incomprehensible, tedious, and rather frightening God, for whom one ate lenten food and muttered prayers. Christ was good and kind in a way I could understand easily. Since I knew that they killed Him in the end, I came to anticipate those chapters with impatience and a certain dread.

I don't know why Mimina locked the Gospels away between readings, but undoubtedly the book made a much greater impression on me this way than if I had read it all at once. For me, the God of the Gospels was neither abstract nor mysterious. That night in the garden of Gethsemane, when He told His disciples, "Don't sleep, my hour is near," but still they slept. . . . And all the rest of that poignant story. I lived with Him in my fantasies for several weeks; I imagined Him and whispered about Him when I was alone in my room. What bothered me most was that everyone, absolutely everyone had fled and abandoned Him, even the children who had greeted Him with palm branches and hosannas. They must have been sleeping and unaware. I could not help but intervene. One girl, a good girl, the daughter of a high priest, hears them say how they are going to seize Him (Judas has already betrayed Him), and how they will judge, then murder Him. She tells me, and we run at once to call the children: "Just listen to what they're going to do: Him! They're going to kill Him! And there's no one better than Him on earth!" My imaginary children agree. We take to our heels and race through the garden.

But nothing further happens. I dared imagine nothing further without His permission, and still less did I dare to speak for Him. And it was not from fear, but from a passionate love, almost a sort of awe. I knew He was God—He was God too, just like His Father, but He was much better. I didn't love that other one. I would never have prayed to Christ. What—pester'Him with my complaints? I didn't want His intercession, I wanted to serve Him, to save Him.

Four years later I no longer believed in God; I had parted with that faith easily. I was sorry at first to lose an afterlife, my "eternal life," but I felt regret only when I thought specifically about that wonderful garden in the heavens. Earth became no worse for me as a result. Quite the contrary. At the very time I lost my faith, I was defining my "life to come" on earth. How endlessly it stretched before me then: at fifteen, even one year seems an enormous amount of time. Of my earlier religious beliefs, only Christ remained with me, engraved in my heart. In fact, it was as if I were more closely tied to Him than ever.

How did I begin to acquire a vision of my life to come? It had gradually been taking shape before my eyes, feature by feature, for the longest time; it was still hazy and distant, shrouded in a radiant cloud, but it was undoubtedly my future. It seemed to me that I personally was being pushed to latch onto everything that smacked of the future. I was repelled by the fate that my social position held in store for me. They referred to it casually at Biakolovo: I was to become a governess. I could take anything but that! . . .

*At fifteen, Vera was taken to Moscow and placed in a private boarding school.*

Even before I had revolutionary dreams, even before I was placed in boarding school, I made elaborate plans to escape becoming a governess. It would have been far easier, of course, had I been a boy: then I could have done almost anything. . . .

And then, the distant specter of revolution appeared, making me equal to a boy; I, too, could dream of "action," of "exploits," and of the "great struggle." . . . I too could join "those who perished for the great cause of love." I avidly devoured all such references in poetry and in ancient songs: "Let us clasp hands quickly and vow to nurse to our graves our hatred of the scourge of our homeland." Sometimes I found what I wanted in poems that the author might have meant differently.

Somehow I had gotten hold of Ryleev's poem "Nalivaiko," and it became one of my holy relics.[3] "I know that ruin awaits the one who . . ." and so forth. And I did indeed know Ryleev's fate. Everywhere, heroism, struggle, and revolt were always connected with suffering and death.

"There are times, there are entire ages, when there is nothing more beautiful and desirable than a crown of thorns." That crown of thorns attracted me to those who perished, inspiring my passionate love for them, too. And undoubtedly, that love resembled the love I had felt for Christ when I read the Gospel for the first time. I had not betrayed Him: both He and they were great enough to merit a crown of thorns, but Christ was the best of all. I would seek them out and try to make myself useful to their struggle. Sympathy for the sufferings of the people did not move me to join those who perished.

---

[3] "Nalivaiko," a poem dealing with a Ukrainian uprising, was written by Kondratii Ryleev, one of the leaders of the Decembrist uprising of 1825. With four others he was condemned to death and hanged on July 13, 1826.

I had witnessed none of the horrors of serfdom and had always considered myself one of the poor—at first against my will, with a feeling of deep resentment, and then, later, almost with pride. And when I was living well, I considered that my misfortune, not a privilege.

I had never heard of the horrors of serfdom at Biakolovo—and I don't think there were any. The master's house had no contact with the village except on holidays. After the harvest, refreshments were set up in the courtyard. The "young ones" in their best clothes would come to pay their respects after every wedding. But Auntie never interfered with their farming; Kapisha—as his masters called him—took care of it, and looked after the domestics and the village.

The estate was one of the best organized in the district. The majority of peasants were on *obrok*[4] and went to Moscow— 120–130 kilometers away—to earn their living. Most of the estate's income, aside from *obrok*, came from the cattleyard, the stables, the poultry, the orchard, and the greenhouse. The village peasants had nothing to do with all this; it was handled by the house serfs, who were so numerous that their cottages took up an entire street. Our good relations with these house serfs are proved by the fact that no one ever ran away, and our household never changed. I know for sure that no one was ever punished—I would have learned of it from the children of the house serfs, and would surely have remembered. Perhaps this was a result of Kapisha's gentle regime.

It was easy for me to leave Biakolovo. I did not think then that I would remember it all my life, that I would never forget even one little bush in the front garden, one old cupboard in the corridor, and that the outline of the old trees, visible from the balcony, would appear to me in dreams in years to come. I loved it even then, but life beckoned to me, life in all its immensity, and in Biakolovo I was surrounded by "profound slumber," a stagnant existence that was not for me. Indeed, I had only come to terms with it by admitting that I was "alien." . . .

[4] A yearly fee paid to the landlord in cash, rather than in crops or labor.

That year, the seventeenth year of my life, was filled with the most feverish internal activity; at last I took my fate into my own hands.

*While she was still in boarding school, Zasulich attended evening lectures offered by the radical Ishutin circle, one of whose members—Dmitrii Karakozov—tried to assassinate the tsar in 1866. When she finished school, Zasulich went to St. Petersburg, where she worked first as a clerk and then in a weaving collective. Like other young people, she also became active in the movement to educate workers, conducting literacy classes for them in the evenings.*

I began to attend some classes in teaching by the phonetic method at the Alekseev teachers' college on Vasilevskii Island. One day, the teacher invited seven or eight students, myself included, to his room. "We must talk about what teachers should read to prepare for their own work," he said.

The evening we set for the meeting arrived, and ten of us assembled in his small room. There weren't even enough places at the table; several people sat off to the side on the bed, drawing back the curtain that hid it.

These teachers were very young, no older than I. They hadn't seemed especially smart to me before, and from the conversations they struck up, I could see that they knew very little, even less than I did. So my shyness quickly disappeared, and I began to interrupt—successfully, it turned out. They listened to me and the majority took my side. Someone suggested that we read books on pedagogy; someone else, sitting on the bed, raised an objection to this and I took his side. The advocates of pedagogical reading were quickly defeated. Now, pedagogy is important, but it was more important for these teachers to learn a little about real life. What to read then? Everyone grew quiet for a moment. I began to name things I thought worthwhile: Mirtov's [Lavrov's] *Historical Letters*, which were being published at the time in *The Week*, and J. S. Mill with the Chernyshevskii commentaries, which I was then reading in the evenings, after I came home from work. I had tried to read it when I was still at school, but it went badly then—I was able to understand the book, but it did not interest me very much.

Every book I mentioned met the complete approval of the teacher and the new fellow sitting on the bed, who was one of the more talkative students; the rest were silent. We asked them what they'd already read, and it turned out that they'd read almost nothing. Some had read a little of Pisarev, but no one had read Dobroliubov. I said that my favorite article of Dobroliubov's was "When Will the Real Day Come?"

"And when will it come?" asked one of the students.

I replied that Dobroliubov believed it would come with a generation that had "grown up in an atmosphere of hope and expectation."

"That means us," remarked the man on the bed.

When everyone had left, he came over and introduced himself as Sergei Nechaev, and asked me to come to the Sergeev school.

"What, are teachers meeting there too?" I asked.

"No, they're not, but we must have a talk."

Within a month or two, the entire student body and everyone else interested in student affairs knew Nechaev's name. But this meant nothing to me at the time. And I never got around to meeting him again.

Almost from the moment that some people from Saratov [a province in the southeastern part of European Russia] began to arrive, I heard that there would be student disturbances that year, without fail. Why, over what issues, I couldn't find out—but everyone seemed pleased, and I was ready to be pleased, too.

The actual student "disorders," as they were officially designated, were marked by the arrest of several people and the exile of about a hundred students from St. Petersburg; these did not take place until the spring.

I don't remember how it all began, but I recall that the students were divided into two camps: the "moderates," and the "radicals" led by Nechaev. The moderates were in the majority, but the two groups together constituted only a small minority of the student population. There were about three hundred activists, made up of first- and second-year students at the university, the medical school, and the technical and agricultural academies of St. Petersburg.

*One night around this time, Zasulich spent the night at her friend Anna Tomilova's house. Nechaev happened to drop in, and, finding Zasulich alone, began to tell her his plans for carrying out a revolution in Russia in the near future. Zasulich had difficulty sharing his optimism.*

I felt terrible: it was really painful for me to say "That's unlikely . . . ," "I don't know about that. . . ." I could see that he was very serious, that this was no idle chatter about revolution. He could and would act—wasn't he the ringleader of the students? . . .

I could imagine no greater pleasure than serving the revolution. I had dared only to dream of it, and yet now he was saying that he wanted to recruit me, that otherwise he wouldn't have thought of saying anything. . . . And what did I know of "the people"? I knew only the house serfs of Biakolovo and the members of my weaving collective, while he was himself a worker by birth.

Troubled thoughts flashed through my head.

"Anyhow, you won't refuse to give me your address?" asked Nechaev, who had lapsed into silence.

We had spoken about this earlier, and I seized on it at once.

"Of course not! I really know very little and I want so much to do something for the cause. I don't believe that what you're doing will produce a revolution, but on the other hand, I don't know of any other way either. After all, I'm not doing anything right now, and I'd be happy to help in any way I can."

I don't remember my exact words, of course, but I remember vividly my feelings at that time. This was my first serious conversation about revolution, my first step toward the cause, as it seemed to me then. My surrender evidently delighted Nechaev.

"Then it's agreed?"

"It's agreed."

He walked into another room to say something to someone. I got up, too, and started walking around the room. Then he returned and abruptly announced:

"I've fallen in love with you."

This was unexpected, to say the least. How should I deal with it? I felt nothing at all except amazement, and embarrassment over how to answer without offending him. I circled the room twice more, in silence.

"I greatly value our good relations, but I don't love you," I declared at last.

"That bit about good relations—that's sweetening the pill, isn't it?"

I didn't answer. He made a bow and left the room.

The episode perplexed me. Somehow, it blotted out, even destroyed, the powerful feeling evoked by the conversation that preceded it. I walked around the room a little longer, then lay down on the couch and immediately fell asleep.

The point was that, instinctively, I had totally distrusted his "I've fallen in love." It was somehow unpleasant to think about it at first, so I simply didn't. Later, I became convinced that my instincts had been correct. Both at this time and soon afterwards, abroad and in Moscow, Nechaev became involved in relationships that must have required declarations of love. Just when he was beginning such an enormous undertaking (in his eyes, at least), relying solely on his own resources, it is unlikely that there would have been room in his heart for several "loves" or even for flirtation. More likely, he declared his love whenever he considered it necessary for the cause.

According to the precepts of Nechaev's *Catechism*, a revolutionary was a doomed man: there was no love, no friendship, no joy for him, only revolutionary passion. There was no morality for a revolutionary outside of service to the cause. Everything that aided the revolution was moral; everything that hindered it was immoral. . . . In the same document, Nechaev placed enormous value on the "assistance of women." But as he conceived it, assisting the cause coincided with assisting him, with carrying out his commands. Even at that time,

*Sergei Nechaev*

deceit weighed heavily in Nechaev's calculations. Still, although the precepts provoked both laughter and anger—so
little did they correspond to what actually happened—it seems
to me that the *Revolutionary Catechism* had a real meaning
for Nechaev himself.

Nechaev had probably been thinking of taking me abroad
even before he made his "proposal": I might be able to help
him with various dealings. For some strange reason, he considered me much more aggressive, more self-confident, than
I actually was. My knowledge of languages would have been
useful to him, too. Had I immediately responded to his
schemes with total fanaticism, perhaps he would have asked
me to go abroad without a profession of love. As it was, he
tried to neutralize my tendency to skepticism—even though I
was ready to help—by his declaration. When that failed too,
he postponed his plans for a while. Later, he wrote a letter
asking me to go abroad, but the letter was intercepted and I
found out about it only in prison.

The following morning, Nechaev and I greeted each other

over the samovar as if nothing had happened—as if nothing resembling the previous night's episode had ever taken place.

When he said good-bye, Nechaev told me that while he was gone I might receive letters addressed to other people.

"Whom should I give them to?"

"You'll see when you get them."

Several days passed. I remember that we gave a literary and musical soirée to benefit a fund for exiled students. The singer was Lavrovskaia, a favorite of all the young people at that time. They loved her not just for her voice, but because she was not resigned to her place as an actress: she refused to accept "gifts." The most widely read magazine of the time scolded her for it, but the public gave her standing ovations.

She arrived that evening in a plain black dress with a stand-up collar—just like the costume a "nihilist woman" would wear on holidays. "Celestial clouds, you have no homeland and you cannot be exiled," she sang. Taking this as a hint at the secret purpose of the evening—which was known to everyone in St. Petersburg—the public applauded furiously. They also applauded another performer, Lernovaia, when she explained that although she had refused to attend the party at first, when she found out its true purpose, she wanted to participate come what may. In general, the benefit proved very successful.

Anna [Nechaev's sister] and I went with Tomilova to spend the night at her place. Nechaev accompanied us. Either that day or the evening before, I had heard that Nechaev had been summoned to the Third Section, where they had threatened to arrest him if the student meetings continued. When Anna or Tomilova remarked that he should stop going, he replied that it really didn't matter: they had told him that he would be arrested anyway, whether he went to the meetings or not. Nechaev was very satisfied with the benefit; seizing upon some phrase that the audience had applauded, he assured us that people were ready to demand a republican form of government.

I awoke the following morning before it was light and saw Nechaev standing in front of me with a package in his hands.

"Hide this!"

I couldn't bring myself to crawl out from beneath the covers. "Okay, I'll hide it," I answered, but I didn't take the package he was offering me.

Tomilova, who had come out of her bedroom when she heard voices, took the parcel. Nechaev left immediately, without explaining anything or saying another word. That was the last I saw him—that morning when he stood with a package in his outstretched arms.

The small bundle contained some tightly packed papers. Tomilova wrapped it up in a kerchief and put it in a mesh bag, the kind you take to the baths. She remarked that if it fell into the wrong hands, the lives of several hundred people might be ruined. I took the bag with me to work and kept it next to me all day, never letting it out of my sight for a moment.

As I was walking home in the evening, it suddenly struck me that I had been stupid not to run over and drop it off at my place during the day. I was particularly frightened by the prospect of walking across the deserted bridges over the Neva. Drunkards sometimes accosted you, if nothing worse happened.

And in fact, halfway across the bridge, I was frightened by a man walking quickly toward me. He came up to me, seized me by the collar of my fur, and began dragging me after him.

At another time I would have screamed, and that would have brought help at once, since there was a policeman at the end of the bridge. But with the package I was carrying, I couldn't scream. Silently, I began to pound my assailant with all my might. The bag, half-empty with the heavy package in it, worked like a bludgeon and he released me, cursing. I ran off.

Before I came to St. Petersburg my bravery had scarcely been tested. I used to get frightened easily, although I desperately wanted to be brave. I was satisfied now.

*Nechaev used the address Zasulich gave him to correspond with other radicals in Russia. Through carelessness, one of the letters fell into the hands of the police, and* as a result, Zasulich and many of her friends were arrested. Despite the absence of other evidence, Zasulich was imprisoned in the Litovskii fortress for two years. She was then released—only to be exiled to the far north, where she was forced to live for two more years. In 1873, when she regained her freedom, she enrolled in medical courses in Kharkov and joined a radical group, the Kievan Insurgents.

Then in 1876 she returned to St. Petersburg and began working as a typesetter for an illegal printing press. It was there that she learned of the beating of a political prisoner, Alexei Bogoliubov. "I waited for some response, but everyone remained silent," she explained at her trial. "There was nothing to stop Trepov, or someone just as powerful as he, from repeating the same violence over and over. I resolved at that point, even if it cost my life, to prove that no one who abused a human being that way could be sure of getting away with it. I couldn't find another way of drawing attention to what had happened. I saw no other way. . . . It's terrible to have to lift a hand against another person, but I felt that it had to be done."[5]

Together with her friend Maria (Masha) Kolenkina, she developed a plan: Zasulich was to shoot Trepov, who had ordered Bogoliubov's beating, while Kolenkina was to make an attempt on the life of Zhelikovskii, the prosecutor in the Trial of the 193. Circumstances, however, prevented Kolenkina from implementing her part of the plan.

The evening of the eighteenth [actually the twenty-third—Eds.] Masha stayed at my house. At nightfall I told the landlady that I would be leaving for Moscow in the morning—I had already told her earlier that I might have to go away for a brief time and that my things could be given to Masha if I did

[5] Tsederbaum (Ezhov), S. Zhenshchina v russkom revoliutsionnom dvizhenni (Leningrad, 1927), p. 69.

not return by the end of the month. All these precautions were
necessary for Masha: for reasons of her own she wanted to stay
in my room for some time. I wrote up a request for a certificate
of conduct.[6] Then I lay down to sleep.

It seemed to me that I was calm and totally unafraid of
losing my free life; I had finished with that a long time ago.
It was not even a life anymore, but some kind of limbo,
which I wanted to end as soon as possible.

I was oppressed by the thought of the following morning:
that hour at the governor's, when he would suddenly approach
in earnest. . . . I was sure of success—everything would take
place without the slightest hitch; it shouldn't be hard at all,
and not at all frightening, but nevertheless I felt mortally unhappy.

I had not expected this feeling. And at the same time, I
was not excited, but tired—I even felt sleepy. But as soon as
I fell asleep, I had a nightmare. It seemed to me that I was
not sleeping, but lying on my back looking through the glass
above the door, which was illuminated from the corridor.
Suddenly, I felt as if I were losing my mind. Something was
irresistibly forcing me to rise, to go out into the corridor and,
there, to scream. I knew that this was mad, I tried to hold myself back with all my strength, and yet nevertheless I went
into the corridor and screamed and screamed. Masha, who was
lying next to me, woke me up. I was indeed screaming, but on
my cot, and not in the corridor. Again I fell asleep, and again
I had the same dream: against my will I walked out and
screamed. I knew it was crazy but nevertheless I screamed. So
it went, several times.

Then it was time to get up: we had no watches, but the sky
had begun to turn gray, and someone knocked at our landlady's door. We had to hurry to Trepov's before nine o'clock,
before he began to receive petitioners. We would then be able
to ask the officer on duty in a natural way whether General
Trepov was receiving, and if it turned out that an aide was

[6] "Certificates of conduct," granted by local authorities, were often needed to
obtain a diploma.

receiving, we could leave unnoticed. And before going to Trepov's we had to go to the station.

We rose silently in the cold semidarkness. I put on a new dress; my coat and hat were old. After dressing I left the room: a new cloak and hat lay in the traveling bag, and I would change into them at the station. This was necessary because the landlady would certainly want to say good-bye (I spoiled her with conversations); she would praise the cloak and advise me not to wear it on the road. And tomorrow this cloak would be in all the newspapers and might draw her attention. I had had time to think about everything, down to the most petty details.

*Vera Zasulich*

It was already growing light on the street, but the half-dark station was completely deserted. I changed, exchanged kisses with Masha, and left. The streets looked cold and gloomy.

About ten petitioners had already gathered at the governor's.

"Is the governor receiving?"

"He's receiving; he'll be right out."

Someone, as if deliberately for my sake, asked again: "Is he himself receiving?" The answer was affirmative.

A woman, poorly dressed, with eyes red from weeping, sat down near me and asked me to take a look at her petition— "Is this how they are written here?" There was some sort of discrepancy in the petition. I advised her to show it to the officer, since I saw that he was already looking something over. She was afraid, and asked me to show it to him. I went up to the officer with the petitioner and directed his attention to her. My voice was ordinary—there was no sign of my agitation. I was satisfied. The nightmarish feeling that had weighed on me since the previous evening was gone without a trace. I had nothing on my mind but the concern that everything should go as planned.

The adjutant led us into the next room, me first, and put us in a corner. At this very moment Trepov entered from another door, with a whole retinue of military men, and all of them headed toward me.

For a moment this confused and upset me. In thinking through the details, I had found it inconvenient to shoot at the moment I presented the petition. Now Trepov and his entourage were looking at me, their hands occupied by papers and things, and I decided to do it earlier than I had planned —to do it when Trepov stopped opposite my neighbor, before reaching me.

And suddenly there was no neighbor ahead of me—I was first . . .

*It's all the same; I will shoot when he stops next to the petitioner after me*, I cried inwardly. The momentary alarm passed at once, as if it had never been.

"What do you want?"

"A certificate of conduct."

He jotted down something with a pencil and turned to my neighbor.

The revolver was in my hand. I pressed the trigger . . . a misfire.

My heart missed a beat. Again I pressed . . . a shot, cries . . .

*Now they'll start beating me.* This was next in the sequence of events I had thought through so many times.

But instead there was a pause. It probably lasted only a few seconds in all, but I felt it.

I threw down the revolver—this also had been decided beforehand; otherwise, in the scuffle, it might go off by itself. I stood and waited.

"The criminal was stunned," they wrote later in the papers.

Suddenly everyone around me began moving, the petitioners scattered, police officers threw themselves at me, and I was seized from both sides.

"Where is the gun?"

"She threw it—it's on the floor."

"The revolver! Give up the revolver!" They continued to scream, pulling me in different directions.

A person appeared before me (Kurneev, as I later found out). His eyes were completely round, and his wide-open mouth issued a snarl, not a scream; his two huge hands, the fingers crooked, were headed directly for my eyes. I shut them as tightly as I could, and he only skinned my cheeks. Blows rained down—they rolled me around and continued to beat me.

Everything went as I had expected; the only additional thing was the attack on my eyes, but now I lay with my face to the floor, and they were out of danger. I felt not the slightest pain, however, and this surprised me. I felt pain only that night, when they finally locked me in a cell.

"You're beating her?"

"Already killed, it seems."

"You can't do that! Stop! We must have an investigation!"

A battle began around me. Someone was pushed away; it must have been Kurneev.

They helped me up and sat me in a chair. It seemed to me

that this was the room in which I had presented my petition, but in front of me, somewhat to the left near the wall, there was a wide staircase without landings, which went to the very top of the opposite wall. People were hurrying down it, pushing one another, making noise and shouting. This riveted my attention immediately; how did the staircase get there?—it seemed as if it hadn't been there earlier, as if it were somehow unreal, and the people unreal too. "Perhaps it's only my imagination" passed through my mind immediately. But then they led me into another room and so the riddle of the staircase was never solved; for some reason, I recalled it all day long, whenever I was left in peace for a minute.

The room into which I was led was large—much larger than the first; large desks stood near one of the walls, a wide bench ran along another. There were few people in the room at the moment, none at all from the governor's retinue.

"We will have to search you." A man turned to me, indecisive despite his police uniform. He did not belong to that time and place: his hands shook, his voice was very gentle. There was nothing hostile about him at all.

"You have to call a woman for that," I replied.

"But where will we find a woman here?"

"Can't you find one?" And immediately I thought of something: "There is always a public nurse in all precincts. Go look for her," I advised.

"It will take a while to find her, and you might still have a weapon! God help us if something happens."

"Nothing more will happen; it would be better if you tied me up, if you're so afraid."

"I'm not frightened for myself—you're not going to shoot me. But really, you upset me. I was sick—I just recently got out of bed. What is there to tie you with?"

I had to laugh inside: *Now I've got to teach* him!

"If there aren't any ropes, you can use a towel . . ."

Right there in the room he opened up a desk drawer and took out a clean towel, but he seemed in no hurry to tie me up.

"Why did you do it?" he asked, somehow timidly.

"For Bogoliubov."

"Aha!" I could tell from his tone that this was what he had expected.

Meanwhile, the news evidently had already spread to higher circles. The room began to fill up; one after another, military and civilian bigwigs arrived, and with more or less threatening looks headed toward me. Soldiers, policemen appeared inside the room. My strange (for that time and place) interlocutor had disappeared somewhere, and I never saw him again. But his towel tied my elbows behind my back. A loud, energetic officer was in command. He called two soldiers with bayonets on their rifles, stood them behind me, and ordered them to hold my hands. He went to the center of the room, looked around, and evidently not liking this position, moved to another. As he walked he warned the soldiers: "Be careful, or else she might stick a knife into you!"

My foresight, and consequently my precise plan of action, did not extend beyond the moment of attack. But every minute my joy increased—not because I was in full control of myself (there was the matter of the staircase), but rather because I found myself in an extraordinary state of the most complete invulnerability, such as I had never before experienced. Nothing at all could confuse me, annoy me, or tire me. Whatever was being thought up by those men, at that time conversing animatedly in another corner of the room, I would regard them calmly, from a distance they could not cross.

They left us alone for a few minutes, and the soldiers began to whisper back and forth.

"Can you believe it! The girl is tied, two soldiers guard her, and he says: 'Be careful, she'll stab you!' "

"And where didst thou[7] learn to shoot?" he whispered afterwards, right next to my ear.

There was nothing hostile in this "thou"; it was the peasant way.

"I learned! It's no big deal," I answered, also quietly.

[7] When "thou," the familiar form of "you," is used with persons other than one's intimates, it is usually a sign of disdain or disrespect.

"You learned, but not enough," the other soldier said. "It didn't hit right!"

"Don't say that," the first objected fervently. "You hear— it hit very well. He'll live!"

There was a movement in the group of officials, and they made their way over to my side. The policemen who had been sent to investigate at the false address I gave when questioned had returned.

"No one lives at Sverenskaia Street at such and such a number—the house has been demolished."

"You gave a false address!"

*The jury that sat on Zasulich's case shared her sense of moral outrage and so acquitted her.[8] The tsar refused to accept the verdict and promptly ordered Zasulich arrested again. Liberal sympathizers helped to conceal her from the police until her comrades could smuggle her out of Russia.*

The time after my acquittal was really terrible for me. I had said good-bye to my freedom before my attempt on Trepov's life and thought no further about it. Then suddenly —to my total surprise—I regained it and had to decide what to do with it, and as quickly as possible. In those first few weeks, I was continually surrounded by innumerable strangers, and was quickly forced to learn how to behave in my new situation.

I can remember my first lesson. No more than two hours after I was freed, one young man exclaimed to me: "You must be very happy now!"

"Not very," I replied, and immediately regretted my thoughtless honesty: there was so much amazement, chagrin, even indignation in his "What are you saying!" I hastened to erase the impression I'd made, saying that I still hadn't recovered, that I hadn't gotten used to things yet.

That man had been a radical. I subsequently found myself among people who scarcely knew radicals, for whom I was

---

[8] Jury trials were instituted in 1864 as one of a series of reforms following the emancipation of the serfs in 1861.

something mysterious, unheard of. They were taking risks for my sake, sheltering me in their apartments. At another time I might have taken a lot of pleasure in their company, but given the circumstances, I felt too constrained. So, despite everyone's sympathy, I was lonelier than I had been in the House of Preliminary Detention.

Three weeks after the acquittal, after hiding in several apartments, I wound up at Dr. Veimar's place. Once I looked it over, I felt much better. The apartment was located above Veimar's orthopedic clinic and was supposed to be unoccupied. His brother had taken the key to it, telling the concierge he would use the apartment to study for his exams. There were no servants, of course. I was sharing the apartment with Dmitrii Klements; we brewed our tea over a spirit lamp and a student brought us food. We had few visitors. In order to get to us, people had to walk through the rooms of Madame Rebinder, who lived with Veimar, and she discouraged most guests. Besides Edinka (as everyone called the student), who stopped in several times a day, and Griboedov, who was a good friend of both Veimar and Klements, D. Veimar himself was our only visitor.

Most of the time, I was left alone in the apartment with Dmitrii. From the start he behaved as if nothing at all unusual had happened to me, and so he was the first person that month with whom I felt at ease. During those first days, however, I still had trouble talking, and he left me in peace. He would go into his room and read something there until Edinka brought us food or it was time to have tea.

Our conversations, which began over tea, soon grew lengthy. Klements talked about life abroad and about the Chaikovskii circle,[9] while I spoke about the Kievan Insurgents, a group I'd belonged to earlier. We had in common the fact that neither of us was affiliated with any organization at that time.

Klements began to bring up Switzerland with increasing frequency, talking about the charm of its mountains and the

---

[9] The Chaikovskii circle, which included Sofia Perovskaia, was one of the most important groups to form in the early seventies, and one of the first to organize among factory workers.

pleasure of going climbing: he was going to have to go back once more and fortunately would get to spend part of the summer there. "You should come keep me company!" he said. "What peaks I'd take you to!"

Initially, it hadn't even occurred to me to go abroad; then I got a letter from Ekaterina Breshkovskaia, advising me not to travel, even if people tried to make me leave Russia. "Why should you want to play the role of a retired heroine?" she wrote. I agreed with her completely.

When I told Klements about Breshkovskaia's advice, he protested. "I'm asking you to go to the mountains, not to 'play a role.' No one does things like that there, and you'll only need enough 'heroism' to keep climbing, no matter how steep it gets."

He obviously loved nature passionately, and he knew how to tempt me with its most unusual features.

And I was tempted. Besides, my sentence had been reversed and everyone was insisting that I leave Russia. I was told that some general had offered to escort me abroad in the guise of his wife, and there were other plans too. But experienced people, and Klements among them, thought that the safest thing for me would be to wait for Moishe Zundelevich, who was then in Switzerland, and cross the border in the usual illegal manner. I preferred it that way too. The notion of traveling with a general didn't appeal to me at all.

After my sentence was reversed, Madame Rebinder noticed some sinister doings around the house, and Klements and I moved to Griboedov's. Griboedov liked radicals, making fun of them while helping them out. His house was frequently searched, always without result. On nights when there was to be a search, he told us, certain unmistakable signs would be evident by evening, and he would get a bottle of vodka and some snacks ready. According to him, the police barely even searched—they'd only eat, drink, and wax sentimental: "If only everyone were so understanding! Some people get angry, as if we really wanted to run around at night making searches."

For the time being, Griboedov could guarantee our complete safety. We lived in total freedom at his place and were even able to see old friends who were in St. Petersburg.

Finally, Moishe Zundelevich arrived along with Sergei Kravchinskii,[10] who came directly to the apartment from the station. Sergei was Klements' best friend, but he was nothing at all like him, particularly at that moment. Sergei arrived all aglow, in a wildly enthusiastic mood. Through the prism of foreign newspapers and Sergei's own imagination, my acquittal and the demonstration that followed it had seemed to him the start of the revolution. St. Petersburg had resumed its usual gloomy aspect long before he arrived, but Sergei did not allow this to alter his position: the city was still proving it could be a volcano or a bonfire (I don't remember which), only covered superficially with ashes and ready to flare up at the first puff of wind.

At other times he would try to persuade us that Russian revolutionaries were all a select group of giants, born to lead.

"What are you saying? You're dreaming!" we'd say.

He would respond with a reference to Madame Roland, who complained in her memoirs during the French Revolution that there were no outstanding individuals among her contemporaries. "But to us they're giants," Kravchinskii said. "And I'm sure that I see our radicals now in the light that posterity will see them, too."

Klements was only two or three years older than Kravchinskii, but he treated Kravchinskii as a father does a beloved child, calling him "Bluebird" because of his flights of fancy. Although we remained friends for years abroad, I never again saw Sergei in the same state as during those few days we spent together in St. Petersburg.

Five days later we were on the road. We made it to Switzerland without the slightest difficulty—if you ignore the fact that we arrived in Berlin the day after the shooting by Nobiling,[11] when all the Russian friends of Zundelevich and

---

[10] Olga Liubatovich writes in more detail about Sergei Kravchinskii. See p. 146.
[11] On June 2, 1878 (New Style), Karl Nobiling attempted to assassinate Emperor Wilhelm I of Germany.

Kravchinskii were anxiously expecting an invasion by the police. There was no apartment we could go to, and we had to spend several hours in some park waiting for our train.

On our way to Geneva we stopped for a few days in Bern and I met Anna Epstein, or Annie, as all her friends called her, and as I soon did too. She was Klements' wife, as he had informed me, asking me not to tell her that I knew: later on she would tell me herself, but she would feel shy at first, and take it out on him.

Later, when Dmitrii was in jail, Annie told me that he had traveled abroad during this period mainly for my sake.

"She's a person," he had said, "who from morning till night thinks only about which bough she'll be hanging on. Nothing good can come of it, and I'm determined to use the mountains to cure her."

"When Dmitrii was living in Switzerland himself," Annie told me, "he often resorted to that cure for his own emotional turmoil. If terrible news came from Russia, or he got really depressed, he'd head straight for the mountains, even in winter (although then of course he wouldn't go to the most deserted ones)."

Annie was a remarkable person in her own right. Both she and Klements had been members of the original Chaikovskii circle, and had been a great asset to it while it was active. She was Jewish, the daughter of a smuggler. Knowing the techniques from childhood, she was the first to arrange regular, safe passage across the border, both for people and for printed matter. She had not been attracted by the idea of serving the Russian people, whom she did not know; for her, "the people" meant poor Jews. But she loved the Russian socialists with all her soul for the dangers they faced and the suffering they endured, and she did all she could to lessen those dangers and ease that suffering. Her other specialty was establishing ties with prisons, and there she displayed both persistence and a proficiency that approached genius.

Unlike the majority of radicals of those days who were forced to sunder their family ties, Annie and her mother maintained the closest friendship (her father had died long ago). Her mother not only knew what kind of work she was doing, but herself assisted in that unselfish smuggling. In this she saw nothing wrong, but she did force Anna to swear that she would never convert or marry a "goy." The fear that her mother would find out about her relationship with Klements forced Annie to conceal it for years.

She died in the nineties, after suffering through the reactionary calm of the eighties. During that time her active love for those who needed her—which was the essence of her nature —had no natural outlet. If there was a misfortune in any émigré family, if someone was dying, or losing his mind, or taken ill, Annie was there. She would concentrate all her energies on that family; she would work, bustle about, bend over backwards to help. ("She'd use her own skin to make someone else a jacket," Klements once said about her.) But then misfortune would pass, the family's life would return to normal, and Annie, who'd managed to become deeply attached to that particular family, would feel she was no longer needed and was once again an outsider and superfluous. In the last years of her life, she was increasingly drawn toward home, to her mother: there, at least, she would not be superfluous. But she would have had to petition to return; she could not have lived at her mother's under a name other than Epstein.[12]

We were obliged to stay in Geneva for a couple of weeks before we could get away to the mountains. It took all my obstinacy and Klements' most energetic protection to avoid succumbing to the "posturing" that Breshkovskaia had predicted. By this time, almost all the Russian émigrés had become anarchists, with close ties to anarchist groups in Switzerland, Italy, and, to some extent, France. Everyone had assumed beforehand that I, too, would be an anarchist, and that when I arrived abroad the anarchists would benefit greatly from my

[12] Since Annie was married to Dmitrii Klements, that was the surname registered on her passport.

sudden international notoriety. But at the time, my notion of anarchism was as vague as my notion of social democracy. The Russian press carried no information about such things, and the accounts in those foreign papers I'd managed to get hold of were too fragmentary. Now, suddenly—on the second or third day after I'd arrived—I was confronted with the following plan. The Parisian anarchists would set a day and time for my arrival in Paris and prepare a welcome of at least several thousand people. The police might intervene, but would not be permitted to arrest me.

I refused in no uncertain terms, but they kept assuring me that it was necessary, that I was refusing only because I didn't understand foreign ways. Klements took my part at once, defending me very energetically, but when we were left alone he began to defend the plan.

"I know you well enough, but it would never occur to them that you've come to hate your fame so much it makes you gnash your teeth. The plan itself is innocent enough; given your fame, nine out of ten people would consent to it with pleasure."

When we'd finished with that plan, another rose to confront us: I must write an open letter against the German Social Democrats, putting them in their place. I don't remember now exactly which paper was supposed to print the letter, but everyone expected it to be copied, quoted, and widely distributed.

Klements had a negative reaction to that one, both because of the plan itself and out of consideration for my peculiarities; he felt that you shouldn't criticize a party that you didn't really understand. And of course, even without Klements, I would never have agreed to write about things I was ignorant of. I would not have gone to Paris either, but it would have been really unpleasant to stand alone against the mass of people who wanted me to go. With Klements I felt that I was in good hands.

At last we set off for the mountains. One émigré had settled with his family in a mountain chalet near a small village in the Rhone valley, and he invited us to stay with them. Foreigners, who came pouring into Switzerland in the summertime, would never go near such a deserted place. There wasn't even a paved road leading up to the few houses scattered over the mountainside; only a well-beaten path, similar to our Russian country roads, led up to the chalets. There were no dwellings at all above those chalets, only shelters for shepherds in the high pastures. Klements liked that, too. On principle, he only climbed mountains that were "not listed in Baedeker's guidebook" and were consequently unsuitable for foreigners, who did not visit them.

We spent the night at the chalet and the following day set off, after asking the postman about the peaks and passes nearby.

We walked at random, following no predetermined plan, trying only to wind up by sunset on an open eastern slope, and as high as possible. Actually, we never met a soul, and might have avoided everyone if we hadn't occasionally followed the sound of cowbells to find a shepherd, who'd sell us as much cream as we wanted, and sometimes cheese, too, for a few kopecks. We'd ask him about the neighboring mountain passes and plan our next excursion. I turned out to be extremely good at the rock climbing we had to do. We would roam about like this for three days at a time and then descend to the chalet, rest for a couple of days in civilization, store up everything we needed, and after that depart again.

It was more than the beauty of the landscape that moved me so profoundly. In those deserted, almost untouched mountains that Baedeker had ignored, I found myself in another kind of world, and my intense feeling of freedom grew stronger with every passing hour. I was liberated from everything that oppressed me—from people, but most of all from myself. All my unresolved questions and painful thoughts disappeared. It wasn't that I looked at them differently, I simply gave up thinking altogether while I was there. "Later there'll be time" —and for the moment I abandoned myself entirely to the impressions of that other world.

Zasulich returned to Russia in the summer of 1879, as Land and Liberty was breaking up. Rejecting the growing emphasis on assassination as a primary means of political struggle, she joined Black Repartition. Its program proved impossible to implement, however, and along with most of the other leaders of Black Repartition, Zasulich returned to Switzerland early in 1880.

In 1883 she became one of the founders of Emancipation of Labor, the first Russian Marxist group. She spent most of the next two decades writing and translating (including some of Engels' work). She described the rhythm of her life in a letter to her comrade Lev Deich:

"I have a tiny room exactly like the ones I usually rent in Geneva. An iron stove, incredible disorder, and all the rest, as always. I get up late, around ten, even eleven sometimes. I immediately brew myself coffee—very strong—with sugar if possible. After I drink it I throw myself into my writing, stopping from time to time (whenever I'm having trouble) to roll myself a cigarette and pace around the room. I do this until 4 or 5 p.m. Then I either go out for something to eat, or, if there is anything left over, I'll cook a steak, eat, and lie down with a book for an hour—or longer, if I get carried away. I don't write anymore, but I think things over and rewrite. There's tea on the stove, and from time to time I sip some. At nine I have coffee, then work until 2 a.m. Then I lie down with a book.

"I don't talk for months on end (or only to myself, in whispers) except in shops 'Give me a pound of this.' I go to Geneva once a month, sometimes less: I'd go more if I had to.

"So there's my life! I see no one, read no papers, and never think about myself."

Zasulich later joined the Russian Social Democratic Labor Party and served on the editorial board of Iskra, its journal. When the party split in 1903, she affiliated with the Mensheviks.

After the revolution of 1905, Zasulich returned to Russia where she remained, supporting herself by translating. By 1917 she was too ill to take an active part in the revolution, and she died two years later, at the age of sixty-nine.

# PRASKOVIA
# IVANOVSKIA

When the People's Will declared all-out war on the state, it attracted the veterans not only of Land and Liberty, but of various currents and phases of the populist movement. Many of its members came from the south of Russia, where the movement was organizationally loose but extensive and highly militant: Odessa and Kiev, in particular, were probably the two most important centers of armed struggle during 1878. Praskovia Ivanovskaia's political career was typical of the "southerners." She had lived underground since her brother's arrest in 1876, working alone or in ad hoc organizations. She had gone "to the people" both in the factory and in the fields, apprenticed herself to learn a trade, and participated in various attempts to free imprisoned comrades. In 1878, she was one of the organizers of the first armed demonstration in Russian history. By the time she joined the People's Will early in 1880, she was a professional revolutionary in the full sense of the word.

Ivanovskaia became a technician in the People's Will, a typesetter, and diligently performed the monotonous unending chores in the party's underground press. Although she never gained the public reputation enjoyed by Vera Figner or Sofia Perovskaia, for example, she was greatly respected by her comrades, who placed the highest value on self-sacrifice and dedication to the collective good. Vera Figner remembered her as someone whom "absolutely everyone" loved, a woman with "an attractive face in the purely Russian style and a voice of marvelous timbre; her warmth, simplicity, and sensitivity charmed everyone with whom she came in contact."

I was born in Tula province in 1853. Mother died when I was young. Father, a village priest, was a man of abstract interests, never much concerned with worldly affairs, and after Mother's death, he withdrew even more from his children: somehow, he never gave much thought to us. Philosophical reflections served him poorly in running the household, and my childhood was one of neglect and grim poverty. We grew up like weeds in the field, without the slightest supervision.

Still, there were some positive aspects to the way we were reared. Although we sometimes went hungry and were poorly clothed, we were always free, always ready to explore new paths. This early independence taught me to love freedom deeply, and to rely solely on my own resources in difficult situations. Another advantage to our economic position was that it didn't set us apart from the people around us. Like the vast majority of clergymen's families, we essentially lived the lives of the middle stratum of peasants: village priests went into the fields with their scythes on their backs, wearing rough, homemade cotton shirts; they plowed the land themselves, carried manure to the barren soil themselves, and harvested the grain themselves; and the fact that their lives were the same as everyone else's around them made relations with their parishioners easier and more natural.

As a rule, priests' sons studied in the seminary, returning during summer vacation to help their fathers with the field work and threshing, which was done with chains, in the age-old manner. Daughters languished at home with their parents —barely literate, waiting for the opportunity to become mothers or deacons' wives. No doubt, this deadly existence would have claimed all the children in our family, too, save for a purely fortuitous circumstance that greatly altered our lives. Early in the 1850's, an amnestied Decembrist warrant officer, Mikhail Andreevich Bodisko, had taken up residence on an estate he'd acquired near our village. He immediately became close friends with my father, and some years later, thanks to Bodisko's financial assistance, my sister and I were able to enroll in the Tula church school.

What joy we felt in leaving our poor home! But our ecstasy, our childish little dreams, were destined to be short-lived. The Tula boarding school resembled a monastery. The stench of the lamps nearly suffocated us, and the meager food they gave us was barely enough to keep children alive. The program in the sciences was very weak. Still, the wave of new ideas of the sixties found their way to us, penetrating the stone walls of our cloister.

First, vague news of the Nechaev arrests in Moscow trickled in. Shortly thereafter, my brother Vasilii, a student at the Medical and Surgical Academy, appeared in Tula with another young man. They helped form a number of groups and study circles and, along with some local students, set up a library and reading room stocked with illegal literature: the journal *Forward!*, works by Chernyshevskii, Lassalle, Lavrov (his *Historical Letters*, which had appeared in 1868, had become enormously popular by now)—all the books that the government had ordered withdrawn from circulation. The radical circle of our school's senior class used the books extensively, sometimes borrowing them over summer vacation. The books were kept in special bookcases and loaned out very carefully: someone the librarian knew had to be responsible for them. More often than not, people charged them out on notes signed by me.

The spirit of radical protest appeared among the student body, hitherto quite meek and submissive, during my last year at school. There were protests against rude treatment by the school authorities, against the ban on "free-thinking" literature, against the inadequate children's rations, which were depleted still further by pilfering. Our naïve religious faith turned to skepticism and protest against regulations bearing the scent of the church. We were seeking to defend our rights as individuals, and we had to enter into battle openly and boldly. Of course, we hadn't evolved any clear political convictions yet: we were too young and foolish, we had awakened only to the consciousness of human rights, and our protests and denials were simply expressions of this mood.

Nevertheless, it was during this period that we became engrossed in the struggle of the Paris Commune. I still remember the day our headmistress walked into the senior class room, extremely upset, carrying an enormous French newspaper edged with a black border of mourning. Line by line, she read the story of the tragic end of the great struggle to our hushed class.

One evening very shortly before graduation, when we were all assembled for prayer in the great hall, we heard someone imperiously ringing the bell in the corridor—a sharp, unpleasant sound. Then, like a ripple in a brook, a suppressed whisper moved through the sedate rows of praying girls: "The gendarmes are here! The gendarmes!" The headmistress, who was presiding over the prayers, turned purple and rushed headlong for the door. Five minutes later, there was no trace whatsoever of gendarmes in the deserted corridor: they had come to arrest "the student Ivanovskaia," but apparently the "witch" (as we called the headmistress among ourselves) would not permit them to create a scene that might shame the school. She hurried over to their offices herself to discuss the meaning of this extraordinary event, which had violated all regulations and disrupted the simple routine of our school life.

In the morning, the class woman escorted me to the gendarme administration. They started their interrogation by referring to some notes which had been found in the possession of the librarian for our illegal collection—the notes I had signed to take books out. After they concluded their questioning, the gendarme colonel boastfully informed me that they'd arrested the librarian and some girls from the *gimnazia*, as well as an older person—my brother in Moscow—in connection with the Nechaev case.

As it turned out, our juvenile arrests brought no serious consequences: neither my brother nor any of us in Tula was detained. To my amazement, the headmistress expressed no indignation over our unprecedented free-thinking. On the other hand, the school's rector tormented us at length, declaring menacingly that my brother was a "revolutionary of the worst sort," that his path inevitably led to prison, the fate that awaited me, too, if I didn't break off with the "nihilists."

But it was too late to "break," and there was no one to break with. To reject the influence of good books, the books that gave us a taste for a larger, brighter life, and that put us on guard against the stifling, humdrum existence around us— that was equivalent to suicide! The sense that there was a better way to live had gradually become part of our souls. And not only through reading—we felt it whenever we looked at the injustice all around us, at the downtrodden, benumbed masses. Our souls pined for truth and justice.

Between 1871 and 1873, a group of students from our school—few of whom could count on any money or assistance —initiated a movement for women's education, a movement to achieve freedom and independence. As I matured physically and acquired a little knowledge, I had dreamt increasingly of going to St. Petersburg to enroll in the newly opened Alarchin-skii courses for women, and now, after graduation, my sister Alexandra and I went to the capital to do just that. The Alarchinskii courses, which were headed by prominent pro-fessors, were set up on strictly democratic principles: it was not a program solely for the upper classes; rather, everyone who was fresh and alive passed through its laboratory, as water passes through sand. Furthermore, students got together in circles and organizational groups to "go to the people"—some immediately, others later on.

*Ivanovskaia's autobiography provides no further details about her life in St. Petersburg between 1873 and 1876. In the spring of 1876, she passed an examination at a gimnazia (secondary school) and was offered a teaching position in a liberal zemstvo. Before making a final de-cision, she visited her brother in Moscow.*

My brother Vasilii urged me not to rush into the *zemstvo* job: he had extensive plans to install radical teachers in the Baranov "palace schools."[1] His chances of success seemed

---

[1] Well-equipped model schools set up in Vladimir province by a factory owner named Baranov.

very good, and since the vacancies wouldn't open up before the fall, I would have the whole summer to do as I pleased. I decided to spend the time in Odessa, where I could find factory work without showing my identity papers, which marked me as a member of the intelligentsia. Maria Subbotina, a frequent visitor to my brother's apartment, gave me the address in Odessa of the Khorzhevskaia sisters.[2]

Before I left Moscow, I loaded up with illegal literature in Vasilii's apartment. I was instructed to leave part of my cargo in Tula for the seminary and *gimnazia* students there and to take the rest on to Odessa with me. However, soon after I left the city, Vasilii was arrested by the gendarmes, who descended on him like hungry jackals. He had been betrayed by a worker, a man who visited his place every day and had of course seen us collecting and packing up the illegal literature and discussing its destination. The gendarmes threw themselves on my trail, hoping to overtake me and catch me red-handed at my father's house, since my route passed close to his parish.

In fact, I did stay at my father's place for a few days. There I found my younger brother Ivan, who had graduated from parochial school and was preparing to transfer to the seminary. Without my knowledge or permission, Ivan proceeded to make a thorough survey of the literature in my suitcase, select for himself some proscribed brochures, and hide them away. The possibility of such a prank, which soon brought the most unfortunate consequences for the entire household, had never occurred to me. I myself was far away by the time the gendarmes reached my father's place, but they rummaged through the whole house and courtyard, finally uncovering the pamphlets my brother had hidden in the garret. They arrested Ivan and brought him to Tula, where they put him in a cell along with the ordinary criminals. The poor lad got a real "taste of the marl" (a deep pit for dogs). Incarcerated for more than a year in his stinking cell, his experience of prison

---

[2] Both Maria Subbotina and Alexandra Khorzhevskaia belonged to the original Fritsche group in Zurich. Later they became defendants in the Trial of the Fifty.

conditions left him with a lifelong hatred for those who oppress others.

As for me, I arrived safely in Odessa, and with the help of my connections—the Khorzhevskaia sisters and Mikhail Eitner —found it relatively easy to make contact with the radical organizations of the south. Eitner first brought me to meet the "tower people"—a group who lived in a tower at the top of a house. Getting to know them was a great help in orienting myself among the multitude of radical circles, communes, and "loners" of Odessa. It became all too clear that there were three major, distinct socialist groupings: the partisans of propaganda, the Insurgents, and the Ukrainian nationalists.

Before I'd been in Odessa very long, I received the sad news of my brother Vasilii's arrest in Moscow. I was obliged to go underground. This was not an unpleasant step in Odessa, since the city was extremely "democratic"—conditions were relatively free: one could live there and find factory work without a residence permit or identity papers. I took advantage of this freedom almost immediately, starting work at a rope factory on Bolshaia Arnautskaia Street.

I got up very early that first Monday morning, so early that the street was still deserted by the time I reached the factory gates. The factory buildings themselves were invisible from the street, blocked by the long, high stone walls—gray, ugly, mottled with obscene graffiti. The factory hadn't come to life yet: I found no one at the gate, which resembled that of a prison. Then the workingmen began to approach, sleepy and sullen, singly and in groups. The wicket gate opened to swallow them up and then slammed shut again, as if of its own volition. Finally, the women workers arrived—late, hurrying, adjusting their clothing on the run. They dived behind the gate, and once more the street was utterly deserted.

I knocked timidly. An eye appeared at a small window in the gate, and a voice shouted: "What do you want? A job? Come in." With no formalities whatsoever, I was led to the lower level of the factory, which reminded me of an enormous shed. It was crammed full of coils of rope, old and new, around which clusters of young girls and old women were bustling. Some insignificant character took my name, and I was led to a group of workers sitting cross-legged on the floor, surrounded on all sides by old rope.

The air was dense throughout the lower level, where old ropes were untwisted and pulled apart and new ropes were covered with canvas. Sometimes we were sent up to the second floor, where wagons carried us swiftly around outstretched ropes, which we lubricated with soap and resin. There was no dawdling here—the slightest carelessness could end in tragedy: I myself saw a youth lose three fingers in an instant. We workers ate and drank our tea sitting on dirty coils of rope; after dinner, we curled up on them like kittens and slept. No one brought dinner to the factory: we simply bought hunks of lard or olives and white bread at the factory gate for five kopecks and took turns bringing boiling water from the tavern.

The air in the building was thick with resin and soap, and the resin quickly saturated all your clothing: within two or three days, every new worker had acquired the factory's distinctive odor, and within a week, there was no way you could get rid of it. The local landladies didn't like to rent rooms to rope workers—they spread their stench through the whole house.

The women were paid twenty-five kopecks a day; the men, as I recall, got thirty or forty. Most of the women workers were totally rootless: as many of them told me, they had nowhere else to go but the streets. Some had come to work there so as not to burden their families. In short, women were driven to the rope factory by the most pressing need, by the cruelest misfortune. Only women in this situation would put up with the ubiquitous rudeness, the men's disrespectful treatment of them, the pinches and searches as they entered or left the factory.

All the women workers were illiterate. They would have been eager to learn, but when was there time to teach them? After a brief dinner, they caught up on the hours of sleep they'd missed in the morning by curling up on the filthy ropes.

By the time we went home, the sun was the thinnest of crescents, sinking into the sea. On holidays, the women couldn't study in their quarters even if they'd wanted to. How, then, could I conduct propaganda among these women, who were so cut off from everyone and everything? Perhaps if I'd remained at the factory longer than two or three months, I might have been able to get something going: a few girls were becoming interested in reading and had begun to drop in at my apartment, and in time I might have been able to propagandize and organize them. But I found conditions at the factory too difficult and depressing to continue working there.

On my days off, I generally visited the "tower people" at home or met them at the seashore. During one of these visits, I ran into Galina Cherniavskaia, an old acquaintance. We exchanged thoughts for a while, then suddenly expressed the identical desire: to go work somewhere in the countryside, for the summer, to experience agricultural labor firsthand, to immerse ourselves in the people and see how the vast peasant world actually lived.

Since we knew the steward at a large estate in Tavricheskaia province, we decided to go there. We prepared for our trip by gathering information about our route and the kind of clothing we would need. We had to stock up on coarse linen, Russian sarafans, and cotton kerchiefs; we needed thick boots for protection against poisonous insects and thin felt for bedding. I can remember the love and tenderness Galina devoted to buying, sewing, and fitting the clothes she would wear in the countryside. Born into a gentry family that had formerly been wealthy and influential, she had never experienced real need. Her upbringing had been delicate, and she knew nothing about the less attractive aspects of manual labor. Not that she'd avoided it: it was simply remote from her life, and she'd had no real contact with it.

The two of us traveled first to Kherson by steamboat, wearing our city clothes. There we spent the night with a family we knew, and in the morning took a boat up the Bug River. I remember how Galina kept dropping her hands into the water as we moved along, bathing her face and offering her damp skin to the fiery rays of the southern sun in an effort to rid her complexion of its whiteness and delicacy.

Immediately after docking, we set off for our summer work. The estate was thirty kilometers away, in a steppe district that was as thinly populated and as boundless as the sea. As far as the eye could see, there was nothing but the farmstead and its large buildings—the barns, granaries, and manor house. Not a building was to be seen in the area where we were to work, not a tree, not even a stunted shrub—only sturdy, reed-like grass brightened by flowers of various kinds. The rye and wheat stretched out in an endless green cover toward the distant horizon, billowing like a limitless emerald sea.

We had planned our arrival for a holiday, when no one was working, so that we'd be able to rest after the long, tiring trip and get our bearings in the unfamiliar place. There was the additional advantage that the foreman had the day off: his wife registered us under our fictitious names, without asking for our identity papers (which were inappropriate for manual laborers[3]), for "the term"—that is, from May to the Festival of the Protection of the Virgin in the fall. Our total salary was to be seventeen rubles.

Our appearance on this Ukrainian estate aroused some curiosity among the other workers, since we were Russians. It didn't last long, however: we explained to whoever seemed interested that we'd lost our positions in the city when our master left town, and that we'd decided to try to learn to live in the country and do peasant work, thinking that it might be easier and more pleasant to work outdoors, in the wide open spaces.

"You'll find it harder, not easier," we were told. "The work's tough here, the houses are filthy, and the food's plain."

"It doesn't matter," we replied. "We'll see. If we don't like it, we'll go back to the city."

On our first day, we joined the other women workers in

---

[3] Identity papers recorded an individual's social station. Cherniavskaia, who was born into the gentry, would have come under suspicion immediately, had she shown her real papers.

some pretty filthy work: shearing sheep. We performed this monotonous task in a large covered shed, saturated with the smell of sheep. Some of us sheared, while others picked burrs and all sorts of trash that had gotten caught in the wool. Filthy brown wisps filled the air, blinding us, and our hands got covered with a sort of sticky, greasy film. Gloomy silence reigned among the workers.

After we'd spent a few days working in the shed, the lady of the manor dropped by—or flitted in, to be more precise. In those miserable surroundings, she seemed so young and elegant, so full of life and joy, as she went from worker to worker, chattering gaily. Finally she stopped next to Galina and me. She looked curiously at Galina, who was sitting cross-legged on the ground, and asked her two or three questions: evidently she'd met Galina elsewhere under different circumstances, but she expressed no surprise and gave no indication that she recognized her, other than showing somewhat more interest in her than in the others.

Either because the lady intervened, or strictly by coincidence, we were soon transferred from the foul shed to a distant work site in the broad steppe, the realm of green fields. We were assigned to hay mowing.

At four in the morning, as the sun's rays were just beginning to spill over the steppe, the overseer would wake us, kicking the legs of those who wouldn't get up immediately. At the camp, the steward assigned us to the various sectors. In the morning, we froze from the bitterly cold dew, which drenched our clothing up to the waist. Staggering along, still half asleep, we worked as automatically as robots, gradually warming up a bit. At ten, we returned to camp for breakfast, which lasted around half an hour. Despite the camp hubbub, some people preferred to nap instead of eating. Our food was of rather poor quality—very plain and unappetizing. In the morning, they cooked us a watery gruel made from wheat and water with a dose of salt, or buckwheat dumplings as big as cobblestones—one or two of these would satisfy the hunger of even the greatest glutton. The meal was poured into a wooden trough, from which you'd pull the dumplings with long, pointed splinters. We got the same modest fare for lunch and dinner. On religious fast days, they occasionally threw some salted fish into a borscht, but the fish was scrawny, not very fresh, and left an unpleasant taste in your mouth. The workers' dissatisfaction was generally expressed in private grumbling, but they also took out their enmity on the cooks— the line of least resistance, although in fact these shameless cooks were guilty of violating the rules by stealing from the provisions that were sparingly doled out from the master's storehouse.

After our brief breakfast, we returned to work. As the day wore on, the heat became so intense that you wanted to take shelter in any available patch of shade. A few lucky people got under the carts that brought our food for the lunch break, but most of us had to lie on our backs under the sun's burning rays. The sun was so strong that the backs of most of the newly arrived vagabonds were practically covered with swollen blisters; later, as their skin toughened up, the burns went away. We women were often so exhausted from the heat that we lost much of our modesty: when we reaped and bound the hay, we wore only our shirts, since that made it a lot easier to work.

During the busy season, there were no set limits to the work day: if the steward wished, it could last for sixteen hours or more, with only an hour off for lunch. Actually, the work itself was lively and gay, although Galina and I found it difficult and alien.

In the evening, after the sun had set, we returned to camp. The fire would be going and dinner waiting. Some people filled their stomachs with the plain, unsatisfying food and fell asleep on the spot, scattered around camp. Everyone slept under the open sky, harassed by mosquitoes and subject to the bites of other enemies as well: the black spiders, whose venom could make your whole body swell up. Wool or felt bedding was the only protection against these creatures.

After dinner, the young folks started playing, singing, and dancing; they embraced, kissed, and fondled in front of everyone, too. Frequently their revelry lasted far into the night, disturbing the quiet and preventing some people from sleeping, but no one raised a voice in protest against the young folks' tumultuous pleasure. The people who were somewhat older, a sedate crew, would sit around in a circle after dinner, chattering on about one subject or another. All you had to do was find a place in the circle and start talking about some unfamiliar subject—another country or a different people—and a group of listeners would form around you immediately. These manual laborers had an enormous thirst for knowledge, although hardly a dozen in the whole camp were literate—during the entire time we lived there, we never saw anyone with a book or newspaper. For the most part, people were absorbed in the daily concerns of their wretched lives.

At first, people found it rather strange to hear ordinary girls—manual laborers like themselves—speak of many things they'd never heard or even thought about. They became most interested when the conversation touched upon the land: this immensely important topic was dear to every heart. Everyone was united on this issue; they all felt the need for land most acutely, and this provided us a way to reach even the simplest peasant.

However, we didn't actually conduct socialist propaganda; it was clear that we were still an alien, incomprehensible element in a world we scarcely knew. In order to merge with that "world of darkness"—that living denial of all knowledge and cultural values, a world in which for centuries the people had lived virtually in caves, working far too hard—we would have to surmount incredible difficulties, renouncing all the comforts and joys of life and inflicting on ourselves a rigorous, monastic existence. Brief contact with the peasants' world was not enough: you had to make yourself comprehensible to it, gain acceptance, for only then could you merge with it. Of course, our difficulties were compounded by the repressive political system of Russia and the peasants' own fear. They reacted to all radical talk with caution, distrust, and sometimes the most natural incomprehension. Frequently our evening talks ended with the peasants saying: "That's our fate—so it's been written"; or, "We're born—we'll die."

In fact, we were rarely able to talk at all: after the day's work, our limbs shrieked with weariness, our exhausted bodies demanded rest and peace. On holidays, the whole camp scattered. The lazybones who stayed behind slept uninterruptedly all day long.

One day, the chief steward noticed how exhausted Galina and I were—particularly Galina, who wasn't used to physical labor—and he transferred us both to weeding in the melon fields.

One of our new overseers was an old soldier who had served under Nicholas I. He stood straight as a stick and was abnormally serious, but he didn't push us too hard. He was very talkative, and his calm, philosophical attitude toward his duties would not allow him to be very strict with us. He had a passionate love for singing, and the girls were able to take good advantage of this weakness.

The second overseer was a different matter: a slimy city slicker, superficially polished, fairly intelligent, but incredibly impudent. He thought himself superior to the rural "small fry" and had no respect for anyone. The insolent fellow believed it his duty to get as much pleasure as he could amid the ignorance and lawlessness of the countryside. Although he really had no business at all with our group of women, he was forever insinuating himself among us, grabbing at our breasts. The girls shied away from him like horses from a wolf. He was restrained neither by the presence of the elders, nor by his responsibilities to his masters, who knew about his disgraceful conduct (even the steward warned him about his improprieties).

One day, a sudden downpour forced us girls to stop the weeding. Our entire crew crowded into the guard's hut, where we settled down in rows on the ground, talking and joking among ourselves as we waited for the rain to stop. We didn't even notice that the overseer was in the hut too, until he suddenly swooped down upon the knees of the girl in front of Galina. Everyone stopped talking and turned to Galina, as if they expected her to do something: in the camp, we two were considered morally strict, stout-hearted Russians. A second or two passed, then Galina struck the fellow with such dexterity and force that he sailed backwards, his nose plowing up the ground as he rolled head over heels out of the hut amid the shouts and laughter of the girls. This was his first rebuff, and it encouraged everyone who suffered from his habitual, brazen insults. Previously, some people had reacted rather indifferently to his lewd behavior, while others had been paralyzed by the fear of any creature in authority. After this incident, however, the man never again tried to insinuate himself among us. He appeared in our camp only infrequently; and eventually, he was driven from the estate altogether.

As we got to know the Ukrainians firsthand, we learned that certain of their customs which didn't seem inherently reprehensible occasionally brought dire consequences. For example, almost every girl was "going steady" with some boy: they petted and slept together—so long as their love affair didn't go too far. But should a girl get pregnant, it was generally she alone who was censured by those around her, cruelly and categorically, for her weakness and inability to protect herself. The girl bore all the consequences of the couple's mutual sin.

On our first night at the camp, some boys approached us with timid, ingratiating requests to spend the night together; subsequently, one or two made shameless efforts to thrust themselves upon us. Galina and I declared that we Russians didn't accept such customs, and we'd fight anyone brazen enough to try anything. All the older peasants took our side, and they advised the young men to leave us alone. "Grab a stick, girls," they told us, "and smash the snout of anyone who tries to touch you. We'll come help." That evening, they loudly announced to the entire camp: "Hey, boys! Keep your hands off the Russian girls! Their people don't share our customs. If you lay a hand on them, you'll feel our fists!" The consideration and sensitivity of these simple folk moved us deeply.

We had been hired to work four and a half months: after the grain was harvested, we were supposed to stay on through the fall. But toward the end of our term, Galina became utterly exhausted by the backbreaking work, fell ill, and left for Odessa.[4] Late in the fall, when the fields were brown and rain was sprinkling down like fine dust, I returned to the city as well.

By this time, virtually the entire radical community was scattering. Many of the southern populists had already begun to lose faith in the efficacy of socialist propaganda among the peasantry, and they were increasingly searching for new paths, new ways to win the right to live in freedom. Amid the general uncertainty, I decided to learn a trade—cobbling—and I moved to Nikolaev, where I'd found a good teacher.

My apprenticeship was cut short, however, by some alarming news: my two sisters, three brothers, and most of my friends had been arrested in Moscow. I was particularly troubled by the arrest of my two younger brothers, who were still only children—one of them scarcely ten years old. They had been living with my older brother, a doctor who worked for the Moscow *zemstvo*, and were arrested along with him. Although they were released within a couple of weeks, they were on their own, with no money and no place to go—they had literally been thrown out onto the street. I had to go to Moscow; it was unavoidable. Thus, my dreams of labor "in union with the people" ended; life's demands frightened them off.

In Moscow, Ivanovskaia participated in an unsuccessful attempt to free Olga Liubatovich from prison. Subsequently, she took part in her older brother Vasilii's successful jailbreak on January 1, 1877. Everyone involved in this escape was obliged to leave Moscow, and Ivanovskaia returned to the south. Her autobiography gives little information about her activity for the remainder of 1877. The narrative resumes early in 1878.

4 Later, Cherniavskaia, like Ivanovskaia, joined the People's Will.

On January 30, 1878, in the course of a police raid, Ivan Kovalskii and others staged armed resistance in Odessa.[5] My sister,
who had recently been freed on bail, and I were with friends
in Petrovsko-Razumovskii when we read the stunning news.
Everyone became extremely agitated as we read and reread
the article. "This is for real!" people exclaimed. Five or six
days later, a telegram arrived from Odessa: "Please do not
delay your departure to your relatives." This summons came
as a complete surprise to us, and we could think of only one
explanation: some of the "tower people" had resolved to do
everything possible to liberate Kovalskii.

When we returned to Odessa, we found that communications had already been established with Kovalskii and the
precise location of his cell determined. There was a realistic
hope of freeing him: all we had to do was make a tunnel to
the prison wall that adjoined his cell. Kovalskii was notified
of the plan and agreed to it, and we immediately took an
apartment opposite the prison, planning to begin tunneling
as quickly as possible. Our hopes were abruptly shattered,
however, when he was transferred to another cell, on the
second floor. We had to sit back and wait for the trial.

As the weeks and months passed, the authorities made preparations for Kovalskii's court-martial.[6] The revolutionaries, in
turn, began to prepare their response to a possible death
sentence: warnings bearing the seal of the "Executive Committee"[7] were sent to the prosecutor and judge, and copies of
proclamations were mailed to people everywhere. Two defense
counsels came from St. Petersburg; meanwhile, various technical preparations were being made. Public interest in the
trial grew with every passing day, and the mood among the
revolutionary youth of Odessa became highly charged. Finally,
the trial began. The court-martial delivered its verdict on

---

[5] Kovalskii, an ardent proponent of armed resistance to the authorities, was
involved in the operation of an underground press in Odessa.
[6] Special courts had been established to deal with cases involving attacks on
public officials.
[7] The group referred to here is not the Executive Committee of the People's
Will, but rather a small armed group that operated in the south of Russia
during 1878.

July 24: Kovalskii was to die. This was the first death sentence, the first bloody act in the latest phase of the revolutionary struggle.

Upon hearing the sentence, the sea of people that filled the streets swelled in a wave toward the courtroom building, seemingly intending to burst in and wrest away the condemned man. But then the Cossacks and gendarmes, lances atilt and swords bared, forced their way into the dense human mass. For a time, everything merged together; then the crowd disappeared into the evening mist.[8]

The next day, the authorities struck in earnest, as they had planned. The military forces encircling Odessa began the devastation around daybreak, and their operation was comprehensive and merciless. With no place to transfer their captives, the police crammed all the city's Houses of Detention to the rafters. Our own apartment was cleaned out completely: not a soul escaped the roundup.

*Ivanovskaia was released from prison after three months. To avoid further harassment and prosecution, she went to Rumania, where her brother was living in an émigré colony of Russian radicals. She does not elaborate on her political development during this period, but early in 1880, when she returned to the north of Russia, she joined the People's Will. The party put her to work in its underground printing plant.*

The apartment was to be staffed by Nikolai Kibalchich and me (alias the Agicheskulovs) and Lila Terenteva (alias Trifonova), who was to pose as a poor relative working as our servant. As was often the case in this kind of operation, we didn't know each other beforehand, although I had met Lilochka Terenteva in Odessa. Generally speaking, the title of "socialist," with the addition of "revolutionary," served as sufficient guarantee of comradely kinship, intimacy, and readiness for sacrifice of all sorts. However, occasionally people

---

[8] This was the first armed demonstration in Russian revolutionary history, and two people were killed in the clash. Kovalskii was executed on August 2, 1878.

found their apartment mates too incompatible, even though they were fellow radicals, and categorically refused to live with them; and since it was best to be cautious in establishing a fictional "family," Lila and I asked for a prior meeting with the man who was going to be living with us.

We went to this "trial inspection" in a mood of pleasant anticipation, making somewhat more of the situation than was warranted. Young, vivacious, and impatient, Lilochka pestered me with questions constantly: "What's he like? Nice, intelligent, serious? Where's he from?" All the way to our meeting, we fantasized, speculated, and made conjectures about the stranger.

As it turned out, the meeting with Kibalchich was quite cold and restrained, consisting of a brief exchange of opinions on the setup of the apartment and the number of workers. The warmth and friendliness one would expect at a meeting of people of the same faith and ideas were lacking. More than that: the feelings we developed toward our reticent future apartment mate were not altogether positive ones. True, Kibalchich seemed quite proper, much older than his years, and this inspired our respect. But his exaggerated pallor and utterly unchanging expression made him appear unpleasantly lifeless, dull-witted, slightly indifferent to everything—an impression that was heightened by the locks of dark hair that fell, straight as icicles, over his high forehead. Every now and then, however, his beautiful blue eyes would flash, brightening up his face and relieving the languor habitually exhibited there.

As Lila and I walked back from the meeting, she blurted out her judgments of Kibalchich: "There's a fine roommate for you! What a sloppy fellow! And to live and work together in a complicated situation, when you need a lot of discretion and sometimes quick wits, too. . . . Well, it'll be interesting to see how things work out."

Subsequently, we completely reversed our unfavorable opinion of Kibalchich. We had formed our rash judgment merely because we failed to observe in him the noisy outbursts of enthusiasm common to other people—such behavior was alien to this bookish, very contemplative man. True, Kibalchich didn't share the illusions harbored by most of the young people of the time, but he wasn't a pessimist in the ordinary sense: his words radiated hope. Nikolai had offered his energies and knowledge to the People's Will in 1879, after his release from prison, where he had suffered agonies during the harshest period of the reaction, enduring prolonged solitary confinement. Prison had drained him of all color. At rare moments, the bitterness seemed more than he could contain; he remarked to us that sometimes he was seized by the desire to throw a lit match into a powder keg.

Although none of us had any notion of the printing trade, we began work in the party's printing plant as soon as we received the articles for the newspaper. Technical difficulties frightened us very little; it had been resolved that there would be a free press in the heart of our homeland, come what may. Annushka, who posed as the "servant" in a previous press operation of the party, was assigned to instruct us in the basic techniques of printing. She gave us a few demonstrations, then left us to our own devices, correctly assuming that the necessary habits and skills would come to us as we worked.

We did make mistakes, however, as we were just beginning work on the *Leaflet of the People's Will*, and this sent us into a rage. We got the first pages set, inserted them into the frame, and began printing. The roller glided smoothly and quietly over the type. But when we lifted off the sheet, we found it was covered with the oddest collection of symbols— a regular series of black lines clearly and intelligibly spread across one column while bald patches and muddled zigzags decorated another. All our collective wisdom, our rearranging and cleaning of the type, helped not a whit—we couldn't comprehend the machine's secret game. Infuriated beyond words at this lifeless thing that was torturing us so cruelly, we stopped work. The next morning, Alexander Mikhailov[9] ap-

[9] Mikhailov was one of the leaders in the People's Will. His constant concern for the strict observance of conspiratorial practices earned him the nickname of "concierge."

peared, looking anxious. He examined everything in a stern, proprietary manner, placed the glass columns under the legs of the couch, diligently cleaned the type, spread new ink . . . alas! To no avail!

The next morning, he brought over a metal worker who belonged to the party, and this man quickly and skillfully adjusted the fickle machine. The far-sighted Mikhailov, who wanted to renovate and expand the press as quickly as possible, wasn't satisfied with the situation, but we were able to resume work. Things went smoothly and without interruption, and the first issue of the *Leaflet of the People's Will* saw the light of day on June 1, 1880. Party members and the reading public received it joyfully, while the Okhrana [a branch of the political police] greeted it in their usual fashion.

We intended to start setting type for the second issue as soon as we were finished with the first, without taking a breather. However, as was often the case, the party's journalists began to suffer from overwork, or else lacked the proper mood; and since our activity was bound up so closely with that of these intellectual workers, we had to call a temporary halt. This plunged us into a depression. But Alexander Mikhailov, whose sharp eye never missed a lapse in party operations, detected the gloom engendered by our idleness and assured us emphatically that henceforth everything would be arranged properly, that we had no need to become depressed.

Actually, Kibalchich took no part whatsoever in the printing work. He would leave the house at ten in the morning, carrying a briefcase and wearing a rather faded top hat, and usually return late in the evening; it was rare that he made it back for dinner. He was engrossed in devising a new type of air engine,[10] and he spent hours on end working in his room. Now and then, he dropped into the room where we worked—not to help, but rather to relieve the tension of intellectual

---

[10] Kibalchich was one of the party's experts on explosives, and his work apparently suggested to him the possibility of building a propulsion system for a flying machine—an "air engine." After his arrest, he continued to work on his plans in prison. He requested the opportunity to discuss his ideas with technical experts before his execution, but the government refused to permit this.

activity and straighten out his back, which was eternally bent over his books. Sometimes Nikolai would refer, ever so briefly, to his long imprisonment and his relationships with the so-called "rabble"—that is, the ordinary criminals. As our life together continued and we got used to this peculiar man, this lethargic philosopher, we came to understand him better; and he, too, came much closer to us. His learning rendered him alien to all pettiness, all philistinism and conceit. He was habitually calm and melancholy—except when Vera Figner visited our apartment: then Nikolai suddenly became so gay and talkative that he was unrecognizable.

By August 20, 1880, we'd finished the second issue of the *Leaflet*. Alexander Mikhailov appeared around this time to announce that our "family"—which had actually become quite close-knit—had to be reorganized: the philosopher Nikolai wasn't suited to serve as the proprietor of a printing operation. (A much more probable explanation is that Kibalchich had become necessary for another kind of project.)

Although Mikhailov's decision was unequivocal, it was two months before Kibalchich actually left us. We watched him change during that period, watched him become more and more distant. He was increasingly immersed in his demanding work, and spent fewer and fewer nights at home. We came to feel that our printing work was irrelevant to him, although out of tact he did try to be attentive to the rest of his "family." At times, these efforts failed and provoked our laughter, which instantly brought him back to reality. One small incident from this period comes to mind.

One day, when Lila and I were deeply involved in urgent work, Nikolai suddenly proposed that we all have some tea.

"Put up the samovar and have it alone this time," Lilochka answered. "The samovar's in the kitchen; you'll find everything you need there."

Nikolai stopped in the doorway, dumfounded. Spreading his hands in a helpless gesture, he said, with a hint of indignation: "Well, you know, that's not *man's* work!"

The outburst of laughter that greeted his statement made his bewilderment complete.

"All right, all right," he said, "but I don't know anything about this stuff." Since neither of us budged, he walked
off into the kitchen to try to solve this problem of woman's
work.

Before long, a racket began to issue from the kitchen:
water was roaring out of the faucet, and apparently something
had fallen down and was clattering around the floor. It
sounded as if a large bear had gotten in and was on the ram-
page. Lilochka dropped what she was doing and rushed headlong to the rescue. She found Nikolai standing there, at a loss
amid the confusion he'd created.

"There's no need to make all that noise," I heard Lilochka
tell him laughingly. "You should live in the wilderness and
be a hermit!" As they were putting things in order, I heard
her declaiming in her cheerful, tender voice, "From the beginning of my life I loved gloomy solitude." After a while, Nikolai walked out—sad, embarrassed, and covered with coal
dust.

On September 20, we finished printing No. 3 of the *Leaflet*.
We prepared to liquidate our apartment and move immediately to a new, larger place. The long-delayed personnel
change was to be carried out, too.

On our last day together, Nikolai asked us to take a walk
with him to Gostinny Dvor [the merchants' arcade] to help
him buy a new overcoat—a "respectable" one, as Alexander
Mikhailov emphasized. For some reason, all the details of
this little business expedition are indelibly impressed on my
mind. Perhaps the extraordinarily lovely autumn weather was
affecting Nikolai, because he was inexplicably talkative, cheerful, and playful all the way there. When we got to the arcade,
we walked up and down the rows of stalls and selected a coat
with great care. Nikolai put it on immediately, and for greater
stylishness, bought a walking stick and gloves. As we strolled
back home, I remember him suddenly stopping in the middle
of the sidewalk to inspect his elegant attire. Apparently he
was completely satisfied, because a broad, childlike smile
spread over his pale face.

"Now, that's how 'Mr. Agicheskulov' should look," he said. "Nobody would recognize me now."

The next day, we parted with Kibalchich forever.

After we moved to the new apartment, our work resumed at a lively pace, despite the difficult political situation—in particular, the fact that the vast, well-organized police apparatus was devoting considerable attention to the search for illegal printing presses. As far as possible, the party made it a rule to use only proven people, or else members of the central group itself, to staff illegal apartments and carry out dangerous work. Accordingly, Mikhail Grachevskii, a man well acquainted with revolutionary activity, was made the head of our fictional family and proprietor of the press. However, in two or three days, a stranger appeared in our apartment—a rather odd creature who slipped in unnoticed, like a foundling. With a hint of swagger, he introduced himself simply as "Bratushka."[11] The party had placed him with us to learn the operations of a press and become a competent typographer. Bratushka worked with obvious reluctance for several days, then abruptly stopped, giving us to understand in no uncertain terms that this work was as necessary to him as the priest's incense to a corpse. He would get up in the morning, drink his tea, and around noon make his appearance in the room adjoining our work room. There he would spend hours on end, sunk deep into the couch, whistling or singing in a melancholy fashion. As a matter of conspiratorial practice, unregistered residents of the apartment were not allowed to go outside during the day, and so Bratushka spent all his time with us, on the sofa. Whenever we invited him to stretch his muscles and join in the work, he delivered his tiresome retort for all to hear: "I was born to be a Stenka Razin, a Pugachev. My place is among the people, in the midst of a rebellion. I'll never accommodate myself to 'moderation.' My hands will never be soiled by any kind of dirty work."

Bratushka wasn't a bad person, and of course it was in-

11 "Little brother."

conceivable to us that he would intentionally wreck our operation. All the same, the idleness of this "orator" became positively intolerable to us, and his tendency to indiscreet, childish outbursts made him a great risk to our security, so we urgently requested that he be removed from the press.

*In fact, the entire operation soon had to be moved once again. The rhythmic sounds of type dropping into the chest disturbed a retired general living directly above the press, and he sent the superintendent down to investigate the "water leak" that was ostensibly producing the noise. Nothing incriminating was discovered, but the group decided it was best to take no unnecessary risks.*

The printing staff as it was reconstituted after our move comprised a very cohesive group of people with long service in the party. For example, the articles were brought to us by Grigorii Isaev, who had been a regular visitor to the first press. Energetic, cheerful, and serene, Isaev always enlivened the group. At the same time, he was sternly conscientious; according to him, serving the revolution inevitably meant restricting your personal life. "Personal renunciation," he would say, "doesn't mean renouncing one's identity, but rather renouncing one's egoism." All of Isaev's life forces and human aspirations were directed to the revolutionary cause— it absorbed him completely. When he observed other people tending to falter in their dedication to radicalism, he hastened to straighten them out as best he could. Nothing could make him retreat. "Our task, our supreme task, is to gain justice for our Russian people," he frequently repeated.

Isaev had been away for some time, and when he resumed visiting us at our new apartment, we were struck by the fact that he constantly wore a glove on one hand. We could sense that there had been some serious incident, some tragic accident that had mutilated his fingers, but we were all reluctant to ask him directly.[12] When he set type, he always

---

[12] I learned that when Isaev was in Odessa, a test tube full of mercury fulminate had exploded in his hands and ripped off three fingers. When he was brought to the hospital, he told the medical authorities that a machine had cut off

pressed his forearm and elbow against his chest; most of his former dexterity was gone. Still, Isaev was a most diligent and skillful worker, and when he was in St. Petersburg, he was our most frequent visitor.

Alexander Barannikov—"Semyon," as we called him—was another regular visitor.[13] In radical circles, he was justifiably known as a "knight without fear or reproach," the most devoted soldier of the revolution. As a youth, he had been trained in a strict military school. Out of that deforming experience, out of the rubbish of institutional life, he had drawn what was of value—concern for the weak, enviable tact in all matters, and, particularly, an unfailingly gentlemanly attitude to women. I remember those tedious work nights when, to dispel our fatigue and keep us awake, Semyon would start recounting fantastic tales of his flight from the Orlov military school or of his numerous other adventures; then sometimes Lila would softly and tenderly sing her favorite song. Those nights slipped away like sand in an hourglass, gently and imperceptibly. How fine and joyful it was!

One day, I recall, Barannikov made a rather untimely appearance at the apartment. Ordinarily so cheerful and straightforward, he now exhibited an unfamiliar, businesslike seriousness; there was something self-important and official in his manner. He invited everyone into one room and assumed a Mephistophelian pose, leaning against the door frame. In the name of the Executive Committee of the People's Will, he rapidly enumerated, point by point, the simple regulations governing our rights and duties. We were indifferent to the former, and the latter had become rooted in our consciousness over time: we were not to write or receive letters from anyone, communicate with people outside the press, or attend meetings, get-togethers, and the like; we were to live as if there were nothing and no one around us—to reduce our existence

---

his fingers at a factory. Since he asserted from the start that it was his own fault and that he wasn't going to make any claims, they somehow believed his story.—Ivanovskaia. (See p. 48.)

[13] After Alexander Mikhailov's arrest on November 28, 1880, Semyon became our regular contact with the party center.—Ivanovskaia.

to the life and work that went on within the walls of our apartment. We knew full well the enormous obligations we bore by virtue of our revolutionary consciousness—to act with utmost care, so as to protect the apartment and the people involved with it.

After Barannikov finished reciting these stern regulations, he abruptly changed back into the familiar, unaffected Semyon. "Whew! I've run on," he announced animatedly, as if he'd just thrown down a heavy load. "I don't like these official business talks."

For our sakes, one precious exception was made to the prohibition on seeing friends: once a week (on Saturday evenings, as I recall) and in the intervals between printing jobs, we visited Sofia Perovskaia's apartment. She shared the place with Andrei Zheliabov, and when we stayed late, we saw him, too. However, sometimes he didn't even notice our presence as he walked past Sofia's open door: he simply went into his room, flung off his clothes and shoes, and dropped onto the bed like a felled tree, as if he had but one invincible desire—to sleep.

To us, the visits to Perovskaia were like a refreshing shower. Sofia always gave us a warm, friendly welcome; she acted as if we were the ones with stimulating ideas and news to share, rather than the reverse. In her easy and natural way, she painstakingly helped us to make sense of the complicated muddle of everyday life and the vacillations of public opinion. She told us about the party's activities among workers, about various circles and organizations, and about the expansion of the revolutionary movement among previously untouched social groups. Perovskaia spoke calmly, without a trace of sentimentality, but there was no hiding the joy that lit up her face and shone in her crinkled, smiling eyes—it was as if she were talking about a child of hers who had recovered from an illness.

There were many occasions when Perovskaia reaffirmed for us the value of the work we were doing. During one period in particular, when all of us were depressed, Lilochka began bothering Sofia for a more dangerous party assignment. Lila was younger than the rest of us and the fighting spirit was very strong in her, but it was more a kind of childlike greediness that prompted her request. A shadow fell across Perovskaia's weary face, as she carefully heard her out, then she walked up to Lila and tenderly stroked her ardent head: "Don't think, Lila," she said sadly, "that the press is any less necessary and valuable to the party's work than throwing bombs."

As time passed, we became confident that the printing plant was absolutely secure. One unforeseen incident, however, and we were thrown back on guard.

It was long past midnight, and Grachevskii was sitting around in the large room, which was virtually empty. The windows were wide open. Outside, it was silent and deserted; the night was utterly dark. Suddenly cabs came clattering down our lightly traveled street—louder and louder, closer and closer, until they stopped at our front door. Mikhail walked over to the window to get a look at the gentlemen who were arriving so late. The darkness was impenetrable; all he could make out were the sounds of careful movements and quiet conversation. A group of people walked away from the cab, continuing to talk softly. Then, suddenly, there was an almost imperceptible flash of an electric lamp: apparently they were searching the wall for the number of the house. Aided by the fleeting ray of light, Grachevskii clearly saw gendarme uniforms and aiguillettes—there was no doubt about the purpose of these night visitors. The measured tinkle of their spurs stopped for a moment as they entered the front door, then resumed as they began to move up the stairs. The footsteps approached, the sounds became clearer. By this time, we were all pressed against our front door, as if frozen in place. Gloomy and resolute, Grachevskii was preparing a defense: a bomb lay in the anteroom; he held the wick in one hand, matches in the other. Everything could be over in an instant: if the gendarmes pressed the door bell, if there was the slightest pressure on the door itself . . .

But the tinkle of spurs continued to move up the stairway: stepping as carefully as burglars, the gendarmes passed our landing. Then, ever so gently, Grachevskii opened the door a crack and listened. The sound diminished, then died out altogether, and we dispersed to our beds, reassuring each other with the plausible assertion that the foul night melodies of gendarme raids always began with ascending spirals, that they weren't launched from above.

In the morning, the handyman who brought the firewood up to our apartment informed Lilochka of an extraordinary incident, the likes of which he'd never seen: "Last night the gendarmes were up there at the students' place looking for something," he said. "They didn't let the superintendent sleep all night. What a terrible thing!"

Before long, the dark forces of the Okhrana initiated an all-out offensive against the revolutionary movement—in particular, against the Executive Committee of the People's Will.

At ten o'clock on the night of February 25, 1881, we heard our doorbell ringing nervously. No one would have come at that hour unless there was an emergency. An indistinct figure slipped silently through our door, as if he were being pursued. It was Grigorii Isaev. He lit a lamp—now we could see that his hand was shaking violently—and headed toward one of the back rooms, which had curtains on the windows. His face was pale; he seemed to have aged in recent days.

"They've arrested Semyon and Kletochnikov," he said in a voice devoid of expression.

Semyon—so bold and resourceful in dangerous situations! And Kletochnikov, the party's peerless protector, the idealistic guardian of its interests![14] It was enough to drive one to despair.

Two days later, on February 27, Andrei Zheliabov was arrested, and Perovskaia had to abandon their apartment. It was Grachevskii, upset and stammering, who brought us the news of this loss. He'd gotten the key to Sofia's place, and

[14] See p. 52.

we had to clean it out immediately. The task wasn't the least bit dangerous or even difficult, because our place, which everyone acknowledged to be secure, was very close to hers. Our printing "family" went as a group to the apartment we knew so well. It was all very quiet and peaceful. By the faint light of flickering candles, we collected the most incriminating items; then, casting one last glance around the apartment, we softly locked the door behind us and slipped away, unobserved, with our parcels. We returned home feeling profoundly satisfied that we had completed our mission successfully.

Grachevskii left our apartment early on the twenty-eighth, parting with us warmly and informing us that we shouldn't expect him before the following morning. He lingered a bit, as if trying to recall something he'd forgotten, then said: "How can one know who'll be the lucky one? Perhaps tomorrow there'll be none of us left." He spoke these words firmly, confidently; there was no trace of sadness or anxiety in his voice.

Thirty hours later, two thunderous explosions shook Russia, announcing to the whole country that the People's Will had carried out its death sentence on the tsar.

Intoxicated by the arrests of central figures in the party during the preceding days, the government—and the tsar himself—had failed to hear the rumblings of impending doom; more accurately, they hadn't wanted to hear them. It would scarcely be an exaggeration to say that if all but one member of the Executive Committee' had been arrested, even then the sentence pronounced by the party on August 26, 1879, would have been carried out. It was inevitable. The honor of the country demanded it; the honor of the party demanded it.

Grachevskii returned home at ten o'clock on March 1, looking as if he were drunk: his eyes were glazed and sunk more deeply than usual into their sockets, his cheeks were hollow, his skin a pale shade of green. Reeling slightly, he walked silently to his bed and sank down on it without undressing; there he remained, motionless, until the morning of March 2.

In the evening, Grigorii Isaev brought for immediate printing the Executive Committee's proclamation on the execution of Alexander II and its letter to Alexander III. The letter was of enormous interest to us, as it was to society at large. The first printing was ten thousand copies, and as the demand kept increasing, additional printings followed.

*In the weeks following the assassination, the People's Will was decimated by arrests. Sofia Perovskaia, who had coordinated the attack on the tsar, was recognized on the street and arrested on March 10; Nikolai Kibalchich was captured a week later. Along with Andrei Zheliabov, Gesia Gelfman, and two of the bomb throwers, Nikolai Rysakov and Timofei Mikhailov, they were tried for their role in the assassination and, on March 29, sentenced to death.*

On April 1, Grigorii Isaev's involvement with the press ended, as he was arrested on the street. In order to determine where he lived, the authorities summoned all St. Petersburg building superintendents to the offices of the civil administration, where Isaev was being held. Our precinct began to report at 9 a.m. on April 2. Accompanied by his assistants, our fat superintendent set off for the inspection at a leisurely pace. There's no need to describe the anxiety and impatience we felt as we waited for them to return: Lilochka, for example, incessantly invented pretexts to go down into the courtyard and check whether they'd gotten back. Finally, they returned, took off their holiday clothes and identification tags, and set about their work.

Before long, the handyman appeared at our door with the firewood. Apologizing for being late, he proceeded to inform Lilochka about the extraordinarily significant event of that morning: the authorities had called in all the superintendents of the precinct to try to identify a certain man, either as one of their residents or as someone they knew.

"Well, so?" Lila asked impatiently.

"Who knows! No one from our precinct recognized him;

the gentleman was a complete stranger. It's terrible how curious people are—they kept milling around like a herd of animals at a water hole."

Subsequently we learned that in the afternoon, the police had begun admitting every passer-by to "take a look" at the suspect. Isaev eventually became like a man possessed, maliciously ridiculing these "volunteers." For example, when a self-important merchant who resembled a cuttlefish walked up to Isaev, the suspect greeted him: "Well, hello there, hello! How are you?"

The cuttlefish goggled, dumfounded.

"Don't you remember?" asked Isaev. "Those illegal books I brought you to hide, have you forgotten?!"

Later, two students who knew Grigorii walked right up to him and silently exchanged expressive glances with him. Through these young women, we learned that the police had stood the exhausted Isaev on a chair in the middle of the room, and by evening, he was so unsteady on his feet that two men were needed to hold him up—he was virtually draped over their shoulders. Finally, around midday on April 3, the

*The examination of Isaev*

superintendents of Voznesensk precinct got their turn, and the show ended.

April 3—a day every Russian would remember forever. We went over to Isaev's apartment, which the Okhrana was still doggedly seeking. Everything we were to remove had been packed up in two large bundles. We had been given an address for the things, the name of the person who would receive them, and a password to use. One at a time, we walked out of the apartment. The large courtyard was empty, totally still; the streets were dead—no movement whatsoever.

The people at our destination had probably been alerted that we were coming, because as soon as we rang the bell, the woman of the house unlocked the door herself. Altogether unexpectedly, she turned out to be someone I knew, an old schoolmate from the Alarchinskii courses. She was very cordial: without a trace of awkwardness, she accepted the bundles and invited us in to rest for a while. The conversation immediately turned to the trial of the "people of March first," the regicides. She had known Kibalchich, who was to be hanged that day, and his magnificent demeanor during the trial had enraptured and amazed her; as she thought of his fate, she clasped her head in her hands and began to sob, bitterly and uncontrollably.

As we walked slowly back home, feeling the effects of all that we had experienced in recent days, we suddenly noticed a crowd moving toward us from Semenovskii Square. Soldiers, dashing songs, bravura music. . . . Everything became clear. Lilochka covered her eyes with her hand and said, her voice filled with grief: "More than anything, I would have liked to die there with them." With a movement of her head, she indicated the square where the regicides had just been executed.

That same day—April 3, 1881—the Executive Committee of the People's Will published a proclamation on the occasion of the execution, giving notice that the party would continue the struggle and calling upon all of society for assistance.

St. Petersburg was intensely agitated in the wake of the trial.

The excitement was universal during those fleeting spring days, but of course, like differently shaped mirrors, everyone reflected events in his or her own particular way. Nonetheless, the fact that the party's actions had forced everyone to think, to emerge from the profound lethargy that had engulfed them for so long, made us rejoice: even if we had outraged some people, at least we had affected their conscience.

And yet, the public did not respond to our appeal of April 3: confused, passive, it allowed the government to devour the People's Will without a trace. The party carried on the struggle alone, with its isolated, dwindling forces. But even as it was perishing in the unequal battle, it was demonstrating clearly to everyone that the social-revolutionary movement was the moral victor—not the tsar, not the Okhrana, not the bureaucracy. And the fact that this was generally recognized meant that the tasks and goals set by the People's Will were correct and historically inevitable. By striking a blow at the heart of the state, the party had cried aloud, not only to our compatriots but to the whole world, as well: "Russia and the Russian people need political freedom. We need the complete liberation of our country!"

Once begun, the campaign to destroy the People's Will gathered momentum like a rock rolling down a mountainside. Doors were smashed, bombs exploded, people perished— everything around us came tumbling down. April brought a continuation of the terrifying, uninterrupted arrests that had decimated the leadership of the party. At times, our own situation seemed puzzling: most of the party was behind bars, but we printing workers were still at large, as if we led a charmed life.

But the end eventually came for us, as it does for all things in life. On May 2, Lilochka left the house after dinner and for the first time failed to return by the time the three of us customarily reassembled at home. The hours passed, and we finally ran out of plausible explanations. Apparently she'd been arrested somewhere. A cruel gloom enveloped us.

*The trial of "the people of March first"*

---

Steps had to be taken. First of all, Grachevskii went off to consult with the other party members. He returned with unequivocal instructions to abandon the apartment immediately; there was no possibility of saving the press. He slowly set about sorting through the various papers: the most important manuscripts and the notebooks summarizing the information which party traitors had given to the police went into a briefcase;[15] we placed the remaining piles of accumulated papers in the stove, taking care to ensure that the burning sheets wouldn't fly up the chimney on to the roof and attract the attention of firemen. The darkened apartment suddenly seemed cold and gloomy. We moved around softly, without speaking, as one moves in a house where someone has died. Our minds were on the terrible human losses suffered by the party and the disintegration of its well-run operations.

Early the next morning, we were awakened by the piercing

[15] The party had obtained this information through Kletochnikov, its agent within the political police administration.

ring of the doorbell. Grachevskii delayed for a bit before going to answer the door. It was the handyman who always serviced our apartment, now somewhat abashed, since he hadn't come for a routine household chore.

"Well," he began, "I'm supposed to ask you if you're all at home."

"And where would we be going?" Grachevskii asked in turn. "We're home, we're home, there's my wife." Mikhail pointed to my room, and the handyman got a glimpse of me through the open door. Reassured, he explained the reason for his early visit: they'd received an order from the authorities to check whether all residents were in their apartments.

Two hours later, we abandoned our empty, devastated nest. Of the people who had worked in the illegal press, only Grachevskii and I were able to leave of our own volition. All the others, with whom we had so often shared the dangers and the long nights of labor, had been snatched away at the stormiest point of the struggle—they were captives, lost forever in the deepest gloom. For them, life was over.

Without losing a minute, Grachevskii went to a barber shop and had his beard, mustache, and eyebrows removed. He left the city on the first train to Moscow.

*Ivanovskaia, too, went to Moscow, where the survivors of the People's Will had established a new underground press. A wave of arrests soon ended this undertaking, however. In September 1882, on a mission to Vitebsk, where the Executive Committee had assembled still another printing staff, Ivanovskaia was arrested.*

*The Trial of the Seventeen—members of the People's Will who were accused of involvement in the assassination of the tsar—took place from March 25 to April 3, 1883. Ivanovskaia received a death sentence, which was commuted to life at hard labor. After three and a half months in the Petropavlovsk fortress in St. Petersburg, she was sent off to Kara, eastern Siberia.*

*The following introductory paragraphs and letters (for which no addressee is given) were published in 1923.*

Political prisoners sentenced to hard labor weren't in fact taken out to work the gold deposits of Kara—we weren't even allowed to carry our own firewood and water into the prison. Strictly isolated from the other nearby prisons of Kara, the compounds for "politicals" had their own special personnel. The administration was headed by a commandant invested with broad powers. There were gendarmes to keep watch inside the political prisons and detachments of soldiers who ordinarily stayed outside, except when there was a hunger strike or suicide by poison: then the governor or governor-general who appeared inside the prison for an inspection invariably surrounded himself with a cordon of armed soldiers.

Political prisoners were permitted to correspond with relatives only by postcard. They allowed us to write the cards ourselves, but we couldn't sign them with our own names. The messages were terse: "Your sister received fifteen rubles and your letter of 20 January. Your sister is very worried by

*The hanging of the regicides*

your silence and wonders where you are at present. Your sister kisses and embraces everyone. Kiss your little ones. (Signed) Lt.-Col. Masiukov, Commandant." Of course, these few lines conveyed nothing to our families and friends back home, and so we were always on the lookout for opportunities, however indirect, to communicate more fully. For example, we sometimes smuggled letters out with people leaving the prison for the exile settlement: encoded letters made by dotting the pages of books, or else letters written on pieces of white calico, which we then sewed into worn articles made of heavy gray institutional cloth. Of course, when relatively safe opportunities presented themselves, we simply wrote and sent long letters. Unfortunately, few of these mementos of the past generation have survived: some were lost or destroyed on the road, and the ones that were received intact were often placed in people's basements, to protect them from police searches, and there they rotted over the years. However, the few pages from my correspondence that have been preserved will give the reader a picture of a small part of our life in those penal tombs, which shattered the lives of hundreds of ardent young people, turning human beings into the living dead. The letters were written between 1885 and 1888.

# I

Long ago I promised to write in detail about our life in Kara, and I hope to keep that promise with this letter. I know absolutely nothing about life in the Shlisselburg fortress in St. Petersburg or about the people interred there; I'd appreciate any information at all. Not a soul has left there yet—at least, no one has made it to Kara. Everyone, or almost everyone, who's come to Kara after the trials of recent years spent the "probation" period in Petropavlovsk fortress, and the stories you hear about that experience literally make your hair stand on end: those who had to endure it for long wound up as living corpses. Before the administration could send them on to Kara, they had to be brought on stretchers to the House of Preliminary Detention to recuperate. They were fattened up a bit and given medical treatment courtesy of the state, then dispatched as soon as they felt a little better.

Of the women, Tatiana Lebedeva and Anna Iakimova suffered most during the "probation" period. However, since Iakimova had an infant, she was eventually granted certain privileges: they improved her food and allowed her to sew things for the baby. Although she was put in a separate building and given no books, caring for the child filled up her time. As for Lebedeva, she was sick the whole time, and no one paid the slightest attention. Like all the "probationers," she developed terrible scurvy. It got so bad that she was lying around like a corpse, all puffed up—she couldn't eat, because her teeth had loosened up and her gums were swollen, and she was indifferent to everything, barely conscious. They called in a doctor, who did nothing more than order a lemon to supplement her food—which she couldn't eat anyway. Only through the auspices of a priest, whom she'd called in for this purpose, was Lebedeva able to get the Bible and a few books of that sort; earlier she'd asked for books and had been turned down. The attendants ("uncles," they were called) treated the prisoners very crudely, addressing them as "thou," and the only official who would talk with them in their cells was the warder; the others refused on the grounds that convicts had no right to submit complaints or requests. Protest was out of the question: the prisoners had been separated in such a way that they knew nothing about each other. As for hunger strikes, they could have nearly starved to death before being noticed.

Lebedeva spent more than a year under these conditions, and one can only be amazed that she was able to survive, given her bad health. I myself had thought she was dead, and I was astonished by her appearance when she arrived in Kara: she'd recovered so well on the road that you couldn't even tell she'd been sick. However, under the conditions at Kara, her symptoms quickly reappeared, and she became seriously ill during the winter, even though she was immediately put on the regimen for a sick person—that is, she was given better food, one of the better cells, and no heavy work.

The Kara prison most resembles a tumble-down stable. The dampness and cold are ferocious; there's no heat at all in the cells, only two stoves in the corridor. The cell doors are kept open day and night—otherwise we would freeze to death. In winter, a thick layer of ice forms on the walls of the corner cells, and at night, the undersides of the straw mattresses get covered with hoarfrost.

Everyone congregates in the corridor in winter, because it's closer to the stoves and you get a warm draft. Since the cells farthest from the stove are completely uninhabitable, the people who live in them carry their beds into the corridor. Of course, there are "heroes"—people who crave whatever temporary solitude they can get: numbed from the cold, they stay in the solitary cells. As Natalia Armfeld has often said, "It would be possible to endure the cold, if you didn't have to take your hands out from under the blanket. Oh, my dears, if only someone would invent tongs that would mechanically snuff out your candles and turn the pages of your book!"

I've been one of the temporary residents of the corridor, and I can say that the accommodations weren't particularly comfortable or quiet. Cooking, bread baking, and all sorts of washing were done there: at the table, someone would be reading recent periodicals, while right next to her, there was someone making chopped meat for the sick people or sloshing underwear around in a trough. Last winter, however, we drew up a "constitution" for ourselves. Since the cold made it impossible to do any studying in the cells, and since the bustle in the corridor had been preventing all but light reading there, henceforth we would have two days a week of silence, when the corridor would be used exclusively for reading. Anyone who wanted to strike up a conversation had to move off into one of the distant cells and speak softly, since the partitions were thin and loud talk could be heard everywhere.

Everyone has been very satisfied with the constitution, and violations are extremely rare. Usually, transgressors are reprimanded immediately and quiet down. There are occasional exceptions, however. Sometimes, after observing the constitution all day long, everyone gradually begins to feel the need to talk. No one wants to be the only person to break the silence, but finally someone perceives the general mood, and she has only to open her mouth for an uproar to break out. The samovar is heated up, and a sumptuous "feast" begins.

Whether it's due to the hunger or the cold, the samovar always plays an important role in our "feasts." Whenever there's a public event—the arrival of letters from back home or mail with recent news from the men's prison, for example— we heat up the samovar, even at night (in fact, many people like that best of all—the samovar at night is an event in itself). Tanichka Lebedeva, who's been keeping the accounts for us—she's the "elder" here—considers herself duty bound to grumble a little whenever this happens, assuring us that people will get excited and eat too much of our stock of sugar; but no one listens to her at such times.

During the day, they lock only the prison gates (outer and inner), but in the evening, they lock the entrance to our living area, as well. Each cell is scarcely big enough to accommodate two narrow beds and a tiny table between them. The windows of the cells are small and set right up near the ceiling, like those in the stables of poor estates; as a result, there's very little light. In the corridor, only the section that has the window gets any light; the other part, which is blocked off by the stoves, is pitch dark.

All our meetings take place at the dinner table, near the window. We generally read newspapers and journals together. Once a week—sometimes less—they bring the books we've requested from the library, which is located in the men's prison, about fifteen kilometers away. They're delivered by a mounted Cossack, who sometimes drops them out of the bag on the way over, losing them forever.

I'm very sorry that I don't have the pictures drawn by Natalia Armfeld. She does humorous sketches of our prison family life and poems and cartoons to commemorate all the notable events here, such as a visit by some feeble general or other important personage.

Out here, the best commandant is the one who visits a prison least, and since the women's prison is rather remote, we get visited less often than the men do. We've had four different commandants since I came here. None of them has been here much, except for this last one, who likes to engage us in conversation—partly to gather useful information, partly just because he's senile and verbose. He's a pettifogger and likes to play nasty tricks on the sly, so that they can't be pinned on him. In general, he's a laughingstock both to the prisoners and to his subordinates.

Last summer, someone reported the commandant for allegedly allowing prisoners to write *too much* on their postcards! As a result, the flow of correspondence was stopped completely for a while: all letters were turned over for examination to the Irkutsk gendarme administration, which was henceforth to control correspondence. But soon the authorities perceived that this plan was exceedingly stupid—in fact, they themselves would find it inconvenient—and so the old procedures were restored. The net result was simply that they forced us to sit here for some months without mail, a very painful loss for us. News from home is the unfading light of our lives. Letters— even the most ordinary, trivial letters—bring us indescribable pleasure. We wait for the Cossack who delivers these words from home as if he were a messenger from heaven. Even if only one person gets a letter, there is universal rejoicing.

By the way: you probably know about the Transbaikal governor's new circular, which prohibits sending money to people in Kara. It's totally preposterous: it says that it's unnatural to help anyone but the closest relatives. I think that it probably resulted from some report made by the commandant.

I won't say anything about the material conditions here; enough's been written already. Anyone who takes an interest in Kara knows how bad things are in both prisons, and how important it is to help maintain the health of the prisoners. I think no circular can prevent people from helping us, if their desire is genuine. Those who help merely for the sake of appearance will find this latest obstacle very convenient, as will those who simply express their intention of helping but never do.

So far, I've only written about the women's prison. You'd get a clearer and more detailed idea of the men's prison from someone there, but perhaps I can describe the externals for you. Their situation is much worse than ours, because they're locked up together with about twenty people to a cell. True, they say the cells are larger and more comfortable than ours, but it's a terrible thing to be so cramped, especially for anyone who's been in a solitary cell for a long time. They've made various "constitutions" so as to disturb each other as little as possible and make their common life more bearable, but still, you know, twenty people! What's more, they're allowed to go out and walk around for only an hour or two a day, and even then only under strict guard—in addition to the gendarmes on duty, there's a mass of armed soldiers lined up in the courtyard. Many of the prisoners walk around in irons.

Everyone released to the exile settlement writes sad letters about the situation, and that shouldn't surprise anyone; it must be a terribly difficult time to be living there. But I'll write about that some other time, when a suitable opportunity presents itself. Our lives are spent waiting for something to happen, and for the appearance, ever so rare, of misdirected travelers.

## II

Not long ago, "free command" was introduced here. Since such terms exist only to describe our situation here and are probably incomprehensible to you, I'll tell you what this institution is all about. Two years before you're scheduled to be released to the exile settlement, they let you out on "free command": you live in unlocked quarters, without constant supervision, but twice a day the gendarmes come by to make a check. Back in the 1860's, the first political prisoners exiled to Kara had the right to get out on "free command" after serving a "probation" period, but under Loris-Melikov's administration, that right was withdrawn from "politicals." It was restored only recently, in 1885.

And even now, the whole business of "free command" is uncertain for political prisoners. It's an inalienable right for the regular criminals; furthermore, married convicts are never kept in prison at all, if their wives have accompanied them. It's true that for us politicals, a man can get on the command sooner if his wife is with him,[17] but the command is nothing you can count on: it's a special privilege, contingent on good behavior, the petitions of relatives, etc., and if something goes wrong with even one person, it'll be totally abolished for all of us. Right now, there are only seven men and four women on the command. The women live two kilometers from us, on the shore of the Shilka River.

Our prison sits in a hollow among dark, densely forested knolls, near the mouth of the Kara, a small stream that is filled with gold. We can see the surrounding landscape—the wilderness, ringed with untamed mountains—only through the narrow chinks of our windows. The whole world beyond is cut off from us by those gloomy mountains and the forest, grown old in its primordial isolation. The men's prison compound is fifteen kilometers away, in a fenced-off circle in the Lower Kara gold fields.

Willy-nilly, people swiftly decay in the tomb that is Kara. There is an inescapable feeling that for many of us, life is irrevocably over; still, one must marvel at the spiritual courage with which we all endure our slow deaths.

Not long ago, my good friend Grigorii Popko died from consumption here in Kara. Almost everyone who falls ill leaves us for the other world, that world where, supposedly, there is no sorrow, no sighs, no tuberculosis. Today we learned that people are coming down with scurvy in the men's prison because of the wretched food. So little money has been coming from relatives that the men are able to supplement the state ration by at most two rubles worth of food a month per person, tobacco and tea included; they don't have any sugar at all. Things will get worse, too—they'll have to satisfy themselves solely with what the state gives them. Our homeland

---

[17] There appears to be no instance in nineteenth-century Russia in which a man followed his wife into exile in Siberia.

is forgetting us, its true and devoted sons [sic]. Can it be that it is finally going to feed us to the wolves?

In 1898, after fifteen years in prison, Ivanovskaia was re- leased to an exile settlement near Lake Baikal. Four years later, she was transferred to Chita, eastern Siberia. In 1903, at the age of fifty, she escaped, feeling the need "to get closer to life, to size up the new currents" of the liberation movement. She joined the recently formed Socialist Revolutionary Party, a populist group in the tradition of the People's Will, whose Combat Organiza- tion carried out attacks on oppressive officials. Assuming the role of an illiterate servant in one of the party's con- spiratorial apartments, in 1904 she played a part in the assassination of the hated Minister of the Interior, V. K. Plehve, whose ruthless policies extended not only to the revolutionary movement, but to national minorities and the liberal opposition as well. "The conclusion of this affair gave me some satisfaction—finally the man who had taken so many victims had been brought to his in- evitable end, so universally desired."

After the assassination of Plehve, Ivanovskaia went abroad for a brief rest, returning shortly after the mas- sacre of workers on "Bloody Sunday" (January 9), which marked the beginning of the Revolution of 1905. Despite a "strong desire and careful plans to carry a lighter burden on my shoulders," she resumed work in the Socialist Revolutionary Party's Combat Organization. The organ- ization was betrayed to the police, however, before carry- ing out a series of assassinations it had planned, and Ivanovskaia spent most of 1905 behind bars. Late in October, after a massive general strike had forced the regime to make constitutional concessions and grant am- nesty to a large number of political prisoners, she was released.

Along with her sister, Ivanovskaia went to the Volga province of Saratov and in 1906 took an active part in the election campaign for Russia's first legislative assembly, the State Duma. Her autobiography records one last encounter with the police. In 1907, gendarmes appeared at her house and attempted to arrest her for escaping from Siberia back in 1903. Once again, she evaded them: "I left by the back door." On this note, Ivanovskaia's autobiographical essay, written in the USSR in 1925, ends.

# OLGA
# LIUBATOVICH

Olga Liubatovich was born in Moscow in 1854. Her father, an engineer by training, was a political refugee from Montenegro. Her mother was the daughter of a gold-mine owner and possessed, Olga writes, "a level of culture rare for those times: she had studied in the best French boarding school in Moscow and had spent time in the company of a number of writers at the home of one of her school friends." She died when Olga was in her mid-teens.

Liubatovich got her early schooling in Moscow. In May 1871, along with her sister Vera, who was one year younger, she went to Zurich to study medicine. Francisca Tiburtius, a Swiss contemporary, has left a vivid description of Olga Liubatovich as she appeared during those years. Waiting for some friends at an eating place frequented by Russians, she chanced to see

> an enigmatic being, whose biological character was at first all but clear to me: a roundish, boyish face, short-cut hair, parted askew, enormous blue glasses, a quite youthful, tender-colored face, a coarse jacket, a burning cigarette in its mouth—everything about it was boylike, and yet there was something which belied this desired impression. I looked stealthily under the table—and discovered a bright-coloured, somewhat faded cotton skirt. The being took no notice at all of my presence and remained absorbed in a large book, every now and then rolling a cigarette which was finished in a few droughts.[1]

[1] J. M. Meijer. *Knowledge and Revolution: the Russian colony in Zurich* (1870–1873). Assen, the Netherlands, 1955, p. 59.

Both of the Liubatovich sisters became active in the Fritsche women's circle in Zurich (in Figner's memoir, Olga appears as the "Shark"—a nickname she acquired because of her voracious appetite—while Vera was "Wolfie") and both subsequently returned to Russia as members of the Pan-Russian Social Revolutionary Organization. In the spring of 1875, Olga Liubatovich took up work as an unskilled factory hand. She conducted socialist propaganda among workers in Moscow and, later, Tula, where she was arrested under circumstances described by Figner on page 30. It was nearly two years before she and her comrades appeared in court. Finally, at the Trial of the Fifty in March 1877, Liubatovich was condemned to nine years at hard labor. The sentence was subsequently reduced to simple banishment, and Liubatovich was transported to a small town in Tobolsk province, western Siberia.

Held under minimum security in a private house rather than a prison (a common arrangement), Liubatovich was able to place her medical knowledge at the service of the local population, among whom she promptly acquired a reputation as a miracle worker. Her fiercely independent attitude repeatedly brought her into confrontations with the authorities: at one point, she successfully resisted a search of her quarters for three days by barricading herself in and convincing a party of besieging gendarmes that she had a gun and was prepared to use it (actually, she was armed with nothing more than a penknife and some kitchen utensils). Then, in July 1878, Liubatovich concocted a "suicide" for the benefit of the police—a note, a farewell letter to her sister, clothing strategically flung on the banks of a rapid river—and, with the aid of a young peasant whom she had converted to socialism, made her escape.[2] Traveling by coach, boat, and train, she managed to reach St. Petersburg, where she hoped to find her comrades and resume revolutionary activity. Her memoirs begin at this point.

---

[2] The details of Liubatovich's life in exile and her escape come from Sergei Kravchinskii [Stepniak]. A *Female Nihilist*. Boston, 1886.

*Vera Liubatovich*

---

It was early August 1878, when I reached St. Petersburg, a free woman. As I stood in the train station, oblivious to the unusual activity and undercurrent of uneasiness among the crowd, my thoughts turned for the first time to the difficulties that confronted me in the capital: I had the clothes on my back, a scant few kopecks in my pockets, and nowhere at all to go. Then, through my reverie, I overheard: "Dead, killed on the spot!" I lifted my head and looked around in bewilderment.

At that very moment, I was approached by an elderly, plainly dressed woman, who looked me over and started inquiring where I planned to stay and whether I had any relatives in the city. I answered that I had no relatives, nor did I know where I would be staying, since I was new to the city. She looked me over again and proposed ingratiatingly that I take one of her furnished rooms: they were cheap, she said, and good, too. I didn't like the woman's stare or her saccharine manner, but, being utterly homeless, accepted her offer gladly—feeling, perhaps, that fate had sent it as my deliverance.

On the way to her place, she complained about how difficult it had become to live in the capital, informing me in passing that some criminal had killed Mezentsev, the chief of the gendarme corps, on the street that morning. I shuddered: this new development made my situation even more precarious, since the police would be searching the city for the killer.

My new landlady led me to a dark, dirty room and brought in a samovar. I had no tea, so I drank hot water with some of the bread that I bought with my last five kopecks. After a while, I went out to wander around the city. There I was in St. Petersburg on August 4, the very day Mezentsev had been killed! One question absorbed me completely: Would I be able to find any of my old comrades?

Totally unfamiliar with the city, I wandered for three whole days without success. My bread disappeared quickly, and I found myself on the verge of starvation, barely able to drag my body around. With her long experience, the landlady immediately sensed that I was penniless, but she continued to treat me kindly: once or twice, she even brought me tea and a roll. But no sooner had I appeased my hunger on one such occasion than I was approached by the building's porter, who insolently suggested that I get acquainted with some young men living in the roominghouse. I was dumfounded. The notion that I was a young woman, and that men could be interested in me as such, was totally alien to me; I saw myself as a homeless fugitive, nothing more. After a moment, I came to my senses and sent the porter on his way. I hastily threw on a kerchief and raced out to continue the search for my comrades. At last, fortune smiled on me: I found the lawyer Bardovskii home from his *dacha*.

Bardovskii had defended the Subbotina sisters at our trial, the Trial of the Fifty. He had been remarkably warm and sympathetic toward all of us: during his argument for the defense, he became so emotional that the judge was obliged to interrupt the proceedings for a few minutes to enable him to calm down. Now, as I was searching for my comrades, the memory of this incident led me to him instinctively. And now, kind and impetuous as ever, Bardovskii immediately invited me to stay at his place, although he knew me only by sight. I thanked him sincerely but declined the offer, reluctant to endanger someone who really was not part of the movement.[3] He then gave me Sofia Leshern's address.

I virtually flew to her place: we had never met, but I felt there was an intimate bond between us, forged by common adversities and prison. Leshern was home, and she greeted me like a long-awaited sister. She suggested that I leave my furnished room and move in with her for a while: the tiny apartment actually belonged to Alexandra Malinovskaia, a young artist, but she had given Leshern the run of the place while she was away in the country.

That evening, about fifteen people—all of them strangers to me—came over to the apartment. It was at this gathering that I first met Sergei Kravchinskii, who was to become like a brother to me.

There were a number of people in the room by the time Kravchinskii walked in, but I felt my attention shift involuntarily to his strong, manly figure and distinctive face. He carried a top hat and was dressed like a gentleman; his Napoleonic goatee made him look like a foreigner. Although several other women were present, he walked directly toward me and extended his hand in a free, comradely gesture.

"I know you by hearsay," he said. "Perhaps you've heard about me, too." He introduced himself.

"Yes," I answered, thinking: how could I not have heard about one of the pioneers of the movement "to the people"? He was older than me and had more experience among the people; I regarded him as a senior comrade. Although I was extremely shy with people in my youth, we somehow struck

---

[3] As it turned out, my caution didn't save him. Bardovskii was arrested on July 25, 1879, falsely charged with harboring me; he had probably talked carelessly about my visit. The arrest, which took him totally by surprise, proved too great a shock for him to bear, and he soon became mentally ill. —Liubatovich.

up a sincere, unconstrained conversation; and as we talked, I glanced freely at his open, bold face, a face in which ugly, irregular features and broken lines became beautiful. We became friends immediately.

Gradually, our animated conversation attracted some of the others over to us. Apart from Kravchinskii, it was Valerian Osinskii who made the strongest impression on me that evening. As was the case with many revolutionaries of the seventies, Osinskii had been led into political activity by his reverence for suffering. His first, brief contact with prison resulted from an attempt to enter the courtroom during the Trial of the Fifty. As he now confessed to me, his overriding desire had been to get a look at us, the "Moscow Amazons," who had grown up in baronial mansions, sampled all the charms of free intellectual work in the universities of Europe, and then, with such courageous simplicity, entered the filthy factories of Moscow as ordinary workers.

Kravchinskii and I continued our discussion, which had turned to my biography of Betia Kaminskaia, a comrade who had committed suicide. Sofia Bardina and I wrote the piece in prison, and it had recently been printed in *The Commune* [*Obshchina*], a journal published abroad. Kravchinskii asked me—since I had worked in a factory with Kaminskaia—whether the rather pessimistic impressions permeating Kaminskaia's descriptions of her factory experience had not, in fact, been colored by her own individual peculiarities.[4] I told him that I shared Kaminskaia's pessimism, and a heated discussion about "the people" developed. Although Kravchinskii's own experience of propagandizing among the people had been comparatively unproductive, like everyone else's, he remained a great enthusiast. He believed that the time would come—perhaps soon—when the Russian people would grasp what we'd been saying to them and would begin to fight for their freedom with all their might; in the meantime, our own task was to clear the path for them by waging a struggle against the govern-

---

[4] Kravchinskii was referring to the fact that Kaminskaia had had a nervous breakdown in prison while awaiting trial.

ment—without abandoning propaganda activities, however.

"According to you, it's difficult to carry the masses along with us," said Kravchinskii. "Well, what do you have to say about the Chigirin affair?"[5]

I didn't know a thing about the Chigirin affair—it had taken place while I was in Siberia—and so Kravchinskii animatedly acquainted me with that attempt made by Stefanovich and Deich, posing as commissars sent secretly by the tsar, to organize a peasant uprising against the nobility and local officials. I decided that I didn't like this imposture. True, it might actually stir the peasants to a rebellion more readily than the honest, frank propaganda practiced by the rest of us. But I believed it was dangerous in that it could serve to strengthen the myth of the "tsar protector" sincerely concerned with the welfare of his people.

I did feel, however, that our movement had no choice but to give up the idealized notion of *le peuple souverain*, a proud, powerful people conscious of their rights and capable of relying solely on their own resources. The others present shared my feeling, and a wave of sadness passed over our faces. Yes, we had hoped to find a people conscious of the "rights of man"—that was to be the higher moral sanction of our politics. Instead, we found an amorphous mass, a slave-people who occasionally produced some powerful individuals, but on the whole were immersed in a deep, lethargic sleep. And so, to avenge that distortion of human nature, we revolutionaries had drawn our swords against the state. First idealism, then pained outrage—that is the entire psychology of the classical, or "heroic," period of our revolutionary history.

To dispel the pall that had enveloped the group, Osinskii enthusiastically told the story of Stefanovich's and Deich's escape from Kiev prison. More discussions followed, one

---

[5] During 1876–1877, Iakov Stefanovich and Lev Deich (later of Black Repartition) composed and circulated fictitious tsarist manifestoes calling upon the peasants of the Chigirin area to organize secret militias in order to seize the nobility's land and redistribute it among the people. They organized about a thousand peasants before the conspiracy was uncovered and smashed by the authorities.

reminiscence led to another, and we sat around talking far into the night. And if some law-abiding St. Petersburger had chanced to peek into the crowded room, nothing in our appearances would have suggested to him that we were a band of the country's most important conspirators. Nothing in our dress, our gestures, or our restrained speech resembled the banal dissoluteness and abruptness that society called "nihilism" and associated with revolutionaries. This stylized "nihilism" actually had dominated the student circles of the 1860's, but by the seventies, it had disappeared completely—at least, in the large cities, and certainly among serious revolutionaries.

The evening concluded with a detailed account of the assassination of Mezentsev. I was struck by Kravchinskii's persistence in emphasizing to me that, although Mezentsev was walking with another man, the murderer had met him face to face, rather than stabbing him in the back. Only later did I learn that Kravchinskii himself was the assassin.

A few days after the party, Kravchinskii came by with his close friend Nikolai Morozov, whom he introduced as "our young poet." Morozov blushed like a girl. Apart from his literary work, he was one of the party's most ardent advocates of partisan revolutionary warfare—terrorist struggle—and he was always heavily laden with guns, nearly bent over from their weight. He was above average in height, with large, pensive eyes and very delicate, miniature features. His body, thin and frail, seemed undeveloped, and his weak, high-pitched voice reinforced my image of him as a sapling that had grown up far from fresh air and open fields. He seemed very young to me, and unwittingly I adopted an almost patronizing manner. Strangely enough, this made us feel closer to each other.

Morozov had repudiated without regret the privileges that lesser people cling to so tenaciously. He quit *gimnazia* shortly before graduation in order to plunge into the growing movement "to the people." Clothing himself in a coarse caftan and bark shoes, he traveled over nearly all of Great Russia, talking with the people and distributing revolutionary pamphlets. Inexperienced and impetuous, he ignored all precautions; he

*Sergei Kravchinskii*          *Nikolai Morozov*

was eventually seized and turned over to the authorities by the peasants themselves. His father, a large landowner, disowned him, and since relatives were the only visitors permitted in prison, Morozov found himself a forgotten man, abandoned by everyone. For more than three years he mourned the vanished illusion of a people's revolution with his bloody tears. It is hardly surprising that, after the courts finally released him, he made a religion of partisan struggle. Yes, he became an apostle of terrorism; the ideal he preached was of an equal duel between the forces of revolution and the state.

About a week later, I had my first, unforgettable meeting with Sofia Perovskaia.

I had spent the night at Malinovskaia's apartment; in the morning, Masha Kolenkina came over. Around noon, a modestly dressed young woman appeared at the door. Her striking face—round and small, but for the large, childlike forehead—stood out sharply against the background of her black dress, trimmed with a broad white turn-down collar. She radiated youth and life.

Perovskaia introduced herself and greeted us in the open, direct fashion of an old friend, although she had never met either of us. We clustered around her: obviously, she was pleasantly excited about something. The rapid walk to our apartment had left her breathless, but she immediately began to tell us the story of her escape at the railroad station in Novgorod—a simple story, but it made me tremble.[6]

The night before, she had lain covered up on a couch in a women's compartment of the train, watching her guards settle down on the threshold for the night and planning her escape. At first, they would give a start and cast anxious glances over at her whenever they heard a bell or the noise of a passing train; but finally, as they satisfied themselves that Perovskaia was sound asleep, they became oblivious to the sounds around them and sank into sleep. Then, as quietly as a shadow, Perovskaia got up, arranged some clothing on the couch to resemble her sleeping figure, put on a kerchief, took off her shoes, and stepped over the sleeping guards. She walked out of the standing train onto the platform without being noticed; then she crossed the tracks and hid in some bushes to wait for the train to St. Petersburg.

An hour passed, each minute as long as a year; the barking of the watchdog, the rustle of the leaves—every sound made her tremble. But finally, the train became visible in the distance, finally it came to a stop right in front of her—she was saved! She jumped on without a ticket.

By morning, Perovskaia was in St. Petersburg. She went to the apartment of an old friend, who sent her in turn to Malinovskaia's place, where she found Kolenkina and me. And now, ecstatic and free, the torturous waiting behind her, she began to breathe easily among comrades of kindred spirit.

The news of Perovskaia's escape spread quickly through St. Petersburg, and in a few hours Kravchinskii—one of her old comrades from the Chaikovskii circle—hurried over to see her. His attitude to this child-woman (for that's how she looked)

---

[6] After the Trial of the Hundred Ninety-three, orders were issued to rearrest those who had been acquitted. Perovskaia was captured by the police as she was traveling to her mother's estate.

was striking: it reflected profound respect, a kind of restrained worship, but was altogether consistent with their comradely relations. "She's a remarkable woman," he told me later. "She's destined to accomplish great things."

Kravchinskii's conversation with Perovskaia focused on the news from the Kharkov central prison. He had brought with him the pamplet "Buried Alive," which he had compiled from information sent by the prisoners. With murderous realism, it described their humiliation and suffering, and I saw Perovskaia's face, one minute so radiant, dim when Sergei began to read us passages: for one thing, Ippolit Myshkin—a son of the people and a powerful revolutionary orator, whom Perovskaia virtually worshipped—was among the comrades incarcerated in Kharkov.

Perovskaia decided to leave for Kharkov immediately. Kravchinskii's reminders that our comrades' suffering hadn't gone unpunished, that Mezentsev had paid for them with his own life, did not comfort her. Her friends pleaded with her to stay in St. Petersburg for a while instead of rushing right off, since escape from the Kharkov prison was all but impossible. Perovskaia was not to be swayed: she was still full of faith that the prisoners could be helped. But in the end, she gave in to our requests and agreed to stay in St. Petersburg for a little while.

Perovskaia spent the next few days taking care of pressing business and helping to bring some of her old comrades into Land and Liberty. Kravchinskii decided to commemorate her stay in St. Petersburg by assembling her closest comrades and taking a box at the opera, where Meyerbeer's *The Prophet*, a great favorite in revolutionary circles, was playing. Generally speaking, revolutionaries didn't frequent the theater during this period, but Kravchinskii was always fond of tempting fate. (For example, knowing how intensely the police were searching for me, he took delight in strolling down the most crowded streets of St. Petersburg with me on his arm.) And since the organization hadn't been hit by arrests, despite the recent police raids in the city, everyone went along with his brave fancy.

We went to the theater in small groups. Eleven people were assembled in the box—each of us extremely "illegal"—and we spent the evening under the spell of the music, enjoying the sensation of danger that is usually so ineffably fascinating when you are young. During intermission, we joked and laughed about the situation: what pleasure it would give the government to capture this whole nest of "malefactors" at one time—although this was, of course, the last place they would look for us! Still, the danger was there, and many of us felt it hanging over our heads.

On this occasion, fate continued to protect Perovskaia. She left safely for Kharkov the next day.

All the people I've mentioned in these pages were, or soon became, members of Land and Liberty, and shortly before I fled the country, I joined the party, as well.

Land and Liberty had first begun to take shape back in 1876 in the form of a small group known among revolutionary circles as the "Troglodytes." They earned this nickname by their secretiveness, which was frequently artificial and excessive: even the members who weren't being sought by the police used false identity papers and concealed their addresses from their closest comrades. Many of them moved out into the provinces, working as paramedics, district clerks, midwives, or craftsmen in order to establish roots among the peasants. But the activity of these "countryfolk," as they became known in the movement, proved to have only the most indirect relationship to the life-and-death struggle against the government.

In 1878, the group's complexion started to change. There was an influx of experienced people—former members of other political groups who had just been released from prison, survivors of the trials of the Fifty and the Hundred Ninety-three, and people who had been active in the south of Russia —and early in the year leaflets in the name of the "Executive Committee" began to appear, bearing a seal that pictured an ax, a dagger, and a revolver. By the second half of 1878, the group—now officially known as Land and Liberty—had become a force to reckon with.

*The seal of the Executive Committee*

---

There was a wave of arrests that fall, shortly after Perovskaia left for Kharkov, but the group was able to start publish-
ing its own newspaper, *Land and Liberty*. Kravchinskii and
Morozov were the managing editors, and they invited me to
join them—probably in order to involve the female element
of the party in the paper. I agreed and started to take part in
the editorial discussions at Kravchinskii's apartment. As it
turned out, my participation was short-lived.

One day we learned that there had been a major police raid
on the apartment of two unidentified women, that one of
them was armed and had resisted, but both had been arrested
and the police had laid an ambush at their place. None of us
had the slightest doubt that the search had been at Malinovskaia's, and that Masha Kolenkina[7] had done the shooting:
Masha had resolved not to relinquish her freedom without a
fight, and she was never without her revolver. It was possible, too, that she fired on the police to give Malinovskaia
time to destroy incriminating documents: Malinovskaia made
passport stamps, so vital for conspiratorial work, and many
people might have perished if the police captured important
specimens or authentic identity papers.

At the time, I was living at Olga Natanson's place without
a residence permit. It was imperative that I leave immediately.

[7] See p. 78.

That night marked the beginning of a difficult period for me
—wandering around a city I still didn't know, moving from
one apartment to another, subjecting hospitable strangers to
risks. I wasn't accustomed to this kind of life, and I wearied
of it. Finally, after discussing my situation with friends, I
decided to go abroad for a while, until the first wave of government persecution had ebbed. I parted hastily with my new
comrades, who had become as dear to me as the ones I'd
lost not long before. Nikolai Morozov saw me off at the train
station, promising to write regularly.

I had no passport, and so I had to depend on Jewish smugglers
to cross the border. It was inherently a difficult operation—
all the more so for a woman. Fanny Lichkus (Kravchinskii's
wife, as I learned later) traveled with me to Vilno. Although
she was only a student, twenty-three or twenty-four years old,
she arranged the crossing very skillfully. At Vilno, she entrusted me to a reliable smuggler, an ordinary Jewish man
with the traditional sideburns. I put myself in his charge without a murmur.

The two of us traveled in a third-class car overflowing with
the Jewish poor. The clamor of the multitude of children, the
screeching of the worn-out, disheveled women, the men bustling around, patiently fussing over their skittish families, the
buzz of the gutteral tongue I couldn't understand—all this, in
a dirty, poorly heated railroad car that reeked with the re-
mains of dried fish and onions, made my head spin.

We finally reached Vilkovishi at twilight of the short winter's day. I stepped off the train with my guide; he silently
picked up my small suitcase and motioned for me to follow
him. We walked over to an enormous, high wagon, the likes
of which I had never seen. Four or five bare boards were laid
across the back as seats, and men and women were clambering
up the spokes of the wagon wheel, shoving each other to get
places. Again I heard the distinctive buzz of voices, the loud,
hoarse music that frightened me so on the train. Somehow I
managed to hide in the first seat I found—the most un-
comfortable—and the journey began.

A young Jew in a lined lapserdak,[8] muddy and soiled, sat in the coachbox, a long whip in his hand. He urged on two large but ill-fed horses, who laboriously pulled the packed wagon (there were at least fifteen of us, I thought) down the paved road. Snow-covered fields spread out all around us; from time to time, the thatched roofs and swaying fences of wretched villages emerged from the shadows of the night. We stopped at several roadside inns, where bundles were thrown down; sometimes, after long, shouted negotiations, people got off and the wagon moved on, I knew not where, blanketed by the darkness. At last, far into the night, we rumbled up to one such inn and my companion got off. A fat, elderly woman covered with a large, tattered shawl that blew freely about in the night wind came out to meet us. My companion said something to her in Yiddish; she responded with a nod of her head. He grabbed my valise and quickly helped me down from the wagon, which dragged off to deliver the last passengers.

As I stepped into the entrance hall, I was met by a burst of drunken voices, swearing loudly and distinctly in my native Russian. My heart began to pound, even more violently than it had that night several months before when I lay waiting in the deserted Siberian forest for the man sent by my comrades to help me escape. True, there I risked meeting the beasts and brutalized vagrants of Siberia. But this hospitable inn gave off the stench of a drunken den of iniquity, and my heart pounded and pounded, oblivious to the commands of my will.

Paying no attention to my uncontrolled trembling, the proprietress led me through the passageway, closing the door to the room on the left, where the drunken throng was reveling, and conducted me to a cold, closetlike room on the right. The room was virtually filled by the plain, unpainted bench in the corner and a high bedstead, with dirty chintz bed curtains and a pile of featherbeds. The proprietress suggested in broken Russian that I undress and get into bed. At first, I stubbornly refused, but then she started telling me that the

---

[8] A traditional style of overcoat worn by Orthodox Jews.

carousers across the hall were border soldiers, that they might well walk into my room, and so it was absolutely essential that I hide in the bed. It was impossible to persist: I wrapped myself up in the dirty featherbeds, and the horrible, sleepless night began.

The room wasn't locked, and people came in several times during the night, whispered about something, and walked out again. Someone wound up sleeping on the bench in the corner, snoring. The drunken orgy lasted until dawn. Through the squeals of the women and the scandalous cursing, I heard snatches of a plaintive Jewish song, sung by a drunken young woman with a cracked voice; the quivering, childlike notes sometimes moved me to the point of tears. Finally, the noise died down, as everyone either fell asleep or dispersed.

I peered through the chink of the bed curtains. The window of my room looked out on a dirty courtyard, crammed full of junk and enclosed with a high fence; I was locked in, with no other escape than the common door. I began to wait resignedly. I had long since lost the childhood habit of praying, but now that forgotten mood seized my soul. I felt like a helpless sliver of wood, tossed on the terrible sea of life; my freedom, my honor, my fate were in the hands of these poor, crude, ignorant people, with their life of night orgies. I knew that the miserable few rubles promised them for my safe crossing meant virtually nothing, that in this operation their conscience was my only protection; and so my prayers were to strengthen that conscience.

The innkeeper came in when it was fully light. She covered my head with a checkered, secondhand woolen kerchief, advising me to hide the little fur cap I'd been wearing. "A soldier we know is on duty," she said. "You can cross now."

Although I was not yet out of danger, I began to breathe more easily as soon as we stepped outside. The two of us walked side by side, our steps measured and calm, toward a narrow bridge over a stream; my traveling companion of the previous day walked ahead of us, carrying my suitcase. I watched him cross the bridge and leave my things in a proper-looking building next to the stream; then the innkeeper and I approached the bridge. For some reason, we weren't able to cross immediately. The soldier said something to the inn-keeper—a signal, apparently. We had to move away and wait for something, and I began to get upset. Finally, after about twenty minutes that seemed like an eternity, we approached the bridge again. The soldier looked me over searchingly; I returned a forthright glance. Evidently he found nothing suspicious in my expression or appearance, because he let me pass without a word. There were no guards on the German side, and I proceeded directly to the building alongside the stream (a hotel, as it turned out) and picked up my things. The Jewish man who had carried my baggage was waiting there, and I gave him some small change (I'd been warned that generosity was dangerous in a border crossing); he grate-fully tipped his cap and left me to myself.

A seat had been reserved for me in the coach that was leav-ing for the railroad station later in the day. As it turned out, I was the only passenger. The solitude didn't frighten me, though—I felt wonderful. Seated comfortably on the soft velvet seat, I dozed off, worn out by the anxiety I had been experiencing since the previous night. Late that night, the coach rolled up to the railroad station. I bought a third-class ticket and set off for Switzerland, where I had spent my happy years as a student not long ago.

The train arrived in Geneva at eight in the morning. I checked my things at the station, got the address of the Russian library[9] from a porter, and headed right over: it was early, but I knew the rhythm of life in Switzerland and was sure that even a Russian institution would be open by this time. I wasn't mistaken. I looked through the book listing the library's members and their addresses and quickly discovered a few familiar names, including that of Professor Dragomanov, whom I'd known during my student years. I was certain that I'd able to get in touch with Kravchinskii through him.

---

[9] A library set up by Russian émigrés and containing most of the major works of European socialism.

As I walked to Dragomanov's place, I passed a number of young Russians on the street. Poorly dressed, many of them emaciated and drawn, their faces reflecting anxiety beyond their years, they contrasted sharply with the well-fed local students. They recognized me as one of their people, too—probably by my clothes, which were too heavy for the Swiss weather—and they looked at me inquisitively. I returned a friendly smile: I knew that we were bound to meet sooner or later in the city's intimate Russian colony.

I found Dragomanov at home. The housemaid first brought me into the dining room, where his wife—a pretty woman, but very pale and sickly—was reclining in an armchair; then the girl went to the study to inform "Herr Professor," who was at work on his writing, of my arrival. Dragomanov came in immediately and excitedly started asking me about things in Russia—the professors' circles, the youth, the *zemstvo* people. I proceeded to satisfy his curiosity as best I could, and the time flew by. Dragomanov's wife was very pleasant, but said little: evidently she was suffering from a serious illness that robbed her of all strength. She couldn't even look after her little eight-month-old daughter, and with my own eyes I saw Dragomanov himself change the baby!

Dragomanov invited me to stay in their spare room. I was afraid to inconvenience his sick wife, but she assured me that she would be happy to have me in the house, that my presence would help her forget her illness, and so I agreed. Dragomanov himself made a coal fire in the air stove to heat the room for me: he was trying to relieve the servant, who was preparing dinner, from any superfluous work. I had to wonder at the courage of this man, who was able to reconcile serious literary work with caring for a sick wife and small child.

In an hour's time, I was settled in my new quarters. The room was furnished with the simplicity that was the hallmark of the Russian émigré homes of that period: a hard camp bed, a small, unpainted table, a wicker chair, and that was all. And really, I required nothing more. The small window under the arched roof of my garret looked out on a garden. There was a beautiful view of the distant mountains, and the soft blue tints of the lake were a pleasure to the eye, making one forget everything petty, transient, and superfluous. If only it were a little warmer! I had suffered so much in the un-heated European railroad cars, I had grown so weak from the emotionally draining experiences of prison, trial, and exile! But it proved to be a long, long time before I was able to warm myself—not until the following spring.

*Liubatovich spent about six months in Geneva, where she got to know a number of émigré revolutionaries, including Vera Zasulich.*

In the spring of 1879, the unexpected news of Alexander Soloviev's attempt on the life of the tsar[10] threw Geneva's Russian colony into turmoil. Vera Zasulich hid away for three days in a deep depression: Soloviev's deed obviously reflected a trend toward direct, active struggle against the government, a trend of which Zasulich disapproved. It seemed to me that her nerves were so strongly affected by violent actions like Solo-viev's because she consciously (and perhaps unconsciously, as well) regarded her own deed as the first step in this direction. Other émigrés were incomparably more tolerant of the at-tempt: Stefanovich and Deich, for example, merely noted that it might hinder political work among the people. Kravchinskii rejected even this objection. All of us knew from our personal experience, he argued, that extensive work among the people had long been impossible, nor could we expect to expand our activity and attract masses of the people to the socialist cause until we obtained at least a minimum of political freedom, freedom of speech, and the freedom to organize unions; as far as propaganda was concerned, we of the intelligentsia had done all we could under the circumstances, and far fewer losses would be incurred if the workers themselves continued this activity.

In any event, we all felt that a major historical phase was beginning to unfold. Our comrades in Russia wrote that rev-olutionary feeling was becoming stronger, that the party's cadres were multiplying; they wanted us to return home, and

[10] See Introduction, p. xxx.

they promised to send an expert to manage our border crossing. Stefanovich, Deich, Zasulich, and I decided to go. In order to conceal our tracks from police spies, we moved, along with Anna Epstein, Kravchinskii and his wife Fanny, to a little house overlooking the town of Montreux—Les Avants, it was called. To this day, the month we spent there, drinking deeply of the spring air, has remained one of the best memories of my life.

Sergei Kravchinskii wanted very badly to return to Russia with us, but he could not: Fanny was about to become a mother. She left Les Avants for Bern very soon after we moved in, because she needed good medical care. Sergei was torn apart: on the one hand, Fanny was expected to deliver at any time, and he wanted to be with her; on the other, he wanted to spend these last few days with his friends, whom he might never see again. For our part, none of us were family people, and so we couldn't fully empathize with his position: we wanted to keep him for ourselves a little longer, if we possibly could. But before long Sergei received an urgent telegram and left for Bern. A few days later, we learned that a son had been born to him [sic] prematurely and had died two days later.

Our stay at Les Avants drew to a close. Our escort, Zundelevich, arrived, and two days later we set out by train for Russia. From his store of experience, Zundelevich supplied us with practical advice so as not to attract attention by our dress or our Russian speech. For example: "Please don't pull your hats down over your eyes," he told us, "or I'll have to go through the same thing I did with Kovalik. When I brought her across last fall, she covered up so secretively that people started peering under the hat just to get a look at her face. It was very disconcerting for me."

Zundelevich took us across in two parties: first Stefanovich and me, then Zasulich and Deich. In fact, this time the crossing proved to be extremely simple.

*Liubatovich and Stefanovich proceeded to Lesnoi, a small town near St. Petersburg where many of the members* of *Land and Liberty were spending the summer. As it turned out, almost everyone was at a party congress in Voronezh, where the political divisions within Land and Liberty were being discussed. In the passages that follow, Liubatovich gives her interpretation of the origins and basis of the growing split.*

Arguments and misunderstandings had begun to develop in Land and Liberty at the end of 1878, after Kravchinskii left Russia. The "countryfolk" continued to engage almost exclusively in peaceful cultural work among the peasantry, but the new members, whom they had hospitably welcomed into their organization during the course of the year, took a negative view of propaganda activity as a result of their own experience among the people, and they began to generate a ferment in the organization. The countryfolk could not keep abreast of this ripening revolutionary mood: they were remote from the center of the movement, and communications were difficult.

The conflict between these two emerging factions within the party became particularly intense during the first months of 1879, when Alexander Soloviev appealed privately to certain of the "redder" elements for support in his attempt to assassinate the tsar. They brought the issue of regicide up with other members of the party, and there was violent opposition, primarily from the countryfolk, who maintained that as a rule every terrorist act made work among the people more difficult and brought nothing but harm to the party. For the most part, these countryfolk were the people who split from Land and Liberty several months later and formed Black Repartition.

But really, they had no adequate ideological justification for the split they produced in the party, and they knew it. The program they subsequently developed for Black Repartition included popular rebellions—hence, they couldn't legitimately become outraged by regicide and systematic struggle against the government on the grounds that these actions involved violence. Nor was it pertinent for them to argue that regicide would intensify the repression directed against the peasantry: both Black Repartition and, earlier, Land and Liberty made local rebellions part of their program, even though the reaction in such cases inevitably victimized the peasantry, whereas regicide would have its repercussions primarily in the cities. The break between Black Repartition and the People's Will was less the result of differences in principle than of differences in temperament.

Several days after we got to Lesnoi, the two factions returned from the Voronezh congress. Each held several open-air meetings. Stefanovich began to negotiate very energetically between them, and many people had hopes that he would be able to prevent the split that was developing. These hopes proved unwarranted; what's more, it wound up that some people were even accusing Stefanovich of throwing fat into the fire and accelerating the final break. Sofia Perovskaia, who wanted passionately to exert some kind of conciliatory influence, arrived after the others, and by then it was altogether too late—the split had become final, and yesterday's comrades began shunning each other like strangers.

Stefanovich became the head of Black Repartition, and his friends Vera Zasulich and Lev Deich joined him. But even ardent populists[11] like Vera Figner, who had been working in one of the countryfolk settlements in the provinces, and Sofia Perovskaia joined the People's Will, the group that had taken up arms to defend the people and their apostles. Black Repartition was stillborn; it left no visible traces of its work among the people at the end of 1879 and the beginning of 1880, because no such activity was possible on a broad scale. After a series of failures, Stefanovich, Deich, Plekhanov, and Zasulich returned abroad.

As for me, naturally I joined the People's Will. The comrades in that party had been confident I would: sight unseen, they had invited me to the secret meeting at Lipetsk, where

---

[11] Liubatovich uses the term here to designate the revolutionaries who had hitherto stressed political work among the peasantry itself.

the Executive Committee of the People's Will was formed. I hadn't been able to attend, however, since the meeting preceded the Voronezh congress, and I was still abroad at the time.

The Executive Committee of the People's Will soon began to chart its own course. Its initial plan had been to carry out a number of actions against the governors-general, but this decision was called into question at one open-air meeting in Lesnoi: shouldn't we concentrate all our forces against the tsar instead, it was asked? We resolved that this should indeed be the goal of the Executive Committee. The implementation of that decision engaged the People's Will right up to March 1, 1881.

> The formal decision to assassinate Alexander II was made on August 26, 1879. The Executive Committee quickly moved into action, establishing three separate operations for the purpose of blowing up the tsar's train.[12] All three, including the attempt in Moscow on November 19, proved unsuccessful.

A few days after the Moscow explosion, Sofia Perovskaia appeared at one of the party's secret apartments in St. Petersburg, where she found Grachevskii, Gesia Gelfman, and me. Perovskaia was generally very reserved, but after Grachevskii left and she found herself alone with us women, the words began to spill out and she emotionally told us the story of the Moscow attempt—all the while standing by the washstand, her hands covered with soap. Perovskaia had served as the "wife" in the fictional household established in Moscow. On November 19, it was she who waited in the bushes for the tsar's train to approach and then gave the signal for the explosion that blew up the tracks. But there had been too little dynamite, she told us; how she regretted that so much had been sent to the operation in the south, instead of concentrating it all in Moscow! There was a catch in her voice as she spoke, and her face reflected intense suffering; she was shak-

[12] See the selection by Figner, p. 44.

ing, either from a chill produced by her bare wet hands or from a painful feeling of failure and long-suppressed emotion. There was nothing I could do to comfort her. I felt the failure would take a heavy toll on the party. And I wasn't mistaken.

The following morning, Perovskaia appeared at the apartment where Morozov and I were living to inform us that she'd learned Kviatkovskii's place was going to be raided—perhaps it had been already, she added sadly—and that she was going over to warn him. I offered to go instead of her, but she refused. Finally, Morozov said that he'd hurry over to Maria Oshanina's place and send her to Kviatkovskii's, since the gendarmes had nothing on her.

Perovskaia and I stayed home. We were both upset, and the conversation flagged. Kviatkovskii's loss would be irreparable; he was one of the best-liked and most active members of the party. At last, burning with impatience and knowing that every passing second threatened not only his loss but

*After the November 19 explosion*

the loss of many others as well, I put on my hat and quickly walked out the door, giving Perovskaia no chance to stop me. I told her only that I was going to Kviatkovskii's and that she should convey this news to Morozov, so that in the event of trouble he would be sure to clean out everything illegal and then leave our apartment.

When I reached Kviatkovskii's building, I looked around carefully before going up to his apartment. There was nothing suspicious. The signal[13] wasn't visible from the courtyard, but the thickly frosted windows made it impossible to see anything anyway. I rang his bell.

The door opened too quickly. In front of me stood the portly figure of a police sergeant.

"I must be mistaken," I said. "I was told the dressmaker lives here."

"No, madam, the dressmaker lives across the way, not here. But come in, come in," he invited me insistently. I assured him that I had made a mistake, that I had no business in the apartment, but the policeman wouldn't relent, and I had to obey. He brought me into the room Evgenia Figner had occupied—the very picture of a pogrom: the room had been turned upside down, and stacks of the latest issue (No. 2) of the *People's Will* were scattered over the bed. Neither Evgenia nor Kviatkovskii was around. The pretty face of their young servant—a simple peasant, rather stupid, but a good-hearted wench—peeked out through the kitchen door at the sound of my voice. The policeman roughly pushed her back into the kitchen, and in so doing, perhaps saved me from being recognized immediately as a good friend of her master and mistress. We walked past the open door of the drawing room: everything there and in Kviatkovskii's adjacent study was also in a mess—copper drums, bundles of wire and other materials, and many more piles of the second issue of the *People's Will*. So as not to irritate the policeman, I sat down obediently in Figner's room for a few minutes. Then I began to whine,

---

[13] Often an object (an umbrella, for example) was placed in a window to indicate that it was safe to enter a conspiratorial apartment.

*Sofia Perovskaia*

asking him please to let me go home, otherwise my husband would get very mad and would most likely beat me. Soon the policeman seemed to take pity on me, because he escorted me out of the apartment. But I was going to the police station, not home.

As we walked down the stairs, we passed Oshanina going up. I let her by without a word, then glanced up to see her walk right past Kviatkovskii's apartment: evidently she had grasped the situation and would no doubt hurry back to warn Morozov and the other comrades. This infused me with new strength. I decided to lead the police on for a little while longer before telling them where I lived: by that time, I knew they would find nothing compromising in my apartment, and perhaps I'd be released.

When we got to the police station, I pretended to be so upset that I was incapable of understanding anything or going anywhere. The police officer treated me harshly, but gave me an hour's time to think things over and give them my address.

My thoughts were gloomy as I sat in the cold, empty office, huddled in the corner of a wooden bench. It was painful to lose my hard-won freedom, and to lose it, moreover, through an accident, not directly in the line of action—I couldn't come to terms with that! I was also greatly troubled by the thought of Morozov, whom I'd of course caused much grief by my haste. But I couldn't believe for a moment that a person who had just risked his life working on the tunnel for the Moscow explosion would stay in the apartment all day waiting for me, when he knew through Oshanina that I had been arrested at Kviatkovskii's place.

The policeman came up to me at the end of my allotted hour, threatening to shut me up in Petropavlovsk fortress immediately unless I gave him my address. Although three hours had passed since I left my apartment, I gave him a false address, the first one I could make up, in another part of the city.

They brought me to this section of town; then, after waiting for a new police convoy, we proceeded to the address. To my good fortune, the resident of the apartment I had indicated turned out to be a general. The police became confused. I implored them not to be upset, saying that I had deceived them because I was so frightened of my husband. I then proceeded to act out a serious nervous fit before their eyes, and the police officer in charge of me got flustered. He brought me back to the precinct. Once again, I got a delay to rest, along with a formal ultimatum: either be prepared by 6 p.m. to take them to my real apartment, or else go directly to prison.

I really did need to rest. Playing out this day-long comedy under the weight of my painful thoughts had so exhausted me physically that I could barely walk. But the last and most critical skirmish still lay ahead. The clock struck six. At least seven hours had passed since my arrest, and so I finally gave them the address of my house, saying that I'd tell them the apartment number and my surname when we got there, since I didn't want my husband to be told before I saw him myself. The police officer was willing to go along with this. We went to another police station, which took almost an hour, and then spent some more time waiting for a new convoy of police escorts to be appointed.

Finally we reached my house. I could see that the signal wasn't in the window; that meant the apartment had been cleaned out. Nevertheless, my thoughts were gloomy as I walked up the stairs. The policeman hurried me along, asking "Where is it? Where is it?" We reached my door, and I rang the bell.

The door opened immediately, and to my horror, I found myself face to face with Morozov. I nearly collapsed. Summoning my last resources to keep my self-control, I rushed over to him like an agitated wife and began entreating him not to get mad at me for coming home late with these policemen, explaining that I'd been hoping to prevail upon them to release me all this time.

"How are you, what's happened to you, where were you?" asked Morozov.

"Your wife was arrested at the apartment of the people who blew up the train in Moscow," the police officer announced. "You'll excuse us, of course; we have to make a search of your apartment."

"Please do," said Morozov, showing them into the apartment. "But it's inconceivable to me how this could have happened," he repeated over and over, as if to himself.

I explained out loud that I had mistaken the seamstress's door. He whispered to me: "Don't worry, Oshanina warned me, and I stayed on purpose."

The policeman went through everything but of course turned up nothing compromising. After they finished, they told Morozov: "Your servant's free to go anywhere, but we have to put you and your wife under house arrest until it becomes clear how she wound up where she was arrested."

Morozov declared that he had no need to go out for the time being, and the police left. One patrolman stayed behind in the corridor as a guard.

Alone in our apartment, we hurriedly figured out a plan to break out of this dangerous trap. We called over our landlady and asked her to offer the policeman some tea. He had just come in from the cold, and the temptation proved too great to resist: after a moment's hesitation, he followed the landlady into the kitchen. Covered by her hospitable bustle and the tinkle of dishes, we put on our summer coats, quietly opened the door, and hurried downstairs into the courtyard. Slipping past the concierge as if we were servants rushing off to a store, we made it to the street and caught a cab over to Oshanina's apartment.

After this narrow escape, Morozov and I had to stay off the streets for a while, both for our own sake and everyone else's. And since there was no better place for quarantine than the party's printing plant—the printing workers almost never left the apartment, and it was visited at most once or twice a week by a single comrade—we went over there that same evening. We were greeted with open arms: the printing workers were very weary of their seclusion, and guests were a rarity.

Although our stay was an involuntary one, Morozov and I helped with the work of the press. I was even able to set type —back in my student days in Zurich, our whole women's circle (the Fritsche) had helped set the first issue of Lavrov's journal, *Forward!* There were three women at the press— Sofia Ivanova, Maria Griaznova, and I—and through our common efforts, dinner was cooked up almost effortlessly. At three o'clock, a large copper pot of steaming *shchi* [cabbage soup] or some other soup would appear on the table, and everyone gaily stopped work and hurried over. Sometimes there was a second meat course, as well, and sometimes, on special occasions—a printing job successfully completed, or some good news from the outside—a small bottle of English liquor appeared. The table talk was almost always lively, often gay and boisterous. Although the press workers were isolated, everyone had something to talk about with the group, and the rest periods flew by.

During the three weeks we spent at the press, type was being set for No. 3 of the *People's Will*, which was to include the party's program.

The basic principles had been worked out by Morozov, Alexander Mikhailov, and Kviatkovskii, in June at the Lipetsk meeting that preceded the Voronezh congress. Unfortunately, these principles weren't put into final form after people returned to Lesnoi. There were several reasons for this: time was short; no one foresaw that circumstances would soon change the program outlined at Lipetsk; and finally, the recent breakup of Land and Liberty was fresh in our minds, and we were enjoying the feeling of being tightly united in a practical task, a task that demanded Herculean efforts. Further discussions were held in the fall, at a number of meetings in Kviatkovskii's apartment in St. Petersburg, and then every paragraph of the draft provoked debate. The differences came down to this: What was to be the primary aim of the People's Will?

One side argued for disorganizing the government by means of partisan terrorist struggle, thus forcing it (in accordance with the name of our party) to grant the people the right to express their will freely and without hindrance, to rebuild their fragmented political and economic life on the basis of justice, equality, and freedom—principles that were embodied in the people themselves. This is approximately the formulation that was adopted at Lipetsk.

The other side in this controversy accepted the same methods of struggle. However, they believed that the party should strive from the beginning to capture power for itself by means of a political conspiracy; it would then decree a constitution from above and only then hand over its powers to the people. This formulation came into currency later, in St. Petersburg, chiefly through the efforts of Lev Tikhomirov and Maria Oshanina.

But before we could arrive at a final decision about the program, Kviatkovskii—one of the authors of the Lipetsk draft—was arrested in the aftermath of the Moscow bombing; then Morozov, the most ardent proponent of the Lipetsk principles, was forced to go into quarantine at the printing plant. It was around this time, too, that it became known that Grigorii Goldenberg had betrayed the party,[14] and a number of people found their freedom seriously restricted for the first time. Amid all these circumstances, Lev Tikhomirov got the idea of taking a vote on the program—not by calling a general meeting, but rather by bringing his own version around to members' homes. Comrades with urgent business gave him their proxies, often simply on trust; the newer members of the party, who had joined immediately before Kviatkovskii's arrest, had no way of even knowing the Lipetsk version, since they hadn't been present at the earlier program discussions. By the time Morozov and I learned of the "home balloting," Tikhomirov had already obtained majority approval for his program.

Morozov and I protested Tikhomirov's irregular methods, which we considered a threat to the morale and mutual trust so vital in a revolutionary organization. A general meeting to discuss the situation was set for after the new year. But of course, the program was already in the hands of the type-setters: delaying its publication would mean delaying the whole third issue of the *People's Will*—and regular publication of the paper was, so to speak, a sign of battle-readiness. Tikhomirov had taken this into account—he was confident that everyone would have to reconcile themselves to his *fait accompli*.

In preparing for the general meeting, Morozov and I didn't want to be constrained by the conditions of life at the printing plant, and so, shortly before Christmas, we hastily rented another apartment (using new identity papers), far from our previous place.

Most of the comrades who were in St. Petersburg got together once before the general meeting. The occasion was a New Year's Eve party, held at the conspiratorial apartment that had been rented after Kviatkovskii's arrest. Quite a few people came, but Tikhomirov wasn't among them, as far as

[14] Grigorii Goldenberg was captured by the police while bringing dynamite from Odessa to Moscow.

I remember. We spent the night telling jokes, talking, and singing—everyone avoided the urgent, difficult issues that had come to the fore.

One scene in particular has stayed with me all these years: the preparation of the hot punch. On a round table in the middle of the room we set out a soup bowl, filled it with pieces of sugar, lemon, and spice, and poured in rum and wine. When we lit the rum and put out the candles, the room was magically transformed, as the flame danced around the bowl, flaring up and dying down, illuminating the stern faces of the men clustered around it. Morozov pulled out his dagger, another man followed suit, then a third. They lay the knives crosswise over the bowl, then, impulsively, burst into a powerful, festive Ukrainian melody. The music swelled and grew, new voices joined in, the flame shimmered and blazed with its reddish gleam—as if tempering a weapon for battle, for death.

When the punch was ready, the candles were relit and the hot drink ladled out into glasses. The clock struck twelve. What fate awaited us in 1880? What was in store for Russia? People clinked glasses, squeezed hands, or exchanged comradely kisses, and we all drank to freedom, to our homeland: that this cup be our last drunk in slavery!

Someone suggested we try some spiritualism. Laughing and joking, we quickly produced a large sheet of paper and traced out the letters of the alphabet. We turned a saucer upside down on the paper and seated ourselves around the table. First we summoned up the spirit of Tsar Nicholas I and asked him what kind of death his son, Alexander II, would meet. For a long time, the saucer wandered indecisively. At last we got our response—and a strange one it was: from poison. This unfortunate answer dampened everyone's enthusiasm; it seemed completely improbable. Some of the people present were aware that a bombing was in preparation at the Palace, and even apart from that, everyone knew that poison was not a weapon the Executive Committee of the People's Will would use. We dropped the fortunetelling.

Someone struck up a Ukrainian song again, others tried to sing a Polish revolutionary prayer, someone else attempted a poem put to music: "I saw slavish Russia before the holy altar, its chains clattering, its head bowed; it was praying for the tsar." Finally, we all sang the *Marseillaise*—softly and cautiously, despite the old and universal Russian custom of giving the New Year a loud and joyous welcome.

The evening drew to a close. When it came time to disperse, we left in pairs and individually, so as not to attract the attention of the superintendent, who was lying at the gates to the street, as usual.

Shortly after New Year's most of us got together again for the general business meeting. I had sent around a letter from the printing plant, expressing my fear that the moral bonds between comrades would dissolve if Tikhomirov's mode of action became the general rule; the few people who had gotten to read it told me they'd been favorably impressed. Of course, by this time, the program was already in print, but there was to be a discussion anyway. Elections to the party's Administrative Commission were also on the agenda.

During the debates, the question of Jacobinism—seizing power and ruling from above, by decree—was raised. As I saw it, the Jacobin tinge that Tikhomirov gave to his program for the Executive Committee threatened the party and the entire revolutionary movement with moral death; it was a kind of rebirth of Nechaevism, which had long since lost moral credit in the revolutionary world. It was my belief that the revolutionary idea could be a life-giving force only when it was the antithesis of all coercion—social, state, and even personal coercion, tsarist and Jacobin alike. Of course, it was possible for a narrow group of ambitious men to replace one form of coercion or authority by another. But neither the people nor educated society would follow them consciously, and only a conscious movement can impart new principles to public life.

Tikhomirov refused to deal directly with the question of Jacobinism. The discussion drew to a close, and Morozov demanded a vote on the Lipetsk program: that it be made binding on the organization, since it had been adopted freely, not covertly. Of course, his gesture was hopeless in light of the accomplished fact—namely, that the members had already endorsed Tikhomirov's program at their respective homes—but Morozov set great store by the ideals of the movement and he considered himself morally obligated to raise the issue. A sizable majority of the members present acknowledged that in their hearts they felt Tikhomirov had acted unethically. Nonetheless, they endorsed his *fait accompli.*

At this point, Morozov announced that he considered himself free of any obligation to defend a program like Tikhomirov's in public. I, too, declared that it was against my nature to act on the basis of compulsion; that once the Executive Committee had taken on a task—the seizure of state power—that violated my basic principles, and once it had recourse in its organizational practice to autocratic methods fraught with mutual distrust, then I, too, reclaimed my freedom of action.

As a gesture of sympathy, one comrade nominated me for the Administrative Commission, probably thinking that I had made my declaration in the heat of the moment and that my primary concern was to spare the organization further damage from the kind of behavior practiced by Tikhomirov. I declined, of course—at which point Tikhomirov maliciously announced: "There's no reason to decline; you haven't been elected yet, and what's more, you won't be."[15]

Tikhomirov had his victory, then. His only mistake was this: his action disfigured one of the most brilliant periods of the revolutionary struggle and set a false course for the future. Much more than state persecution or Goldenberg's betrayal of the party, it impaired the harmony of the family of people who had freely chosen to band together in the life-and-death struggle. Inertia moved the party unswervingly toward the main goal: killing the tsar. But after that last, mighty blow was delivered on March 1, 1881, the first Executive Committee perished almost in its entirety; and the

[15] The Administrative Commission did admit its first woman member around this time. This was no coincidence, of course: it was to aid the Commission's moral regeneration. The woman was Sofia Perovskaia, who was responsible, to a considerable degree, for the historic act of March 1—for which she paid with her life.—Liubatovich.

second, reconstituted Committee was unable to achieve anything, despite the substantial number of people it enlisted.

As for Tikhomirov himself, within two months he had begun a gradual retreat from the business of the Executive Committee. More and more, he devoted his time to writing (under a pseudonym) for officially tolerated journals. Eventually, he clung to this sphere almost exclusively.

In mid-January, the press where we had so recently hidden was raided. Fate had saved us—we might easily have been captured along with the printing workers. Morozov and I decided to go abroad for a while. He took an indefinite leave from the Executive Committee, intending to set forth in writing the views that had won acceptance at Lipetsk (without, of course, exposing the internal organizational split). As for me, I had to leave because I was seriously ill: I had recently suffered a severe strain carrying a heavy bottle filled with some sort of liquid up to a fifth-floor apartment. Since then, I had become far too weak for revolutionary work, which requires one's undiminished strength.

It was early February before we got passports and prepared to leave. Our comrade Andrei Zheliabov strongly urged us to stay, but we'd made our decision and, painful as it was, we had to refuse him. Our parting was very warm. "Hurry," Zheliabov advised us. "It'll be carried out in a day or two." And in fact, we had scarcely reached Berlin when the news of the bombing of the Winter Palace overtook us.[16]

> From Berlin, Liubatovich and Morozov went to Geneva, where they spent the remainder of 1880. Her account of this period in her life is extremely brief. It becomes clear in the passages below that she must have been pregnant for the greater part of the year, although she makes no mention of the fact.
>
> It was during this period that Morozov wrote Terrorist Struggle, outlining the strategy of "systematic terror"

[16] See pp. 46–47.

with which the two became identified. He explicitly renounced all efforts to build a mass movement in Russia
in the near future and called instead for the creation of
"a whole host of independent terrorist groupings which,
having recognized one another in the struggle, would

*After the explosion at the Winter Palace*

unite into one general organization."[17] These societies, based on the closest of comradely ties and intentionally kept small, would be virtually invulnerable to police spies; they would maximize the effectiveness of the limited number of revolutionary forces. Moreover, Morozov argued, terrorism was the most selective form of revolutionary warfare, since only the most guilty were chosen as targets.

In January 1881 Morozov finished writing the pamphlet *Terrorist Struggle*, in which he elaborated the principles of the Lipetsk program, and returned to Russia. Never in my life had I felt so sad. Since we were living in Geneva, a cesspool of police spies, I couldn't even see him off at the train station, lest it attract attention to him.

A few days after Morozov's departure, I got word to go to the theater, where I'd be given news from him. This secretiveness surprised and upset me—why hadn't I received a letter directly? I went to the theater and listened nervously, absentmindedly, to some opera or another. At the intermission, a man I knew came up to me and explained, in a confused way, that bad news had come—that it seemed Morozov had been arrested, although this wasn't certain yet.

I nearly collapsed from grief.

Staggering as if I were asleep, I somehow managed to make my way home. I wasn't sufficiently careful when I walked into my room, and I woke up my baby daughter. Her crying finally brought me to my senses, and I calmed down and fed her. But what venom I must have given her along with the milk from my breast, where I would rather have been holding someone else! She cried all night long, and I carried her around the room in my arms, pressing her to my breast. My mind ached, and I felt so, so empty.

At about eight in the morning, I heard knocking at my door. I opened it silently. There on the threshold, white as a sheet, stood Sergei Kravchinskii; apparently he had just arrived on the morning train from Klaran. I could tell immediately

[17] Nikolai Morozov. *Teroristicheskaia Bor'ba* (London, 1880), p. 8.

that he knew everything. "Listen, Olga," he said, "I'll go, I'll free him myself."

"As if one loss weren't enough," I answered, "you want to destroy yourself, too. No, I'll go myself. A woman can get around more easily than a man in this situation, and I may be able to do something for him."

Sergei tried to persuade me to stay, assuring me that arrangements had already been made to send a certain woman we knew and that she would do everything possible. But I had made up my mind, and I stood my ground.

"And your daughter?" Sergei pointed to the baby, as if that would clinch things.

"It makes no difference, even now I can't feed her. I'll leave her with you and your wife in the meanwhile, and we'll decide what's best for her later. I hope to be back soon." Sergei made no more objections.

I hastily began preparing to bring the child to Klaran and then go on from there myself. I didn't have the money for the trip to Russia, nor did I have a passport—it was risky to use my old one. I was fortunate enough to get a passport that same day from a very nice Russian girl who was studying in Geneva, on condition that I use it only for the trip, not to live on while I was in Russia.[18] I got the money I needed for the trip through Gerasim Romanenko, a first-rate comrade who had emigrated from Odessa and was studying law: he obtained a thousand francs, no strings attached, from a wealthy girl student. And so, within hours, I was ready for the trip.

I carefully packed my poor little girl's things in a separate suitcase, keeping for myself only the little silk kerchief that usually covered her head. This kerchief and a photograph taken of Morozov before he left were the only keepsakes left to me from the past.

I went to Klaran alone with the baby. By early morning, I was at Kravchinskii's. Sergei was remarkably thoughtful: he had already obtained a crib for my little girl and set it up in a

[18] I did in fact keep the passport "clean" in spite of all the dangers and ad-
versity I encountered, and got it back to her through acquaintances in 1882,
after I'd been imprisoned.—Liubatovich.

clean, light room. He left me alone with the child. For a long time I stood like a statue in the middle of the room, the tired baby sleeping in my arms. Her face, pink from sleep, was peaceful and filled with the beauty of childhood. When I finally decided to lower her into the bed, she opened her eyes— large, serious, peaceful, still enveloped in sleep. I couldn't bear her gaze. Not daring to kiss her lest I wake her up, I quietly walked out of the room. I thought I'd be back; I didn't know, didn't want to believe that I was seeing my little girl for the last time. My heart was numb with grief.

I said good-bye to my closest friends and left for Russia immediately. Romanenko accompanied me as far as Bern, taking care of me like a nanny. I felt and looked like a sleepwalker, and Romanenko repeatedly urged me to put a more cheerful expression on my face, if only for conspiratorial considerations. "Frankly, I don't care what happens to me. But you'll see," I argued in my defense, "I'll get to Russia all right, even though I look sad. Sleepwalkers get by where people with their eyes open stumble."

And so it turned out. I traveled second-class on a fast train from Berlin. This luxury was not a whim: I was sick. After suddenly tearing my baby from my breast, I wasn't able to get rid of my milk, and it gave rise to an inflammation and fever. I hadn't even considered this possibility before I left Switzerland.

I arrived in St. Petersburg in a weakened condition and got in touch with some old comrades from the Executive Committee. We were still on good terms, despite my differences with them, and I needed to find a man to help me in the town of Suvalki, where Morozov was imprisoned. But it was late January or early February 1881, and by this time the People's Will had suffered heavy losses. At first, Grinevitskii agreed to help me, but the next day he informed me that the organization had assigned him to another, more crucial project, and as much as he wanted to help, he couldn't go with me. I didn't ask what the project was, especially since I'd learned from Vera Figner that the party was in the midst of preparing a

*Gesia Gelfman*

new attack. Grinevitskii referred me to a young man who, he said, knew the area I was going to and could be useful to me.

I had asked Gesia Gelfman, my old comrade from the Trial of the Fifty, to check whether Morozov had been brought to the Petropavlovsk fortress,[19] and just before I left St. Petersburg, I went over to see her.

I still remember the first time I ever met Gesia. It was in Kiev, back in the summer of 1875. I was en route from Odessa to Moscow and Tula, and I stopped in at her apartment, which was used as a mail drop and meeting place. The place was empty, and I settled down to wait for her. I was very tired from my trip, and so finally, with the trusting directness of youth, I lay down on this stranger's bed and dropped off to sleep. Eventually, I was awakened by a kiss. Through my sleepy eyes, I saw the head of a young woman—curly-haired, friendly, beaming with incredible kindness.

[19] Kolotkevich, by whom Gelfman was pregnant, was imprisoned in the fortress, and I knew Gesia was corresponding with him.—Liubatovich.

"Are you Gelfman?" I asked.

"Yes, I'm Gelfman, I've been looking at your peaceful, peaceful face for a long time," she said. "I fell in love with you immediately, and I couldn't resist—I kissed you."

From that moment we were friends. Subsequently, she told me her whole life story. She had grown up in Mozyr (Minsk province). Her father, a prosperous but fanatical Jew, gave her no education whatsoever; Gesia owed everything she had become to her own energy. When she reached the age of seventeen, her father decided—without consulting her—to marry her off. A dowry was prepared. The eve of her wedding came—time for the older women to perform on Gesia the repulsive rituals dictated by ancient Jewish custom. But Gesia's sense of modesty made her rebel, and she resolved to leave home. She grabbed her jewelry and escaped by night to the home of a Russian girlfriend who had promised to help her. Gesia moved to Kiev, where she enrolled in the courses in midwifery[20] so as to be able to make an honest living. She made friends among the progressive youth of Kiev, getting to know Alexandra Khorzhevskaia, one of the Fritsche, in 1875. It was at this time that I met her.

Gesia was arrested in September 1875. Two years later, at the Trial of the Fifty, she was convicted of serving as an intermediary for our organization, which had been engaged in propagandizing and organizing among the youth and workers of various cities of the Russian Empire. She could claim no legal privileges by virtue of her social status,[21] and so she was incarcerated in a St. Petersburg workhouse. In August 1878, when I reached St. Petersburg after escaping from Siberia, Gesia was still languishing in the workhouse. I corresponded with her, and once, after she was transferred to the Litovskii fortress, walked down the street beneath her window. It made her happy to see me free.

In the summer of 1879, Gesia was sent off under police

[20] These were, incidentally, the only courses available to women in Kiev at the time.

[21] Russian criminal law exempted certain social categories of people (especially the nobility) from various forms of punishment.

guard to finish out her sentence at Staraia Russa (Novgorod province). Later that year she escaped, and we saw each other for the first time since our sentencing. She told me that she felt extremely weary after her prolonged confinement, that she wanted to rest. But those were times of feverish activity, and Gesia, like the rest of us, got swept up in the intense struggle. She was a very sensitive person, and her life was one of continuous sacrifice; she had the ability to love.

Now, at what proved to be my last meeting with Gesia, she was sad and looked rather ill, but she buried her personal grief amid the endless concerns imposed by her life as a revolutionary. For that matter, there were few cheerful people in revolutionary circles at the time: every day someone else was snatched away by the police, and the survivors, depressed by these losses, were straining every nerve for a final assault on the regime. Gesia seemed to have a foreboding that she was living out the last days of her freedom, the freedom she had enjoyed so briefly.

The apartment Gesia shared with Nikolai Sablin was used for briefings by the people who participated in the assassination of the tsar on March 1. On March 3 the place was raided by the police: Sablin killed himself, and Gelfman was arrested. A few weeks later, she was sentenced to death. Her pregnancy delayed the execution—dooming her instead to another, more horrible fate. She languished under the threat of execution for five months; finally her sentence was commuted, just before she was to deliver. At the hands of the authorities, the terrible act of childbirth became a case of torture unprecedented in human history. For the delivery, they transferred her to the House of Detention. They gave her a fairly large cell, but in it they posted round-the-clock sentries—a device that had driven other women, women who weren't pregnant, insane. The torments suffered by poor Gesia Gelfman exceeded those dreamed up by the executioners of the Middle Ages; but Gesia didn't go mad—her constitution was too strong. The child was born live, and she was even able to nurse it. Under Russian law, Gesia's rights as a mother were protected, even though she was a convict; no one could take her baby away. But at that time, who would have considered being guided by the law? One night shortly after the child was born, the authorities came in and took her away from Gesia. In the morning, they brought her to a foundling home, where they abandoned her without taking a receipt or having her tagged—this despite the fact that many people (myself included) had offered to raise the child. The mother could not endure this final blow, and she soon died.

Thus ended the life of Gesia Gelfman, who fled from her father's house, filled with indignation at ancient custom, filled with indignation at the trampling of women's rights—only to perish as the victim of unprecedented violence against her sensibilities as a woman, a human being, and a mother.[22]

But this still lay in the future.

After parting with Gesia, I went to meet the young man with whom I was to travel on my search for Morozov. On his invitation, I spent my last night in St. Petersburg at the apartment of some close friends of his, a group of young girls. These kind young girls saw that I was ill and persuaded me to get treatment. They brought me to a hospital in the morning, and I was able to get the advice and medication I needed. That evening, I left for Suvalki.

My task proved to be very complicated. We didn't know a soul in Suvalki. My companion was very young, apparently fresh out of *gimnazia*, and naturally I couldn't bring myself to subject him to any great risks. But he was so inexperienced and behaved so unconspiratorially (probably he thought that I was a respectable lady, "legal" like himself), attracting atten-

---

[22] Liubatovich got the details for this account of the last months of Gesia Gelfman's life in 1882, from women guards at the House of Preliminary Detention and from the district attorney, whom she petitioned (from her cell) for custody rights to Gelfman's child. According to a Soviet biographical sketch of Gelfman, her sentence was commuted on July 2, 1881. She was transferred to the House of Preliminary Detention on August 5 and gave birth to a daughter on October 12, 1881; peritonitis is cited as the cause of her death on February 1, 1882.

The commutation of Gelfman's sentence was substantially the result of public outrage and protest, in Russia and abroad, against the regime's callous treatment of the pregnant woman.

tion to us by his excessively liberal remarks in the presence of strangers, that I became thoroughly angry. He was a novice in the full sense of the word: ardent, selfless, but completely unskilled. For example: we had to make contact with the prison through the guards. Now, as a woman, I couldn't befriend them and buy them drinks at a tavern—but neither could my young companion: he didn't know how. It took us two whole weeks to learn that there was no "Lakier" [Morozov's pseudonym] in Suvalki prison.

Some people told us that he'd been taken to Kovno, and so we traveled there. Again, we knew absolutely no one; again, the same incredible difficulties in establishing connections with the prison. My companion got bored and started frequenting the public reading room, despite my warning that he might run into a spy there. As for me, I spent my time rushing around in impotent depression, hiding from him the grief I was feeling. I tried to establish contacts among the old ladies and tradeswomen of the town, but I couldn't find out anything useful. And so the time passed fruitlessly. February came to an end.

Then one morning, I awoke to an unusual commotion in the streets. On every corner, small groups of people were standing around, talking about something, shaking their heads. Obviously something important had happened—but what? I went outside. Couriers were tearing madly through the streets. I thought back to the previous evening, March 1, when carriages had been hurrying to the governor's house, which was lit up as for a ball, although there was no sign of a large gathering. Judging from the rumors that were now circulating among the crowd—the sovereign had been killed, St. Petersburg had been blown up, and so forth—the gathering had been a council. Toward noon, the notice of Alexander II's death and Alexander III's accession to the throne appeared, and people started gathering in synagogues and churches to take the oath of allegiance.

Meanwhile, it was becoming increasingly clear to me that it was useless to stay in Kovno any longer. I finally went to the prison myself and asked the clerk whether they had a prisoner by the name of Lakier (I didn't mention that he was a political prisoner) who had been transferred from Suvalki. I was told that they did not, and I could see by the man's face, his tone, and his attitude toward me that he was telling the truth. They probably had no "politicals" at all; otherwise, he would have taken more of an interest in my visit.

We decided to go to Vilna, where we knew people, in order to find out the details of the political situation and to get some names of people in Minsk. My companion's inexperience finally bore its fruit. When we boarded the train, a spy wearing blue glasses impudently began to follow him. Apparently, he knew the spy well from the reading room: as my companion told me, the man always seemed to hang around him. The spy didn't touch us on the train, but he followed hot on our heels throughout the trip. When we arrived in Vilna, I suggested to my companion that we stay in different hotels. I told him, furthermore, that after registering for a room he should make his disappearance immediately.

He stubbornly refused to listen to me: he wanted to see someone in Vilna, so he decided to stay the night in a hotel and go on to St. Petersburg in the morning. I couldn't save him, and it would have been stupid to share his fate. And so, after I checked in at a hotel, I promptly ordered a samovar, left the door to my room unlocked, and slipped out of the building undetected.

I went to an address I'd been given. The residents, a very nice Jewish family, willingly offered me shelter. The young student in the family accompanied me back to the hotel. He got my suitcase and walked out without being noticed; I placed a ruble on the table in the room, left the hotel, and took a very circuitous route back to the apartment. The next morning, we learned that my traveling companion had been arrested at his hotel during the night. His stubbornness cost him dearly: he wound up in Siberia, where he spent some years in administrative exile.

After his arrest, it was risky for me to be seen at the railroad station. However, with the help of a Russian worker, I was able to get a train to Minsk a couple of days later. He put me in a workmen's car, locked the door with a key, and I sat there for nearly half a day waiting for the car to be coupled to a train. Only after we were underway did my worker escort join me in the car.

After I reached Minsk, I no longer had to operate completely on my own, and this made my task easier. I quickly learned that Morozov wasn't in the Minsk prison, either; apparently he had been taken directly from Suvalki to St. Petersburg. I was terribly weary from my fruitless search. All the same, I didn't want to accept defeat, and so I decided to go to St. Petersburg. From previous experience I knew that it was impossible to move around the capital freely without good identity papers, and so I remained in Minsk in order to get the documents I needed. This took time. Meanwhile, I had occasion to mix with the local radical youth, as well as with some workers.

Everyone was still feeling the impact of March 1, and I was often approached for my opinions about the situation: Why was Russia keeping silent? What was to be done? Shouldn't some sort of demonstration be arranged? Some armed attack on an individual or institution? My response was this: "Comrades, count up your forces; they're very meager, I'm sure. I'm afraid that you won't accomplish anything great, only something ridiculous." They would confess to me that politically conscious forces were indeed extremely scarce; then they would lapse into silence. They were beginning to understand that weak, isolated outbursts would not bring freedom, but only new oppression.

At the request of my acquaintances in Minsk, I brought the type for the new People's Will press to Moscow with me—a risky task, but one I didn't want to refuse. A very simple solution presented itself. First I tied up the type in bars, which I packed between layers of rags in a large, bulky, aging leather suitcase. Then I acquired a very elegant hat with bright bows and flowers, bought a fine new summer cape, and went to the railway station—unescorted—with the suitcase. I told the porter to carry it to the baggage compartment. It was so heavy that he let out a groan as he lifted it.

"What've you got in this suitcase, miss?" he asked.

"Oh, it's filled with various metal household utensils," I replied. Seeing my smart, festive outfit, he believed me and left the matter at that. I personally watched him check in the suitcase.

I got to Moscow safely and, with my fine new passport, went straight to a hotel.

The comrades in Moscow advised me not to go to St. Petersburg until the first wave of reaction following March 1 died down. "There are almost no 'illegals' there," they told me. "Besides, for the time being nothing can be done for the people in prison." I decided to go anyway. I gave Anna Korba the receipt for the suitcase, warning her that it had to be a woman who picked it up at the station. I decided to remain in Moscow just long enough to see my family—my father, whom I hadn't seen since my trial in 1877, and his younger children.

Eight years ago I had left the family home to study in Zurich. In the interval, our family unit scattered and the house I grew up in was sold. My sister Vera had accompanied me to Zurich; Tatiana started living alone as soon as she grew up, and was now studying voice and living in the Conservatory apartments; Claudia—barely sixteen—had just married the former manager of my father's company; and my older brother was a company administrator somewhere. Father had married our governess a year before I left for Zurich—less than two years after my mother's death—and was now alone with the new family that was growing up around him.

His business had gone badly. The general depression during the Russo-Turkish war ruined him: he had to stop production at his large, very profitable brickworks in Setuni, near Moscow, and sell his estate. He was forced to return to the Moscow Surveying Department of the Senate,[23] where he had worked

---

[23] The Senate was not a representative institution, but rather a high administrative supervisory body and a kind of a supreme court.

during his youth. He no longer lived in the huge house he had built at Setuni, but in a *dacha* in Petrovskii Park. After finding out his address and letting him know when I was coming, I went to see him there.

I felt sad as I crossed the paternal threshold after these long years of separation. I found Father and his whole family at a carelessly set dinner table—no trace of the former comfort and order. He was surrounded by five small children, the oldest of whom was eight. When he caught sight of me, he sent them out to the garden to play, since he knew that I'd escaped from exile and thus was "illegal." My stepmother followed the children, and I was left alone with Father.

"Good Lord, how you've changed!" he said, clasping my hands and looking at me intently. "Only your eyes are still the same." I threw my arm around his neck. For a long time, I was too overcome with emotion to speak.

"Yes," he continued sadly, when I had regained my composure, "I sometimes blame myself for not being able to restrain you when you visited me secretly in Moscow five or six years back—remember?—just like now, for not locking you in, if necessary, after you admitted to me that you were working in a factory and conducting propaganda."

"I was warning you then, Father," I answered, "so that it wouldn't be too hard on you later on, when other people told you about what had happened to me. You wouldn't have been able to lock me up—I would have escaped from you just as I escaped from Siberia. Let's drop this, you have nothing to blame yourself for. My destiny was decided; neither you nor even I myself had the power to change it. For the sake of your other children, spare yourself. You're worn out and depressed: that's not good."

"Yes, I've had quite a bit to endure, too," he said, almost to himself. He walked over to the window and flung it open. "It's so stuffy in here," he remarked. "If you're not tired, let's take a walk around the park."

As we walked, Father explained to me frankly how his ruin had come about; how, to protect his honor, he had been obliged to give up everything to his creditors. Even those eight thousand rubles my grandfather had won on a lottery ticket and set aside for me until I came of age—money that my father had kept for me despite my conviction in 1877—even that sum had fallen into the abyss. I felt infinite pity for Father; I could see that these admissions had cost him a painful struggle. Father had let me know about the lottery winnings when I was in prison, and I'd been hoping, as I came to see him now, that perhaps something was left for my orphaned daughter.

When Father learned that I had a child and that I'd left her abroad, he became extremely upset. An intelligent and well-educated man, he naturally understood perfectly well that a child born of a mother living underground couldn't be legitimate, and he suffered, both for my sake and for the child's, suffered from my grief and from the impossibility of helping me. He didn't want to reproach me. . . .

"Oh, why weren't you born a boy?" In an instant, that melancholy, too-familiar expression came back to me from my childhood, the expression that used to make me pray quietly to God for hours on end that He might make me over into a boy. . . . Now I understood Father, understood that I had to bear a double burden in life—the heavy burden of a human being, and the burden of a woman, as well. . . .

We wandered around till dusk, talking about current events and about the future. Like me, he ached to the bottom of his soul over the state of his homeland; he, too, longed for it to be free—but he wouldn't condone violence. "Our society must be regenerated morally," he said. "Look at our public figures, the people in our municipal councils and *zemstvos*, they're guided most of all by personal interests and ambitions. . . . That's not the way Russia will be made over."

"I don't even expect anything significant or worthwhile from them," I answered. . . .

It had long since gotten dark, and the park was deserted. Father accompanied me to my hotel, and we parted. . . . My heart was heavy.

The next day, as I was getting ready to leave for St. Petersburg, a comrade from the Executive Committee (Vera Figner, as I recall) came over to tell me that Sofia Bardina's husband, Shakhov, was in Moscow and wanted to see me.

How my heart started to beat when I heard that! Sofia and I might be able to reinvigorate the revolutionary movement. We had been comrades in the Pan-Russian Social Revolutionary Organization,[24] a group that had developed considerable strength through its great ideological and moral unity. Back in 1875, we had laid the foundations for revolutionary workers' associations in Moscow and other cities. Our program reflected in embryo the course of the revolutionary movement in the seventies: from peaceful propaganda to armed resistance and disorganization of the government by means of terror. Many people subsequently told me that the solidarity we had achieved served as a model for the revolutionary organizations that came after us, particularly Land and Liberty. Our group didn't produce a single traitor, thanks to the principle on which it was based: the complete freedom and equality of all its members. Everyone—worker or member of the intelligentsia, man or woman—took a turn at carrying out administrative duties, which were both an obligation and a right. There were no elections. No one was anxious to enter the administration. The administrators had no power; they were intermediaries, and nothing more. But even apart from that, all of us placed a very high value on working directly among the people and doing ordinary manual labor. Although our period of activity was brief—less than a year—our propaganda left very perceptible traces among the people, and our legacy was put to use by those who came after us.

And so, I had high hopes as I went to my meeting with Bardina's husband. But from his first words, I could see that he wasn't really one of us, and I couldn't speak plainly with him about anything. He wouldn't come out and tell me where Sofia was—he only wanted to know whether it was possible to live in Moscow or St. Petersburg. I told him that only people

[24] The group that the Fritsche circle of Zurich helped form.

who weren't being sought intensely by the police could live safely in those cities, and if Sofia had just escaped from exile, he should tell her to take care of herself and go abroad for a while. We parted, and I went off to St. Petersburg.

Later I learned that Bardina did indeed go abroad for some time. But by this time, the revolutionary movement had divided into two distinct camps, and people like Sofia and myself—whose politics had combined a free organization of the people, peaceful propaganda, and armed protest—didn't quite fit in with either. In emigration, she found only members of Black Repartition, and they had forgotten their former spiritual kinship with the rest of us. Bardina found herself abroad without a single close friend. Even that wouldn't have been so bad, but she had deteriorated physically as well. She spent several months in a Geneva hospital, forgotten by everyone. In 1883, there in Geneva, she became convinced that her lost strength would never return, and—like Beta Kaminskaia in St. Petersburg in 1877, Khorzhevskaia in Tomsk in 1886, and Batiushkova in 1892[25]—she took her own life, in the spirit of the stoics of antiquity who preferred freedom in death to slavery in life.

While I was in St. Petersburg, I paid several visits to Rosa Lichkus, the first cousin of Kravchinskii's wife. It was through her that I received Sergei's telegram about my baby's death.

Sergei Podolynskii had asked Kravchinskii to allow him to raise my daughter. Podolynskii and I were friends from my student days in Zurich: he used to love to go boating on the lake and talk about philosophy and science with me, then a girl of eighteen. He later married a Kievan gentlewoman, but after their third child was born, he separated from her, keeping the children himself. Kravchinskii was somewhat hesitant about letting him take my daughter, since she would be growing up without a mother. But Podolynskii was a very kind person; he was a doctor, too, and his wealth would enable him to give all his children a fine education. Since Kravchinskii's

[25] All the women mentioned were tried with the Fifty.—Liubatovich.

own nomadic life couldn't guarantee my child a secure, peaceful home, and since he was unable to communicate with me directly and regularly, he had to decide her fate as he thought best. He finally granted Podolynskii's request.

My little girl was six months old when Podolynskii brought her to his villa in the south of France. She did not survive two weeks with her new foster father: like one of Podolynskii's own children, she died in the meningitis epidemic that was sweeping that part of the country, and was buried in the cemetery at Montpellier. Nor did Podolynskii himself last long. Emotionally drained by the drama he had lived through with his wife, he developed a serious mental disorder and died shortly thereafter in Paris.

Yes, it's a sin for revolutionaries to start a family. Men and women both must stand alone, like soldiers under a hail of bullets. But in your youth, you somehow forget that revolutionaries' lives are measured not in years, but in days and hours.

I sat over Kravchinskii's telegram for hours on end before it fully registered on me that my daughter was dead. I didn't cry; I was numb from grief. For some time thereafter, I suffered torments whenever I walked down the street or rode in a tram: the sweet, happy faces of small children tore at my heart, reminding me of my own child. Dulled by thoughts of her death, I temporarily lost my innate caution. I couldn't look at people easily, couldn't penetrate their thoughts and feelings.

What saved me during this period was the hope, not yet abandoned, of arranging Morozov's escape. I had already made certain preparations and was corresponding with him about a plan when I was approached by Vladimir Degaev, whom Morozov had known earlier.[26] He offered his services and asked me some natural questions: Where was Morozov at the moment? Did I have contact with him? I told him that I was

26 As Liubatovich learned later, Degaev had become an agent of the police.

communicating with Morozov, and that he was in the House of Preliminary Detention. That was enough for Degaev. The next letter I wrote to Morozov, a few days later, was returned to me, and I was informed that he had been transferred to the fortress: I never even found out whether he received my preceding letter, with the news about our daughter's death. Thus, my fruitless efforts to free Morozov came to an end. Betrayal crowned all my other failures.

I still had my own freedom, but it seemed to me that the police were beginning to tail me, and so I moved to Okhta, where I got a place for a few rubles a month. Okhta had this advantage: in order to get into St. Petersburg proper, you crossed the Neva River in a skiff, and so it was always possible to determine whether you were being followed. It turned out that the spies had not yet made their way into Okhta.

After May 1881 there were only three of us living underground in St. Petersburg: Tikhomirov (who had long been avoiding everyone), Tatiana Lebedeva, and me. Tatiana and I got together several times during the period of almost a month that I spent living quietly in Okhta. She complained to me that she had grown infinitely weary of the police following hot on her heels, that her existence seemed unnecessary, and sometimes she thought of giving herself up. She didn't count on getting help from comrades—they were in bad shape themselves, and besides, none of the old comrades were in St. Petersburg, except for Tikhomirov, who wouldn't see her.

This kind of talk terrified me. Something had to be done— I was afraid Tatiana would kill herself. We arranged for her to come to my place, and I gave her directions by way of the Neva skiff. But she was so exhausted, both physically and emotionally, that the slightest unaccustomed effort or unfamiliar path was beyond her strength. She wound up taking a roundabout route via the Liteinyi Bridge, going part way by cab and then approaching my place on foot. As I sat on the little balcony of my garret, watching the street in the fading light of evening, I made out her figure in the distance—and to my great distress, she wasn't alone. Someone was following her every movement: she went into a store and he went after her, she stopped and he did, too. It was a bad sign, but there was nothing to be done. Tatiana could hardly walk, yet she had come to see me; it was obvious she didn't have the strength to go any further. When she got to my place, I communicated my observation to her. She agreed that the tailing was suspicious and was sorry she hadn't taken my advice.

Tatiana spent the night at my place but went back into the city again the next morning. Around noon that same day, two lodgers suddenly moved into the empty room next to mine—a young man who looked like a store clerk, and a woman considerably older than he, with a worn-out, insolent face. After putting their things away, these people unceremoniously knocked on my door on some pretext and tried to strike up an acquaintance. I passed myself off as a private tutor; they started asking whom I taught, what I got paid, and so forth. With some difficulty, I got rid of them and went into the city to inform Lebedeva of this latest development.

Tatiana had just received a letter from the comrades in Moscow, telling her to get out of St. Petersburg. Indeed, there was no other solution to her dilemma—but how to evade the spies who shadowed her? We arranged everything possible for an escape—connecting courtyards, an arcade where there was a shop she could slip through unnoticed—but it was to no avail. They caught Tatiana when she reached the train station. I followed her at a distance and watched the whole scene, powerless to help her.

Late that day, I returned to my place in Okhta. I found my new neighbors half-drunk and squabbling noisily. From the way they acted with each other, it was obvious to me that they weren't a family, but some kind of team of scoundrels. Obviously I had to start thinking about getting out while I still could.

To my complete surprise, Gerasim Romanenko showed up in St. Petersburg a few days later, urgently requesting, through friends, that I meet with him. Romanenko persuaded me not to wait passively in St. Petersburg to be arrested, but rather

to go to Moscow, where many of our people had gathered.
I agreed, preferring to die, as the saying goes, with gun in
hand.

Not that I expected anything important to develop in the
revolutionary movement at this time. When I traveled through
Moscow in the spring, I had heard such comments as this:
"Alexander III must die at the hands of the people themselves, not at the hands of revolutionaries." I had been a common laborer; I knew the people, and I understood how empty
these hopes were now. It made me sad to look at the heap of
appeals that had been printed up—"To the People," "To Society," "To the Officers," and others—for I knew they wouldn't
bring any broad response. True, anti-Semitic disorders were
developing in some places, and there were revolutionaries who
considered this a symptom of a ripening revolutionary mood.
But as I saw it, such wild, ugly manifestations held no promise
at all for the future—they reflected unbridled passions, not a
conscious striving for freedom and justice.

So I agreed to go to Moscow, without knowing what I
would do there—almost certain, moreover, that there was
nothing important that could be done. For me, there was no
one and nothing to save my freedom for, anyway; the winning
of Russia's freedom had been delayed, I felt, for a long, long
time to come.

Before taking the train to Moscow, I kept in quarantine
for a few days at the apartment of a friend of Romanenko's.
To avoid a repetition of Lebedeva's arrest, they brought me two
stations down the line toward Moscow by post chaise, pretending to be going to the hunt. Even these precautions
couldn't save me. The police probably didn't know which
apartment I was staying in, but as soon as I went out, they
must have picked up my trail again, because a police spy and
his wife turned up in my car on the train. They tried to make
friends and persuade me to take a room in the same hotel as
them in Moscow. I pretended to agree, but when we arrived in
Moscow in the evening, I managed to lose myself in the crowd
and get a cab to another part of the city.

My days were numbered, however. One afternoon a few days

after I arrived in Moscow, an agent—the one who had moved next door to me after Tatiana Lebedeva's visit—walked up to me on the street, stopped me roughly, and began shouting for the police. I attempted to hide in a nearby hairdressing shop, but the proprietor, a well-fed German, was standing in the doorway, and he pushed me back into the street. A crowd was collecting. Several people tried to move me away from the policemen who were running up, but I had no place to hide, and there were no cabs in sight. They finally caught me.

I wasn't overly dismayed by being arrested, but I was afraid that someone would be captured at my hotel room. And so it happened: Romanenko went there the next day and was arrested. Fortunately, the news of our arrests spread quite quickly, and no one else fell into the police ambush.

Thus ended my earthly wandering during one of the saddest eras of Russian history.

> The police discovered in Liubatovich's possession a letter from the imprisoned Morozov, urging her not to worry about him but rather to carry on the struggle, even though she was the "sole remaining representative" of systematic terror. Her arrest ended any hope of translating their ideas into reality.
>
> In order to prevent the authorities from concluding that the terrorist movement as a whole had been defeated, Liubatovich informed them that she belonged to a small faction which had split from the Executive Committee of the People's Will. At the same time, she affirmed her complete moral solidarity with the party: "in leaving it, I certainly had no intention of harming my old comrades; on the contrary, I intended to proceed hand in hand with them toward the same goal, so dear to all of us."[27]
>
> In November 1882 she was banished without trial to Irkutsk, eastern Siberia. She spent more than twenty

---

[27] "Doznanie o docheri inzhenera Ol'ga Liubatovich . . ." *Byloe*, August 1907, p. 296.

years in exile, returning to the European part of Russia only after the Revolution of 1905. Her memoirs are dated March 30, 1906, and we know little about her life thereafter. She died in 1917.

# ELIZAVETA
# KOVALSKAIA

Elizaveta Kovalskaia was the only woman revolutionary of her generation to be born a serf. Although her father, a wealthy landowner, did not abuse her peasant mother in the fashion of some Russian noblemen, Kovalskaia became painfully and irrevocably conscious of class inequality and oppression early in life. Years later, she related a remarkable story from her childhood to a comrade, Osip Aptekman: at the age of seven, she had confronted her father and somehow convinced him to exercise his influence to get her mother and her retroactively registered as free citizens. Thereafter, Kovalskaia was raised in a manner appropriate to a nobleman's daughter. When her father died late in her adolescence, he bequeathed her his large estate.

By that time, Kovalskaia was already a committed feminist and socialist. In one of the houses that she had inherited in Kharkov she set up a radical educational center. Until police harassment abruptly shut it down in 1869, it served as the home of a school for working women, advanced courses for women of the upper classes, various political study groups, and small conferences. Over the next few years, Kovalskaia passed through the two most intensive "schools" for the women revolutionaries of the seventies. She was among the first group of women to attend the Alarchinskii courses in St. Petersburg; then, around 1872, she went to Zurich, where revolutionary currents were so strong among the Russian émigré colony. When she returned to Russia, it was as a Bakuninist.

To some extent, Kovalskaia's subsequent activity placed her outside the mainstream of the populist movement. Whereas most revolutionaries of the seventies (the Pan-Russian Social

Revolutionary Organization was an important exception) concentrated their efforts on the peasantry or radical intelligentsia, Kovalskaia generally organized among factory workers. She deliberately shunned the revolutionary groups of the early and middle seventies, for reasons she cites in her memoir. It was late in 1879 before she joined Black Repartition, and as it turned out, she withdrew from the party in a matter of months. Along with a comrade, Nikolai Shchedrin, she went to Kiev early in 1880 and established an independent organization, the Union of Russian Workers of the South.

The program they developed for the Union was based on "economic terror"—attacks on oppressive factory administrators, landlords, and local authorities whom the people encountered in their daily lives. The Union was the most successful attempt of the populist era to link a strategy of armed struggle with a mass organization. At a time when all unions were illegal, when possession of a leaflet could result in imprisonment or even execution, no less than seven hundred workers attended the clandestine meetings conducted by Kovalskaia and Shchedrin—an "enormous number" for that period, as she rightly notes.

---

I was born near Kharkov, an illegitimate child, on the estate of my father, Solntsev. My mother was a peasant, my father's serf. For family reasons, my father utilized his extensive connections in high administrative circles to have my mother and me legally transferred into the *meshchanstvo*[1] of the city of Kharkov. This change took place when I was about seven, but it was made retroactive to my birth. Thus, I was designated on official papers as the "illegitimate daughter of a woman of the *meshchanstvo* of Kharkov and Colonel Solntsev." Different documents give different birth dates for me: one has 1849, another 1850, and a third 1852. I don't know which is correct.

[1] The *meshchantsvo* was a conglomerate social estate of free citizens, roughly equivalent to a lower middle class. It contained such groups as craftsmen, shopkeepers, and soldiers.

From my earliest years, life seemed incomprehensible and cruel to me. I think I was barely six when I became aware that there were landowners and peasant serfs in the world; that landowners could sell people, that my father could separate my mother and me by selling her to one neighboring landowner and me to another—but my mother could not sell my father. Another discovery struck me as equally cruel: children were divided into legitimate and illegitimate, and the latter were always treated with contempt and subjected to insults and mockery, regardless of their personal qualities. The children of the house serfs used to tease me with the dirty word then used to describe illegitimate children.

On long winter evenings in the village, I would quietly make my way into the maids' workroom and hide myself in a corner. There I would listen while the maidservants told each other their sad stories as they sat at their spinning wheels in the light of the blazing stove. Once, one of them took notice of my presence: "Take it from me!" she declared. "You'll grow up someday, too—and then they'll sell you." I was tormented by nightmares: I dreamt that they were selling me.

I don't remember my father selling any of his peasants. But before I was born, he did buy a young, intelligent musician —a violinist, the illegitimate son of some count and one of his peasants. After buying the man, my father gave him his freedom, but he was already ruined, a heavy drinker. He stayed on voluntarily to live with us as the steward of one of my father's estates, and our common situation brought us together. When he was a bit "tight" he would share his experiences with me, a child. His fate made me aware of what lay in store for me.

It was he who taught me to read and write. The first books that I read from his small library were poetry: Pushkin, Lermontov, and Polezhaev. The "Song of the Captured Iroquois" by Polezhaev was my favorite:

> But like an oak ancient and great
> The shafts will not move me
> I shall stand fast and free

> And greet the moment of my fate
> . . . . . . . . . . . . . . . . . . . . . . . . . .
> I will die, but my foes
> Will perish at my death.

I would sing this to a melody I invented, as I wandered alone around the old, neglected garden.

Images of the Decembrists[2] passed through my childhood like dim phantoms. Among my father's relatives, there was a very young officer, a Prince Volkonskii. I don't know whether he was related to the Decembrists in any way, but he taught me the following song about them:

> Not a sound can be heard from the city
> There is silence on the Neva towers
> And only the sentry's bayonet
> Burns with the light of the midnight moon.
> An unhappy youth, the same age
> As the trees, young and blooming
> Strikes up a song in a lonely prison
> And gives out his longing to the waves:
> Father, do not await me with my bride
> Destroy the wedding ring.
> Here, behind the iron bars,
> I can be neither husband nor father.

When I asked who that young man behind bars was, Volkonskii told me how there had once been good people who were imprisoned by the tsar for wanting to change things so that no one could sell people anymore.

I have another vivid memory—of Bagration, a relative of my father's, who was also a prince or a count. We all thought he was crazy; and perhaps he was. His visits were mysterious.

---

[2] In December 1825, a number of army officers, organized in several secret societies, took advantage of the death of Tsar Alexander I to attempt an armed coup. Although the Decembrists, as they became known, differed as to the form of government they sought for Russia (constitutional monarchy or republic), they were in general agreement about the need to abolish serfdom. The coup was smashed and the leaders punished harshly: five were hanged and scores of others imprisoned or exiled to Siberia. They became heroes to succeeding generations of Russian radicals.

I remember the first time he appeared. We were living in the village then. It was a winter night, the middle of a blizzard. The dogs started barking furiously. The footmen ran out into the courtyard; a tall male figure could be seen moving in the light of their lanterns. The maidservant ran anxiously to my mother's room: "Take it down, quickly, take it down!"

My mother hurriedly removed the tsar's portrait from the wall of our living room. A tall old man—hunched and gray-haired, yet young-looking—appeared in the living room. Before he greeted anyone, he searched the walls with his eyes. Then he turned to my father: "Everything's fine here, Nikolai; it's clean, you don't have any of that trash on your walls."

He was particularly affectionate with me. He sat me on his knee and told me about many things that were incomprehensible to me then, and that left me with only another foggy notion of some good people who did not want others to be sold like cattle, and of a tsar who buried them alive. He portrayed the tsar as a fantastic monster who devoured people.

After our mysterious guest left, Father ordered me to repeat nothing of what my uncle had said to me. I obeyed his order scrupulously, proud that they would trust me with any kind of secret.

The emancipation of the serfs in 1861 made a tremendous impression on me. For a long time, I felt literally drunk with joy.

When we moved to Kharkov, my father began to take an active interest in my education: he was preparing to make a lady of me. For this purpose, he hired a Frenchwoman to teach me music and dance, and for the other subjects, a Polish student who had been exiled to Kharkov because of his involvement in the Polish uprising. This student told me enthralling stories of the Poles' struggles for their freedom, and I wept because I was not Polish and could not struggle for my freedom.

At the age of eleven, I was placed in a private boarding school for girls. The founder of the school—a woman of the

1860's, with progressive views—had set it up beautifully. The young teachers did more than give lessons; they were very generous with their time and took a real interest in our development. However, the school was soon closed because it failed to get financial support from the public. In particular, parents had gotten upset when gymnastics were introduced into the curriculum, and we had to dress for them in loose-fitting men's clothing.

When the school closed, I enrolled in a *gimnazia*—although not before a struggle with my father. There I made the acquaintance of a girl who introduced me to the literature of the sixties, and I began to devour greedily the current journals (*The Russian Word* and *The Contemporary*), the poems of Nekrasov, and other books with a definite political orientation. I set up a circle for self-education among the girls. It soon merged with a group of young male students. We concentrated on social issues, but we also read papers on the natural sciences, astronomy, physics, and other branches of knowledge. Chernyshevskii was one of our favorites—particularly his novel *What Is to Be Done?* with its exploration of the woman question.

Toward this time, a new judicial institution was introduced to Kharkov: the public trial. After we finished our schoolwork, our group would race to the court sessions, where we sometimes stayed until midnight. We saw social issues unfold before us, in scenes from real life. Among other things, we saw peasants who had been cheated of their land by the emancipation process being tried for rebellion; and we saw women who, unable to bear their legally sanctioned slavery, had murdered their husbands.

The emancipation of the serfs in 1861 had given rise to the women's movement. Like a huge wave, the movement to liberate women swept over all the urban centers of Russia. I, too, was caught up in it. My father had died soon after I finished school, leaving me a large inheritance. In one of the houses he left me, I organized free courses for women seeking higher education. Iakov Kovalskii, whom I later married, worked with me on this.[3] There were so many auditors for the courses that we had trouble squeezing them all into the house. Kovalskii gave lectures on physics, chemistry, and cosmography; de la Rue, an assistant professor, taught the natural sciences; and we used university students for political economy, history, and higher mathematics.

At the same time, I belonged to the Kharkov Society for the Promotion of Literacy. At the Sunday schools where I worked, I picked out the most capable of the women laborers and invited them to my house on holidays. Gradually, a school for women workers was formed. I read them fragments of Russian fiction and recounted episodes from Russian history; I told them about the French Revolution; but mainly, I conducted propaganda on the woman question.

A men's study circle devoted to social questions met in my house; its orientation was radical, although not revolutionary. Parallel to this group, I organized one exclusively for women who were interested in socialism. A male comrade who had a good grasp of French, as well as access to the university library, made excerpts from source works to help me in compiling papers on Fourier, Saint-Simon, Owen, and other utopian socialists.

On holidays, some village schoolteachers who were friends of Kovalskii came to visit us. We provided them with books and organized small conferences on pedagogy, in the course of which we also dealt with political topics. During one of these conferences, a police officer and his entourage appeared in our house. When he saw the maps and visual displays spread out on the desks, he was taken aback. "All this is fine," he declared; "you're doing useful work and I see nothing illegal in it. But according to the orders from my superiors, all your meetings must cease, and if they don't, I'll have to arrest you all."

We had to stop everything.

---

[3] The author's maiden name was Solntseva; when she married Kovalskii, she became Kovalskaia (the feminine form of the name). She mentions neither the date of their marriage nor the circumstances under which they separated.

Dmitrii Tolstoi,[4] the minister of education, was supposed to visit Kharkov around that time, and we agitated for the right to present a petition to him: we wanted permission for women to enroll in the universities. Meetings were held constantly; I was chosen to the committee that drew up the petition, and also as a delegate to present it. But as it turned out, Tolstoi was very hostile to us: he declared that he would never allow women into the universities.

Although the universities of Russia remained closed to us, the advanced courses for women at the Alarchinskii *gimnazia* were just opening up at that time [1869]. I decided to go to St. Petersburg with my friend Anna Aptekman. Kovalskii also traveled to St. Petersburg to attend a student meeting as a delegate from Kharkov. Before he left St. Petersburg to return home, he introduced us to a medical student named Ginsburg.

Ginsburg paid Aptekman and me a visit at twilight one foggy, wintry day to suggest that we go to an apartment where a number of very remarkable women were meeting. I must say, there was some timidity mixed in with my joy as I walked with him down Vladimir Street. We stopped at a large house across from a church and walked up the main staircase to the second floor. Ginsburg opened an unlocked door, and we found ourselves in a large foyer, decorated with mirrors, palms, and coat stands; it was evidently an expensive apartment. It was noisy in the next room: women's voices could be heard arguing. A very young woman walked over to us. She was short and strongly built, with close-cropped hair, and she wore an outfit that seemed almost to have become the uniform for the advocates of the woman question: a Russian blouse, cinched with a leather belt, and a short, dark skirt. Her hair was pulled back revealing a large, intelligent forehead, and her large gray eyes, in which one sensed exceptional energy, radiated cheerfulness. In general, she looked more like a young boy than a girl. This was the youngest of the Kornilova sisters, Alexandra.

She greeted us pleasantly and led us into a large room where

---

[4] A reactionary official, no relation to the famous writer.

about twenty women, divided into several groups, were conversing animatedly. A few sat quietly, listening. So many women were smoking that it was difficult to breathe in the room. The hostess returned to one of the groups to continue her evidently unfinished argument, leaving us to make our own way in the new surroundings. Ginsburg left at once, without stepping foot into the room: the meeting consisted exclusively of women.

New books, their pages still uncut, lay in heaps on the floor. Glancing at them quickly, I saw Flerovskii's *The Position of the Working Class in Russia*, Vermorel's *The Revolution of 1848*, Mikhailov's *The Proletariat in France,* and others.

I couldn't get my bearings right away: new surroundings, so many unfamiliar new faces . . . books . . . snatches of conversation. I found a secluded corner of the room and proceeded to examine the people present. In the middle of the room stood a tall, slender young girl wearing a red Garibaldi,[5] with a cameo profile, luxurious curly golden hair down to her shoulders, and a strict, proper expression on her face; she could have been taken for a statue of liberty. A young girl, almost a child, was standing near her. Her plain costume set her apart from the others: a modest gray dress with a small white collar that somehow looked clumsy on her, like a schoolgirl's uniform— you could see that she was totally oblivious to her appearance. The first thing that you noticed was her broad, high forehead, which stood out so strongly from her small round face that all the other features were somehow lost in the background.

The blond girl, impetuous and passionate, was on the attack. The girl with the large forehead replied with extreme restraint, but very stubbornly. Looking closely at her, I saw that below the large forehead were eyelids drawn slightly downward toward her temples; her gray-blue eyes seemed rather evasive, but held a kind of stubborn inflexibility. Her expression was distrustful. When she was silent, her small, childlike mouth was tightly shut, as if she feared saying something superfluous.

---

[5] A kind of shirtwaist worn by women, similar to the red shirt worn by the Italian patriot Garibaldi.

Her face was deeply thoughtful and serious; her entire figure exuded a monastic asceticism.

I listened closely and caught the thread of their conversation. The blonde was proving that it was unnecessary to separate women's circles from men's. Her opponent kept asserting that joint circles were impossible, in view of the fact that men, being more educated, would undoubtedly make it difficult for women to think independently. As the argument flared up, despite my striking first impression of the blonde, and despite my weakness for beauty in general, I found myself more and more attracted to the modestly dressed, ascetic young girl. Many interesting, beautiful, gentle faces passed before my eyes, but again and again my attention would return to the girl in gray. Perhaps it was because her unpretentious clothing was so different from that of the others, who were dressed in the particular fashion of that circle of women. Perhaps, too, because this girl resembled one of those stubborn defenders of their faith who carry their cause to the point of self-annihilation—I had been attracted to that type from childhood.

The group began to disperse long after midnight. Alexandra Kornilova, who lived in the apartment, made me stay. When everyone but the girl in gray had gone, she introduced us: the girl was Sofia Perovskaia. Perovskaia suggested that I join a small circle of women who wanted to study political economy, and I agreed.

On the day set for the first meeting, I went to the room of one of the circle's members, Anna Vilberg. I was surprised at how few women were there, and I asked Perovskaia about it: "Why are there so few of us, why didn't you invite Aptekman, who was with me when I visited the other group?"

Perovskaia replied: "We decided to be very discriminating for this circle. We chose only people we knew, because this circle is going to develop into a different kind of group, with different goals."

"But why did you take me and not Aptekman? You don't know either of us."

"Yes, but we had heard of you even before you arrived; we knew about your activities with women workers in Kharkov.

*Group portrait: Sofia Leshern von Gershfeld*
*Alexandra Kornilova*                          *Anna Vilberg*
*Sofia Perovskaia*

---

We still don't know Aptekman. She'll probably be invited later."

We talked at length about how to begin. It was decided to start with J. S. Mill, the edition with the Chernyshevskii commentaries.[6] As it turned out, only Perovskaia and I came punctually to the sessions. The others either failed to come altogether, or else arrived after we had already finished the portion of Mill assigned for the day. Perovskaia would administer sharp reprimands to the latecomers. Olga Schleissner came in for it

[6] Mill's *Principles of Political Economy*.

the most: she was always going somewhere, always in a hurry. Perovskaia took her studies very seriously. She would stop thoughtfully at each idea, develop it, and raise objections first to Mill, then to Chernyshevskii. It was obvious that she was enthralled by intellectual work and enjoyed it deeply for its own sake, not only as a means to an end.

The circle did not last for very long, however. Perovskaia, too, began coming late to the meetings; she was troubled by something and absent-minded. One time when she was particularly unhappy, she abandoned her usual reserve and told me about her unpleasant personal situation. She was very close to her mother, who sympathized with her efforts to break free of the stifling atmosphere of her family life, but her father was furious with her, and their relations were very strained. Now her father wanted to make her live at home. She dreaded this terribly; and now, staying with various friends, she found herself in a semi-illegal position.[7]

Aptekman and I joined other groups besides this unsuccessful one. In every case, the woman question was the center of debate, although other political and social issues were touched upon in passing. Women's meetings were so frequent that we barely had time to get from one place to another. I would see Perovskaia three or four times a day at these meetings, but never do I remember her making a speech (although many people spoke far too often at that time). From her hiding place in a corner, she would inject sharp comments in the rigid tone of a new convert who has little patience for those who think differently.

Just as these meetings and the process of forming circles were reaching their height, just as the Nechaev trial was starting, I grew seriously ill, and the doctors categorically ordered me to leave St. Petersburg for the south. Perovskaia paid me a visit shortly before my departure. "Get well soon," she said. "We have to talk about something very important with you."

[7] Perovskaia did not have the identity papers legally required for a woman to live apart from her family (her father or husband). Her father had not yet reported her to the police, however.

She saw that I was in no condition to listen or speak; I had begun to spit blood, and I was growing quite weak.

Shortly thereafter, I was visited by someone from a circle that included Kornilova, Perovskaia, Aptekman, myself, and many other women. Indignant and upset, she told me: "Imagine! Kornilova and Perovskaia, who have always argued against merging with men's circles, have themselves joined a men's circle. I've come here to find out if we can have a meeting today at your place; we're going to demand an explanation from them." I agreed.

That evening, my room was filled with women. We waited quite a long time for Kornilova and Perovskaia. Kornilova entered with a free and easy, even somewhat defiant attitude; Perovskaia looked embarrassed and depressed, but ready for battle. Accusations flew at them from all sides. The role of prosecutor was quickly assumed by a woman named Berlin, who later became a lawyer. At the end of Berlin's speech, Kornilova responded with the enthusiasm that was characteristic of her, but she was very unconvincing. Perovskaia was more reserved, and replied simply: "We are not going to explain anything to you." She then rose and walked out with Kornilova.

I soon went south, as I had been ordered. When I got there, I started to revive the circles I had organized earlier, but my doctors quickly packed me off to Zurich.

In Zurich I came into contact with various revolutionary currents, especially Lavrism and Bakuninism. I was attracted to Bakuninism, and when my health had improved somewhat, I returned to Russia in order to "go to the people."

Because of my physical weakness, I was absolutely unsuited for the role of a manual laborer. Instead, I took a position as a schoolteacher in the district of Tsarskoe Selo, close to the Kolpino factory, where the young people of the village worked. I quickly came under surveillance for conducting propaganda and illegally distributing revolutionary pamphlets among the factory workers. One day, the *zemstvo* school inspector came to warn me that I was about to be arrested.

I escaped to St. Petersburg, where I got to know some workers and began providing them with illegal literature. My status was semi-illegal, but I managed to avoid arrest by dividing my time between St. Petersburg and Kharkov. Then, during the demonstration that followed Vera Zasulich's acquittal [March 31, 1878, in St. Petersburg], I was severely beaten by the police. I had to spend almost a year in bed back in Kharkov.

After I recovered, I organized several groups—two circles of metalworkers from the factories and a third one composed of young people. My political work was conducted in the spirit of Land and Liberty's program, but I didn't join the party: I wanted to retain my freedom of action.

There were many revolutionaries of the 1870's—Bakuninists, Lavrists, and people espousing other programs—who preferred to work independently, outside any groups or organizations. They had entered an unfamiliar and, to many of them, alien milieu—the people—and they found it extremely inconvenient to bind themselves to the directives of any organization: there would be no freedom of action; in unanticipated situations you would have to try to make your actions conform to the organization's statute—which in many cases had been developed in the libraries of people who were out of touch with real life. Then, too, in revolutionary practice there were frequent conflicts between your own inner morality and the theoretical morality of the group, and you sometimes had to steer a course between them. Of course, an organization did have advantages: it made it possible to get from one place to another more easily, to obtain a passport, shelter, or connections among the local population. But at the same time, there was the enormous danger of being torn away from your work through the slightest carelessness of any member of the organization. This was especially true during the early 1870's, when the enthusiastic novices doing political work paid very little attention to the conditions that prevailed in Russia—the searches, interception of mail, and police "tailing."

But in the spring of 1879, after Governor Krapotkin was assassinated, there was a wave of searches and arrests in Kharkov. I had to flee and go underground for good. I spent brief periods of time in various cities, reaching St. Petersburg in the fall of that year. By this time, Land and Liberty had split into the People's Will and Black Repartition. Firmly convinced that only the people themselves could carry out a socialist revolution and that terror directed at the center of the state (such as the People's Will advocated) would bring—at best—only a wishy-washy constitution which would in turn strengthen the Russian bourgeoisie, I joined Black Repartition, which had retained the old Land and Liberty program.

*The operation of an underground press was a primary concern of every revolutionary party. But the government zealously controlled the printed word in Russia, and obtaining the necessary equipment could be difficult and risky. After Land and Liberty split, its press became the object of heated contention between its two successor parties.*

I recall a very stormy meeting about the printing press which Black Repartition held in one of its conspiratorial apartments. Maria Krylova, who had been serving as the proprietress of Land and Liberty's printing operation, emphatically refused to let the People's Will have the press—she was even prepared to use arms against them, if they took any aggressive action to get it. Georgi Plekhanov[8] was also strongly opposed to giving up the press, but at the same time, in his characteristic manner, he wittily and venomously ridiculed Krylova's plan for "armed resistance." Popov and a few others took their side. Preobrazhenskii, Shchedrin, and I argued for some sort of compromise: we felt it was undesirable to strain

[8] Later an important Marxist theoretician.

relations—much less initiate some sort of armed struggle!—between the two newly formed groups. Finally, it was decided to have Preobrazhenskii and Stefanovich negotiate for the press with the People's Will.

This decision notwithstanding, when I visited our party's secret apartment a few days after the meeting, I found Krylova, agitated and triumphant, holding two large valises and some sort of long stick wrapped up in a curtain: she had acted on her own and taken some parts of the press, for which she now wanted us to find a storage place. I was assigned to arrange this immediately.

I visited the apartments of many of our sympathizers without finding a suitable place. Then, by chance, I ran into an acquaintance of mine—Novikov, a student from Kharkov. Although he wasn't directly involved in the revolutionary movement, he was completely trustworthy, and he never refused his help when it was needed. Novikov introduced me to a Siberian woman he knew very well, a priest's widow. She worked as a housekeeper for a man who owned gold mines. The place was completely secure, and the widow made an excellent impression on me when I met her. The very next day, Piankov and Prikhodko brought a wooden trunk loaded with the captured printing equipment—which I didn't get to see—to her place.

There was an accident not long after the trunk was settled in: a fire broke out in the house. People raced around, dragging things out of the building, but the Siberian woman, who knew that the small trunk was suspiciously heavy, didn't lose her head. She sat down on it, an icon in her hands, and prevented them from taking her things out of the room: the Holy Virgin saves, she declared. The fire was extinguished, and there was no further trouble.

But as it turned out, Krylova hadn't gotten the really essential printing equipment; it was impossible for us to work with what she had taken. Consequently, the announcement of the existence of the new party, Black Repartition, was printed in the *People's Will*—the other party's newspaper—on the equipment that the People's Will had retained.

Our group immediately negotiated to get a new press from a man named Perepletchikov, who had his own legal printing plant in Smolensk, and rented a modest apartment on Vasilievskii Island [in St. Petersburg] to house it. Piankov and Krylova moved in, posing as husband and wife; Zharkov, a typesetter who was on close terms with the former members of Land and Liberty, was summoned from Saratov; and Elizaveta Shevyreva and Pyotr Prikhodko were also enlisted to work at the press.

We were afraid that the printing operation would be discovered if the police tailed our people after they picked up the new equipment at the train station,[9] so we decided to set up another, intermediate apartment. Shchedrin and I—designated as the Krudners, a German couple, on our phony identity papers—rented a small, cheap place in another section of town. We explained to the superintendent that we wanted to open a small locksmith shop. Shchedrin consulted with the man at considerable length as to the best place to hang a signboard on the gates, and we told him we were expecting to receive a machine and other tools within a couple of days; he promised to send us customers. After we were established in the apartment, we often invited the superintendent in and treated him to beer, thereby winning him over completely.

One day, the printing press arrived, and four of the men brought it from the railway station to our place. Shortly thereafter, it was transferred to the apartment on Vasilievskii Island. The heavy cast-iron slab proved to be a great problem: we were afraid that it would attract attention if two people carried it. Tishchenko, who was exceptionally strong, came to the rescue—he simply wrapped it up in paper and carried it like a picture.

Once the press was duly installed in its place, it was necessary to liquidate our apartment without arousing suspicion. Now, at that time, Lev Deich was supposed to go abroad, but it would have been difficult for him to get a passport for foreign travel. We offered to try to get one on the

[9] The police routinely posted spies at railroad stations in hopes of catching fugitives.

basis of our false documents. We asked the superintendent in and told him an elaborate story about an uncle who owned a business in Berlin and had invited us by mail to go work with him; we had already sold out our workshop in parts, we said, and now we needed a passport for foreign travel. We gave the superintendent our identity papers plus ten rubles for the fee, promised him something more for his trouble, and in a few days received a legal passport, which Lev Deich did in fact use to cross the border.[10]

In January 1880, Black Repartition's printing plant was raided: Zharkov, the typesetter, had betrayed the group. Our apartment escaped discovery, however, because he didn't know about it. I had met Zharkov for the first time after he arrived from Saratov, and he made a very bad impression on me. I categorically opposed his participation in transferring the press from our place to Vasilievskii Island. Although some of the people in Black Repartition criticized me for feminine capriciousness, Zharkov was kept out of the operation, and that saved our apartment when he was arrested and began to talk. I don't think Zharkov had joined our group as a provocateur, but this was his first arrest, and he panicked. The gendarmes sized him up and put him to use as their agent. It was his testimony that enabled the police to capture our press and arrest a number of people associated with Black Repartition.

Joining Black Repartition had involved accepting the basic principles of the Land and Liberty program. Those principles had, in fact, guided my own political work previously; my reservations about joining the organization concerned tactics. The experiences of the revolutionaries who had

[10] The procedure described in this passage was standard. Generally, the superintendent's favorable reference was sufficient for the applicants to obtain a passport for foreign travel.

*Police raid on a printing press*

worked in the countryside had not been very successful. From my various approaches to the masses, I had gradually come to the conclusion that two activities should be paramount. The first was *economic terror*. Now, the program of Black Repartition included this, but the party's emphasis was on local popular uprisings. In my opinion, economic terror was more readily understood by the masses: it defended their interests directly, involved the fewest sacrifices, and stimulated the development of revolutionary spirit. The other major task was organizing *workers' unions*, the members of which would rapidly spread revolutionary activity from the cities to their native villages;[11] and there, too, economic terror should be the heart of the struggle.

[11] At this time, most factory workers in Russia were seasonal, returning periodically to their native villages to do agricultural work.

Nikolai Shchedrin, whom I met in Black Repartition, shared my views. He impressed me as a man of enormous energy and great strength of will. Mercurial, always racing around with some new project, Shchedrin was nonetheless discreet, a good conspirator. Together we set about developing a practical program of economic terror and union organizing.

After Zharkov turned traitor, it was dangerous for us to remain in St. Petersburg: he might run into us on the street at any moment. At this time, Shchedrin happened to come across a worker friend who had just come from the Khludov factory in Smolensk. He told Shchedrin about the horrible catastrophe that had occurred there: Khludov, the owner, habitually locked his workers in at night because he was afraid that they would steal his raw materials; a fire had broken out and many workers had been burned. When he heard this story, Shchedrin raced home, extremely excited. "We must begin economic terror immediately," he declared. "This incident can't go unpunished."

Pavel Akselrod was the only member of the central body of Black Repartition still left in St. Petersburg, and we rushed over to discuss the matter with him. When he learned that we intended to plot the murder of Khludov, he got indignant and tried to prove to us that it was an impossible, undesirable, and even harmful project. He proceeded to read us the new program he had drawn up for Black Repartition. It was a very diffuse draft for something in between populism and Marxism—an impossible mixture. I can't reconstruct it from memory, but of this much I'm sure: political objectives had made deep inroads into the populist program, and Western social-democratic methods had permeated its tactics. We found the program totally unacceptable; and I learned later that most of the Black Repartition people abroad rejected it, as well.

At any rate, we had decided to leave the next day for Smolensk. Akselrod saw how stubborn we were about this. Gently but firmly, he declared: "But you don't have the right to act in this way without the consent of the party."

"And where is the party now?" I asked. Almost none of

the party's original members were still around. There were some recently formed groups, but they were very amorphous. Given the difficulties of communicating with comrades abroad, our work would have suffered if we had bound ourselves to them. "In any case," we told Akselrod, "we're leaving the party and we're going to work independently." We exchanged friendly good-byes with him and walked out.

*As it turned out, Shchedrin and Kovalskaia did not go to Smolensk. Instead, they left St. Petersburg for Kiev, where they heard the situation was favorable for their work.*

My first objective when we got to Kiev was to find Mikhail Popov, a member of Black Repartition. I was surprised to hear him confirm what we had been told earlier: "People here don't care much about theory; everyone wants to do revolutionary work, they don't want to be at odds over programs. Yes, unity is necessary; here in Kiev, I'm bringing people from Black Repartition and the People's Will together in one group. We don't allow supporters of the People's Will to sway us much in the direction of political struggle."

What immediately struck me in Kiev was the incredible carelessness I saw. More than that: it was a kind of rejection of conspiratorial practices on principle. The day after I arrived, Prisetskii [a male comrade] came by to take me to a meeting where I was to discuss our program. It was early evening and many people were out strolling. We walked down a long boulevard until Prisetskii pointed out a small, one-story wooden house that faced out on the street: the meeting was in there. From a distance, I could hear the uproar of people arguing: passers-by were peering in the windows of the house. I couldn't believe my eyes. It would have been awkward to turn around and head back home, so I went in.

There was a mass of people in two small, low-ceilinged rooms. It was hard to move, hard even to breathe. All around me, I saw the faces of educated people, ardent and militant. The people I had met in Moscow had struck me as languid and overly rationalistic; these Kievans radiated life, energy, and freshness.

I presented the program Shchedrin and I had developed, which later served as the basis for the Union of Russian Workers of the South. It was essentially this: the goal was to transform the existing order into a socialist system. This was possible only by means of a *popular revolution*. The preconditions for such a revolution existed in Russia: the *obshchina*, or peasant land commune, and the propensity of the Russian people for workers' cooperatives and self-government. If there was to be a revolution in Russia, it could only be a socialist one, because the people would rise in rebellion only for the land; political demands made little sense to them. Any revolution that did not involve the participation of the people— even one carried out by a socialist party—would inevitably be *merely political*: that is, it would bring the country freedom similar to that enjoyed in Western Europe without changing the economic situation of the working people at all. It would simply make it easier for the bourgeoisie to organize itself and thus become a more formidable enemy of the workers.

Now, the peasants and workers of Russia were dissatisfied with their situation, but they lacked faith in their own ability to overthrow the established order, and this prevented them from rebelling. The people had to be instilled with the necessary confidence. Political terror directed at the center of the system was too remote for them to comprehend. *Economic terror* (we called it "democratic terror" then) defended their immediate interests. It involved the murder of the police officials and administrators of all sorts who were in closest contact with the people; its meaning would be clear to the people, and it would involve fewer sacrifices than the strike or local popular uprising. Only this kind of terror could increase the people's faith in *their own* ability to struggle, to organize and overthrow the existing structure themselves. It was virtually impossible for the intelligentsia to do political work in the countryside. It was easier among city workers. As these workers returned to their villages, they would be able to implement a program of action among the peasantry.

It is clear that we parted company here with the People's Will, which was definitely moving toward political revolution. While the powerful blows dealt the established order by the People's Will stunned the upper elements of society and the students, their impact on the workers was small, and they generally made no impression whatsoever on the peasantry. When news of a terrorist act did get through to the people, they often turned it around and misinterpreted it. Shchedrin and I had come to the same conclusions from our own observations. When Soloviev attempted to assassinate the tsar [April 2, 1879], I was doing political work with a group of metalworkers from factories in Kharkov. After they learned of this attempt, they came up to me and declared indignantly: "It's all the work of the nobility, they did it because the tsar freed the peasants." And although I argued with them for a long time, I couldn't fully dispel their suspicions.

After my presentation to the meeting, there was an outpouring of questions and objections, but there was obviously some sympathy for our program. When the meeting ended, I left with Prisetskii. Two people joined us: a very young man, tall and handsome, blond, with large, pensive blue eyes; and a short, swarthy man, with small, regular features, a broad, thick beard, small black eyes set deep under a low forehead, and a whole shock of thick, straight dark hair that fell down to his shoulders. "Well, introduce yourselves," Prisetskii said to us. The blond man was named Polikarpov; he offered me his hand. The dark-haired one did not honor me with so much as a glance; he continued walking alongside us, a stern expression on his face. Prisetskii began to discuss something with him; his responses came mostly in monosyllables. He used peasant speech; every now and then, his deep voice slid off into Ukrainian. He emanated coldness.

After our two companions left us, I remarked to Prisetskii, "What stern workers you have here!"

"And where have you seen workers?" he asked.

"Well, that dark-haired man just now!"

Prisetskii laughed. "Pavel Ivanov's a former student; he was nearly a doctor, all but finished medical school, and now he's 'illegal.' He's a remarkable person."

*Before Kovalskaia could implement her program in Kiev, she was summoned to Moscow to participate in an escape attempt. The attempt never materialized, and in her absence the movement in Kiev was decimated by arrests. Polikarpov, the blond man in the passage above, killed himself after failing in an attempt to assassinate a provocateur.*

When we returned to Kiev in April 1880, we found everyone in a militant, revolutionary mood. The governor-general, Chertkov, was quick to sign death sentences. He had executed one man, Rozovskii, merely for refusing to name the person who had left a suitcase of illegal literature with him, and another, Lozovskii, for possession of an illegal proclamation. All strata of society were aroused and indignant, especially the students. Numerous programs were circulating, and people did not bother to make careful distinctions among them: it was obvious that all they wanted was the chance to do revolutionary work. We established many contacts among the young members of the intelligentsia who had managed to keep out of jail, and there was no problem finding people to accept our program.

We tried to make contacts among the workers as quickly as possible. I managed to get an introduction to two railroad workers. I went to a tiny flat, with cheap and pretentious furniture; there I was met by a man of about thirty-five who gave the appearance of being weary and indifferent. I tried to direct the conversation to the situation of workers in Russia and the ways people could struggle to improve it. He agreed with me completely, but showed no desire to do anything. His friend arrived, a man who seemed energetic and bold. He listened to what I had to say—somewhat patronizingly—and then confidently began to inform me that he "knew for sure" that there was a committee in Russia that was taking care of things so that everything would change in the country; it already knew everything that was going on and was doing what was necessary, and we ourselves shouldn't poke our noses in, we would only mess things up. All my arguments that this had to be the struggle of the *workers themselves* were in vain: it was his unshakable conviction that someone was on their side and would do everything for them. I spent a long evening talking with the two of them and concluded that although they could be trusted, they were sympathizers and nothing more, people who had settled down and didn't want to take any risks.

We had to find other contacts. Using false identity papers, Shchedrin got a position as a draftsman in a railroad workshop. He made some friends there, and soon picked out three young men who showed great interest in his stories. He told them about how workers lived abroad and what sort of revolutionaries were active there, how the Irish were fighting for their freedom, and how Russian workers would be able to win freedom themselves. The three had never previously come in contact with revolutionaries, but they listened and spoke about them with reverence. The executions of Rozovskii and Lozovskii had affected them deeply; they blazed with indignation when they talked about them.

We learned that trouble was already brewing among the workers of the Kiev arsenal, who suffered every manner of oppression. Our friends from the railroad workshop introduced us to some friends of theirs from the arsenal. The situation there couldn't have been more favorable for our purposes.

Before long we were able to hold a small meeting, at which we laid out our program in general terms. The response was completely favorable. We proposed that the Union of Russian Workers of the South be established immediately and political work be initiated at the arsenal in accordance with our program and tactics. Everyone was delighted with the idea. We immediately read them the statute we had worked out. It was very brief, since we anticipated that it would be enlarged and modified by the organization's practice. The members of the central circle were to organize other circles, which would not be informed of the activities of the center but which would enjoy—within the limits of the program—far-reaching freedom of action. The Union's affairs were to be kept strictly secret. We asked simply, were those present willing to submit themselves to these regulations, as well as the program? One young fellow who had read a lot of novels jumped up from his seat and solemnly recited an oath. Others indecisively followed his example. Shchedrin and I hadn't expected such ceremony, but we maintained a serious tone.

This, then, was how the circle that called itself the Union of Russian Workers of the South got started—with only ten people, including Shchedrin and myself. The workers insisted that "Russian"[12] be included in the name. It was scarcely appropriate for the Union, which subsequently attracted an unusually international membership—Ukrainians (the largest group), Russians, Poles, Jews, a Frenchman, an Austrian German, a Saxon, a Rumanian, and a distant descendant of a Tatar.

It was international in spirit, too.

Anti-Semitism was rampant among the workers of Kiev during this period, and the appearance of the first Jew in the Union provoked bewilderment and cold hostility among our workers. One of our best members, nicknamed Gaidamak,[13] stayed after the meeting and attacked me violently for bringing in a "yid." I asked him why Jews were inferior to Russians, and to my surprise, he replied: "They crucified Christ."

"But Christ himself was Jewish," I answered.

Gaidamak had been very religious in his youth. Although he had since become somewhat skeptical, he continued to revere the person of Christ. My answer startled him; he didn't believe me. He spoke to a friend of his, a young priest, who confirmed what I'd said. Gaidamak spent a good while reflecting on this; he assimilated every new idea slowly, but

---

[12] "Russian" in this context refers to the Great Russian nationality.
[13] The participants in eighteenth-century Cossack and peasant uprisings against Polish magnates were known as Gaidamaki.

deeply and firmly. Finally he came to terms with it and proceeded to convince other workers that Jews were no worse than Russians. "Christ himself and all the apostles were Jews," he would argue to the others, "and what a fine religion they made—the same as socialism!"

Little by little, our workers stopped discriminating between Russians and people of other nationalities. The next year, in late April 1881—when Shchedrin and I were in prison—an anti-Semitic pogrom erupted in Kiev. At the very height of the disorders, the Union printed a proclamation and scattered copies among the crowds on the street. "You beat up Jews indiscriminately," it stated, "while you should be beating all exploiters, Russian or Jewish, and not poor Jews." It was written by the Union's workers themselves.

Shchedrin and I worked at a feverish pace; we had to move quickly and strengthen the Union so that it could survive our arrest. For we knew that our days were numbered. Many people in Kiev knew me from my work in Kharkov and St. Petersburg, and I was in constant danger of being recognized on the street; for this reason, I went around Kiev in men's clothing for a while.

A high level of conspiratorial technique was maintained in the Union. We adhered strictly to the practice of never using a person's real name; everyone had a nickname. As a result, arrests almost never involved our workers. We held our meetings at night, outside the city, and we varied the location.

At the first meeting, we proposed printing proclamations stating the arsenal workers' demands and threatening to execute the director if he didn't comply immediately. The proposal was adopted unanimously. One of the railroad workers had friends in a printing plant. He learned to compose there and managed to obtain some type; and before long, the first proclamation emerged from our primitive press—in the crudest form, since we were short certain letters and punctuation marks and couldn't manage to keep our lines straight.

Shchedrin and I collaborated with the workers of the Union's central group on the proclamations, but our role was limited to helping them formulate their own thoughts. We tried to retain their own expressions and uneven style, so that it would be obvious to the administration of the arsenal that the proclamations had been written by the workers themselves.[14] The first two were not posed as ultimata; no time limit was set. The third proclamation was more threatening, and the administration responded by meeting some of the workers' demands: they shortened the work day by two hours and eased the regulations on lateness.[15] Shchedrin and I suggested to the workers that they be satisfied with this for a start, but on their insistence, a fourth proclamation was drawn up, calling for the satisfaction of all the remaining demands.

The Union's success brought such an influx of workers that we had difficulty finding a place to meet. The workers suggested Baikov Grove, which was not far from town. Shchedrin and I would go to someone's apartment around eleven at night, disguise ourselves, and then head for the meeting. We talked to the crowds of tired workers until daybreak, and they listened eagerly, with no thought of rest. The passionate Shchedrin inflamed them with his rapid-fire, emotional speeches. He was very witty, and with his quick tongue he often livened up his audience, exhausted from the day's work, with a joke or some pointed gibe. One worker put it this way: "Shchedrin's like a knout, he lashes you with his words and in spite of yourself, you run where he calls." Unlike many revolutionaries of the seventies, Shchedrin did not make a fetish of the people: despite his youth (he was twenty-three when the courts put an end to his life outside prison walls), he saw all of their defects. Nonetheless, he was always in good spirits, and he cheerfully faced any danger in the struggle to liberate them.

---

[14] Shchedrin and Kovalskaia, meanwhile, wrote a number of leaflets, including "The Trial of the Socialists," "A Constitution Will Give Nothing to the People," "How the Irish Struggle for Their Freedom," and "What Is the International?"

[15] Fines were generally imposed on workers who arrived late to work.

*Nikolai Shchedrin*

We succeeded in organizing about seven hundred workers. We divided them into groups and met with a different one every night, seeing each only once a week. There were rarely fewer than a hundred people at a meeting—an enormous number for those times. We had no specific agenda for the discussions; our theoretical positions simply emerged as we talked about one or another current social ill. There was no need to dwell on how terrible things were in general for workers and peasants; people were already well aware of this. All we had to do was make the connections between this misery and the workings of the established order as a whole, then go back and integrate each specific instance of discontent.

Despite the organization's success, the struggle against the passivity instilled over the centuries was a difficult one. Often workers would listen attentively and then proceed to tell us that things would somehow get done without them. Everyone had his own version of this, depending on his degree of political development. The most sophisticated believed that some revolutionary committee would take the land away from the landlords for the peasants. Others said that the tsar had abolished serfdom and was now fighting the gentry in order to take away their lands and distribute them among the people. Those who had heard about the Chigirin affair[16] believed that the "tsar's commissars" were genuine, and that the nobles had captured and murdered them. There were some, too, who "knew for a fact" that foreign powers (they didn't know which ones in particular) were doing things to better the situation of the Russian common folk. The least sophisticated workers—even the young people—spoke with profound conviction of how "visions had begun," how the Virgin had appeared to their priest, saying: "Pray, for the day of rejoicing will soon be upon you." They believed in the elders who indicated definite dates on which "everything will be turned upside down and all the poor will be exalted."

*Our main task, then, in organizing the workers was to stimulate their initiative so that they would take up their cause themselves.*

Although we often worked together with the revolutionary intelligentsia of Kiev, we would not admit them to our nightly workers' meetings, nor would we bring them into the Union's central circle. They rejected conspiratorial practice on principle, regarding every precaution as cowardice, and that frightened us. Take Pavel Ivanov [see p. 228], the best representative of this milieu: he was bold and decisive, abounding in initiative, and an effective organizer who had established relations with people of every station in life. He was also so unconspiratorial that unless you knew him, you might well have thought him a suspicious character. Once I told Pavel that he, an "illegal" who was obviously tailed by police spies, must not strut around Kiev—in broad daylight, dressed in a red student shirt, hair hanging down to his shoulders—in the com-

16 See p. 151.

pany of our workers. He got indignant. "Why don't you Petersburgers take care of yourselves," he snapped. When Pavel saw a spy on the street, he would wave his fist at the man. After the spy ducked around a corner, Pavel would simply continue on his way, with never a thought of covering his tracks.

*Despite the nonsectarian spirit that generally prevailed in Kiev, the Union's success brought it into conflict with the People's Will, which was also active in the city.*

On one occasion, a couple of our workers brought two people who belonged to one of the worker groups of the People's Will to see us. They were very interested in our union, and I talked with them for a couple of hours. To my surprise, they were completely naïve about the programs of the People's Will and every other group. Again the same story: they saw the People's Will as a powerful party that was preparing to bestow great favors on the workers and poor people in general. In that case, I asked them, why did their workers' circle exist? They replied: "In case some assignment has to be carried out."

"Why do you belong to the People's Will and not Black Repartition?"

"A student from the People's Will made our acquaintance, and so we joined that party."

As they were leaving, one of the workers told me: "Your program is the most suitable for us."

A couple of days later, Pavel Ivanov informed me: "The members of the People's Will are angry, they say you're trying to take their workers away."

"Since we're convinced that our program is correct, naturally we have to propagandize," I replied.

Shortly thereafter, two representatives of the People's Will arranged a meeting with me. I argued with them at great length that no party could have a monopoly on workers, that there could be no question of any exclusive claim. At the end of our conversation, one of them asked me to meet with their people and discuss things in greater detail: his organization had instructed him, he said, to annex the Union of Russian Workers of the South. This announcement struck me as exceedingly naïve. I agreed to go to the meeting, but insisted that some of our workers and some worker-members of the People's Will be present. He emphatically refused: "If the workers are arrested, they'll give everything away." I had no qualms about our workers, but it would have been pointless to continue the argument.

I went to the meeting with Pavel Ivanov. Their side tried to persuade us to renounce economic terror, arguing that this particular form of terror would drive away all the liberals and sympathizers who were aiding them with money and connections. We found this argument totally unconvincing, given our program. On this note, our negotiations with the Kievan group of the People's Will ended.

Although the Union's primary activity was organizing the workers, we also attempted to arrange the escape of three revolutionaries from Kiev prison. For this we needed money. Pavel Ivanov suggested that I make a trip to the Crimea, where the father of the deceased Polikarpov [see p. 228] lived: according to Pavel, he would very likely aid his son's comrades. I was doubtful: in those days, bereaved parents usually blamed their children's deaths on the harmful influence of revolutionaries. Visiting the old people, who had not yet recovered from the recent, tragic death of their beloved son, asking them for money to save some people they didn't know, people whom they may have considered responsible for their son's death— it was an extremely unpleasant task. However, since the Union had no other resources, and since the three in prison were threatened with execution, I had to bring myself to do it.

I took the train to a small station near Simferopol, arriving at dusk. The road had been described to me. I set out with a heavy heart. It was deserted. The distant, mournful sounds of a Tatar song deepened my gloom. I stepped up my pace, wanting desperately to be rid of this painful burden as quickly as possible. Finally I came to a small white house, sitting on a low hill and surrounded by vineyards. A woman stood on the porch, looking attentively in my direction. She was about forty-five and her face—sunburned, calm, strong—bore signs of the grief she had experienced. Tears appeared in her eyes, but she quickly suppressed them.

"We've been expecting you," she said. I didn't know that they had been informed in advance of my visit. "I'll call my husband now."

She brought me into the small parlor, simply furnished, with a low ceiling and freshly whitewashed walls. After a few minutes, a tall old man with graying hair came in. He was laboring to hold himself erect, as if to keep from sagging beneath the weight of his grief. His face showed the same composure, the same strength that I had seen in his wife. He avoided my eyes. "Let's go to Simferopol right away," he said. "I don't have money here, but I can borrow it from someone there; you'll be able to return to Kiev tomorrow." We walked back to the station, Polikarpov setting a quick pace. That evening he gave me a thousand rubles. I took the first available train to Kiev.

*As it turned out, the escape attempt had to be abandoned at the last moment because of an abrupt change in the situation at the prison. Years later, Kovalskaia learned that the authorities had been warned by I. G. Piotrovskii, a trusted friend of the unconspiratorial Pavel Ivanov.*

Notwithstanding the failure of the escape attempt, the Union's activities were expanding. Preparations to start a workers' newspaper were under way. An action combining economic and political terror was in the works: the Union sent a threatening letter to Chertkov, the governor-general of Kiev, who was also an oppressive landlord, and Shchedrin and I assumed responsibility for carrying the project through. The Union had business requiring people to travel. But there was no money. The thousand rubles I obtained from Polikarpov were smuggled into the prison, in case an opportunity for escape arose; and we were left with the small funds secretly sent by my mother for me to live on.

Meanwhile, Shchedrin and I were being tailed everywhere, and it had become almost impossible for us to meet with workers. We had to keep changing identity papers and apartments; we even spent a night in a boat on the Dnieper River. The only solution was for us to move to another city—but there was no money.

We were never without our revolvers, in case the police caught up with us. On October 22, 1880, I picked up my gun as usual, preparing to walk to the library one house away, but Shchedrin stopped me: "It's not worth it to lug around a revolver whenever you go out for five minutes," he said. I reluctantly laid it down on the table.

We had barely made it through the gates of our house before a group of men flung themselves upon us. Although we were unarmed, we resisted, hoping to prolong the struggle and attract passers-by, who would spread the news of our arrest around the city. We achieved our goal: our comrades got word that very evening and took steps so that no one fell into a police ambush.

Never in my career had I encountered the widespread sympathy for revolutionaries that I did at every step in Kiev. Although we were in contact with many, many workers (between seven and eight hundred), we never found a single informer among them, nor anyone who would have testified against us in an investigation or trial. We hid out with people of all different social positions, and no one ever gave us away. No doubt, the Kievan revolutionary intelligentsia, with its open, sometimes even reckless, propaganda deserves much credit for this.

Then, too, I often came across traces of earlier revolutionaries, who had left the best possible memories among the masses. Often when people try to sum up the activity of a group or individual and can point to no immediate, tangible results, they conclude that the activity was a failure. But how can you count all the circles made by a stone when you toss it into the water?

Shchedrin and I were brought before Military Circuit Court the following May, along with the members of the Union arrested after us [January 4, 1881]—among them Sofia Bogomolets and Pavel Ivanov. The articles of the indictment provided for capital punishment.

As I've noted, Shchedrin and I had some differences, both programmatic and tactical, with the Kievan revolutionary intelligentsia, to which Bogomolets and Ivanov belonged. We did have "diplomatic," or "neighborly" relations with them, however, and when a letter was smuggled in to Bogomolets during the course of our trial, she deciphered it and then approached me.

"Tell me," she said, "are you planning to escape if you're sentenced to hard labor?"

"Yes, even if I only get banishment."

"Will you have any outside help?"

"No, I'm on my own."

"Would you be willing to make an escape with me?"

"Yes, all right. But I want to make one condition beforehand: if for some reason it's impossible for us to escape together but I can get away alone, I will. And of course, you'll do the same."

"Well, of course, there's no question about that. Now, if you've made up your mind to escape, I must tell you: I've received a letter from the outside; some people I'm close with are offering to help the women sentenced to hard labor to escape."

"Tell them we're willing."

I trusted Bogomolets completely; I knew she took things very seriously and—unlike some of the Kievans—strictly observed conspiratorial procedures. I felt it would be awkward even to ask about the people who had offered to help us.

In court, I declared that I did not recognize the government's tribunal and would not participate in the proceedings. I refused to have a lawyer or make a final statement to the court. They sentenced me to hard labor for life.

Everyone tried with the Union of Russian Workers of the South was sent off from Kiev together. The men were left at Mtsensk. The women—Bogomolets, Prisetskaia, and I—were brought to Moscow, where we were put in one of the towers of the Butyrskaia prison. After studying our situation thoroughly, I concluded that it was utterly impossible to think of escape.

Bogomolets' husband, who was free at the time, visited her while we were in Moscow. When she returned from their final meeting, Bogomolets informed me: "The Kievans haven't forgotten their promise, but they say it'll be impossible to organize an escape before we get to Siberia."

There was no choice; we had to wait.

Finally, in the fall, we were taken from the prison and put on a train. There we were reunited with the men from our group and met some others who had been brought from St. Petersburg.

The party stopped at Krasnoiarsk. There we found Dolgushin, a survivor from a party of centralists.[17] Dolgushin had suffered through a difficult term in the central prison at Kharkov. Recently, just a few months before he was eligible to leave the prison at Krasnoiarsk for the "free command,"[18] he had assisted in Malavskii's unsuccessful escape attempt. By the time we reached Krasnoiarsk, he was standing trial for this. Dolgushin's wife and baby stayed with him in his cell. His ten-year-old son lived with Dolgushin's father, who was the district attorney in the city.

The Krasnoiarsk prison didn't have enough plates and

---

[17] During the early seventies, Alexander Dolgushin was a leading figure in a small revolutionary group influenced by Nechaev. It succeeded in printing and distributing several proclamations calling for an immediate peasant rebellion. Dolgushin was arrested in September 1873 and sentenced in 1874 to ten years at hard labor.

[18] The "free command" is described in Ivanovskaia's memoir. See p. 139.

dishes to go around, so several people had to eat at the same time from each of the small wooden kegs in which they put our food. I ate with Dollar and Kizer, two workers from our organization, and Dolgushin joined us. He impressed me as a person constantly burning with some inner fire, all the while maintaining an external calm in his movements and speech. Only his dark, rather somber eyes betrayed some kind of profound suffering. His small, slender figure appeared in the common room only at eating times. He made witty, biting remarks, but he never smiled. It was as if some sort of mask had hardened on his face.

The shared keg brought us closer to each other, and I began to ask Dolgushin questions about the city. He understood what I needed. One evening, he invited me to his cell.

"Are you thinking of escaping?" he asked.

"I want to."

"Malavskii's escape broke many of my connections, but I still have a few. If you decide to escape, I'll help."

"I'm not alone," I said. "Bogomolets wants to, also."

"That'll be difficult. It'll have to be you alone."

"But why me and not her?

"You have a life sentence, she has ten years."

I thought things over.

Shortly after this conversation, there was an unexpected and complete change in our group life. One day Bogomolets was summoned to the office to write her letters. She returned all in tears. She told us that Ostrovskii, the warden, had insulted her, but she refused to explain what the insult was, despite all our questions.

Our whole party moved into action. Everyone gathered in one large cell and demanded to see the governor. Dolgushin was waiting for a visit from his son, but when it wasn't granted, he came over to the common cell and joined us. He was unrecognizable: to our amazement, he was young again. His eyes blazed with youthful fervor; the mask had fallen away in an instant.

Our excitement increased. Instead of the governor, a gendarme of some sort came to see us, along with Ostrovskii. While Bogomolets was speaking with the gendarme, Ostrovskii cut in rudely. Dolgushin leaped down from a plank bed and slapped him. This act was totally unexpected, for he was ordinarily so calm.

Ostrovskii and the gendarme ran off in fright. We were dragged to our cells and locked up.

Some of us went on a hunger strike, demanding the replacement of Ostrovskii. After a few days, Pavel Ivanov and I were in such bad shape that the prison doctor went with Ostrovskii to announce to the governor that there might be deaths in the prison. I must admit, this time Ostrovskii, a notorious petty tyrant, asked the governor to satisfy our demands. The governor agreed to send him away for as long as our party was in Krasnoiarsk.

Immediately after our rebellion ended, we were divided into pairs for the journey to Irkutsk. I was teamed with Dr. Veimar, but I declared that I would go only with Bogomolets. The authorities wanted to get rid of us as quickly as possible, and so they allowed me to travel with her.

We were in a state of tension throughout the long journey in the cruel frost; we didn't know where or when our help would appear. Every time we passed someone on the road, our hearts skipped a beat, as we tried to detect clues that might indicate he was our savior. Finally, late one evening we reached Irkutsk.

Weary and freezing, we rode up to a small wooden house on the outskirts of the city: this was the women's prison. A small stream separated it from the main prison. Everything about it was extraordinarily simple: a wooden wicket gate, just as in any typical front yard; at the gate, a sentry with a gun; an ordinary fence instead of a high barrier; a one-story building, ordinary windows except for the grates. A rather large woman came out to the gate to answer the bell—the matron, in a plain dress that gave no indication of her office. I liked the simplicity of the entire situation.

*En route to Siberian exile*

We were brought into a large cell, where we found Eliza-veta Iuzhakova and her baby. She was under investigation for escaping from Balagansk. Soon Vera Rogacheva was brought into our cell; and from time to time, Maria Legkaia stayed there, too. All this made escape more difficult, although the general conditions at the prison were favorable. Finally, Rog-acheva was taken away and Legkaia left. We became friends with Iuzhakova. Since we felt we should not try anything with-out her consent, we asked her opinion: did we have the right to escape and thereby subject her to the inevitable conse-quences? She answered passionately: "It's not only a right, it's the duty of every revolutionary; I'll gladly help you." This gave us a free hand. We began studying the prison conditions and the officers directly responsible for us.

A couple of weeks after our arrival, Kazantsev, the prison doctor, came to our cell. As he examined Bogomolets, he slipped her a letter. After he left, she deciphered it by means of the key she had from Kiev, and then, her face beaming, she rushed over to me: "They're going to help us escape; all we have to do is get out of the prison."

"Do you know them well, the people who've offered to help us?

"Well, I should think so! Of course!"

That was enough for me; I didn't question her any further.

Little by little, I sized up the situation and formulated the following escape plan.

Every evening, the guard who did the roll call entered by way of the kitchen, where the matron was posted. She then walked through our cell and on into the large cell where the criminals[19] were kept. After counting them, she returned by the same route. All this time, both the door between our cell and the kitchen and the outer door to the courtyard were left open. A sentry stood on the street side of the gate—also open. During roll call, the sentries changed and the matron went home to the city for the night. Sometimes, the matron's women friends came to the prison and left with her.

[19] That is, the women convicted of nonpolitical offenses. Political prisoners were segregated from other inmates.

So we had to utilize the roll call to make our escape: I would copy the matron's appearance, Bogomolets would pose as her friend, and we would walk through the gates together. We had to work out something to convince the roll taker that we were in our beds when she returned from the criminals' cell, so we made it a habit to lie in bed, our prison smocks covering our heads, during her rounds. At first she would come over to us and pull the smocks away. We responded with demonstrations of indignation that we "sick people" were given no peace. Gradually, she established a routine of looking at us on the way in and later walking back without touching our smocks. We constructed two dummies to put in the beds and assembled an outfit like the matron's from Iuzhakova's large collection of odds and ends.

Meanwhile, Bogomolets was corresponding with the outside through Kazantsev, the prison doctor. I took no part at all in this; I didn't know and didn't ask whom she was corresponding with. It was arranged that the people on the outside would meet us as we were walking away from the prison and take us to a hideout that had been readied. We would recognize each other by the white handkerchiefs we carried.

Finally, in February 1882, the day we had planned for came. We lay in our beds that evening, dressed to leave the prison, our heads covered with the smocks. When the roll taker came in, I announced loudly to Bogomolets that I hadn't been able to get to sleep at all for the last few nights, and she made some equally loud response. The woman heard our voices and went off to check the criminals. We had only four or five minutes. We jumped out of bed and dashed into the courtyard. Iuzhakova immediately put the dummies in our places and covered them with the smocks.

Now we're at the gates. I stride confidently in front, Bogomolets follows me. We walk calmly out onto the street. The sentry looks at us and says nothing. The roll taker walks away from the prison, close on our heels. She crosses the street and turns left, toward the prison fortress; we turn right, toward the long bridge leading to the city. The sentries change. The new one doesn't know that the "matron" has already left, and he lets the real one out.

We start walking across the bridge. Two male figures are coming toward us. We take out white handkerchiefs: white handkerchiefs appear in their hands, too.

The men pause.

Suppose they're strangers, coincidentally blowing their noses? What should we do? How can we make sure? We slow our pace. The men's forms draw closer. Now we're right in front of them. We step aside indecisively. Then we hear: "We're your people, we're yours, we've come to meet you!"

One of them took me by the arm and the other took Bogomolets. "We'll have to put you in different apartments," they said. Of course, we made no objections. Bogomolets and her companion turned; I and mine went straight, keeping silent for fear that our conversation would attract the attention of passers-by. We walked for a long time, until we reached a tiny hut on the outskirts of the city. A plain young girl met us and brought us into a little room. The entire hut consisted of two small rooms: a tailor lived in one, this girl—his daughter—in the other.

In the light, I saw my companion's face for the first time. I didn't know him. When the girl went out, he introduced himself: "Kozlovskii, a Kievan. I have to run, I can't stay here a minute. We'll see each other soon." We said good-bye.

The girl asked me no questions.

The next day, late in the evening, Kozlovskii brought Bogomolets to the room. "Sofia won't stay without you for anything," he said. "I was forced to bring her here."

Kozlovskii was very tired. As he lay down on the floor and prepared to sleep, he asked us to wake him without fail at 2 a.m., for it was imperative that he be at his post. (As I learned later, he was in the military at the time.)

A few days later, at midnight, Kozlovskii brought an enormous man to our room. He explained that this new person also had to hide out there for the time being, and that he would tell us how we'd be transported from Irkutsk. Once more, Kozlovskii left quickly.

The new man gave his name as Pyotr Fedorov. He said that he'd come to Siberia specifically to aid the escape of "politicals," that he had connections among the coachmen of the civilian postal service,[20] which also carried passengers (there was no railroad in Siberia then). The coachmen relayed travelers the length of the route—"along the string," as it was known. Fedorov expected the coachmen he knew to arrive very shortly, and they would get us all the way to the railroad.

It was terribly cramped in the small room. When Fedorov lay down on the floor to sleep, he filled up the whole room all by himself. We felt like Lilliputians in the presence of Gulliver.

The waiting was agonizing. A great open space of brilliant white snow stretched out beyond the window, the blazing sun and azure sky beckoned with the air of freedom—but we didn't dare step out of our voluntary prison for a minute.

About two weeks passed.

Suddenly one morning the daughter of our host came rushing in, all excited: "Get ready, they're going to arrest you right away!" Soldiers burst into the room after her, their revolvers pointed at us. The police chief walked in behind them. We were put in three sleighs. I rode with the police chief himself.

At the prison, we were conducted to separate rooms in the administrative offices. Later they reunited Bogomolets and me and put us in a small cell with the window boarded up. Bogomolets started to rip away the boards. The guards burst in and someone ran for the warden; he came to the cell with employees carrying a strait jacket. They started to bind Bogomolets. I rushed to wrest her away from them and slapped a guard, Bernhardt. They then called the blacksmith and put me in handcuffs.

Shchedrin, who was locked up in the same prison at the

---

[20] As distinct from the special system that had been established for prisoners.

time, learned that the governor's aide, Soloviev, had ordered our mistreatment. He got Soloviev to come to his cell and proceeded to strike the man so hard that he fell down. Soloviev was infuriated. He had Shchedrin bound to the pillar that supported the cell's ceiling and beat him unmercifully. Shchedrin was then put in the "fox"—an arrangement of manacles on the hands and feet, joined in a continuous circle, that makes it impossible for the prisoner to straighten up. Shchedrin was tried and sentenced to death. But the ladies of Irkutsk took a passionate interest in his fate and got the governor to rescind the sentence. (The governor's wife was related to the Decembrists, and she openly expressed her sympathy for Shchedrin, sending him flowers and wine.) Instead, Shchedrin was chained to a wheelbarrow.[21]

Bogomolets and I were sent to Kara. One full year after our escape, we learned that Kozlovskii and Grabovskii (Bogomolets' companion) had been arrested and exiled. Later we learned that Fedorov had been exiled to Iakutka but had quickly escaped.

Almost a quarter of a century later, when I was abroad, I met V. Alexandrova, and she informed me that she and Evgeniia Subbotina had assisted in our escape. She couldn't explain why we had been recaptured, but the generally accepted explanation was this. The tailor's daughter was intimate with a soldier. She wouldn't let him into her room while we were occupying it, and he suspected her of hiding some other man there. He started to beat her, and then she told him that there were women in the room who had escaped from prison. The soldier immediately reported this to his superiors, and so we were recaptured.

During two decades of Siberian exile and imprisonment, Kovalskaia waged an unyielding struggle against the authorities: hunger strikes, two more escape attempts, a suicide attempt to call attention to prison conditions, a knife attack on a prison official who had administered

---

[21] This punishment was applied whenever there was an official visit or Shchedrin was in transit between prisons.

corporal punishment to one of Kovalskaia's woman comrades. In 1903, twenty-three years after she was sent to Siberia, she was released and went abroad with her second husband.

In Geneva, Kovalskaia joined the populist Socialist Revolutionary Party, but she quit within a month and formed a group of "maximalists"—people who accepted only the "maximum program" of the Socialist Revolutionary Party, which provided for the socialization of all means of production, not just the land. Shortly before the October Revolution of 1917, she returned to Russia. Under the Soviet regime, she worked in the State Archives and served as a member of the editorial board of a journal devoted to the history of the revolutionary movement in Russia. She died in 1933.

# BIBLIOGRAPHY
# INDEX

# BIBLIOGRAPHY

SOURCES

Vera Figner. *Polnoe sobranie sochinenii v shesti tomakh* (Moscow, 1929), Vol. 5.
"Iz pokazanii V.N. Figner," *Byloe*, 1906, N. 7–8, pp. 27–43.
Vera Zasulich. *Vospominaniia* (Moscow, 1931).
Ekaterina Koval'skaia. "Avtobiografiia," in *Entsiklopedicheskii slovar'* "*Granat*," (Moscow, 191-), Vol. 40, pp. 189–199.
"Moi vstrechi s S.L. Perovskoi," *Byloe*, 1921, N. 16, pp. 42–49.
*Iuzhno-Russkii rabochii soiuz, 1880–1881* (Moscow, 1926).
"Pobeg," *Katorga i Ssylka*, 1932, N. 95, pp. 110–128.
Olga Liubatovich. "Dalekoe i nedavnee. Vospominaiia iz O. S. Liubatovich," *Byloe*, 1906, N. 5, pp. 208–46, and N. 6, pp. 108–54.
Praskovia Ivanovskaia. "Avtobiografiia," in *Entsiklopedicheskii slovar'* "*Granat*," Vol. 40, p. 151–163.
"Idilliia," *Russkie Zapiski*, 1916, N. 8, pp. 77–99.
"Pervye tipografii 'Narodnoi Voli,'" *Katorga i Ssylka* 1926, N. 24, pp. 32–56.
"Stranichka i istorii katorgi (Kariiskaia zhenskaia tiurma)," *Katorga i Ssylka*, 1926, N. 24.


SUGGESTED FOR FURTHER READING

Breshkovsky, Catherine. *Hidden Springs of the Russian Revolution.* Stanford, 1931.

Chernyshevsky, N. G. *What Is to Be Done?* Vintage, New York, 1961.

Figner, Vera. *Memoirs of a Revolutionist.* International Publishers, New York, 1927.

Footman, D. *Red Prelude: The Life of the Russian Terrorist Zheliabov.* The Cresset Press, London, 1968.

Kennan, George. *Siberia and the Exile System.* Praeger, N.Y. 1970.

Stepniak-Kravchinskii, Sergei. *Underground Russia: Revolutionary Profiles and Sketches from Life*. London, 1883.
A *Female Nihilist*. B. R. Tucker, Boston, 1886.

Kropotkin, Peter. *Memoirs of a Revolutionist*. Grove Press, New York, 1970.

Leffler, Anna Carlotta. *Sonya Kovalevsky; Her Recollections of Childhood*. New York, 1895.

Meijer, J. M. *Knowledge and Revolution. The Russian Colony in Zurich 1870–1873*. Fernhill, New York, 1965.

Venturi, Franco. *Roots of Revolution*. Grosset and Dunlap, New York, 1966.

Yarmolinsky, A. *Road to Revolution. A Century of Russian Radicalism*. Macmillan, New York, 1957.

# INDEX

# A Note About the Editors and Translators

Barbara Alpern Engel is Associate Professor of History at the University of Colorado and author of *Mothers and Daughters: Women of the Intelligensia in Nineteenth Century Russia*. She received her Ph.D. from Columbia University.

Clifford N. Rosenthal is Executive Director of a nation-wide coalition of financial co-operatives owned by low-income communities. He received his B.A. and M.A. from Columbia University.

# A Note on the Type

This book is set in ELECTRA, a Linotype face designed by W. A. Dwiggins (1880–1956), who was responsible for so much that is good in contemporary book design. Although much of his early work was in advertising and he was the author of the standard volume *Layout in Advertising*, Mr. Dwiggins later devoted his prolific talents to book typography and type design and worked with great distinction in both fields. In addition to his designs for Electra, he created the Metro, Caledonia, and Eldorado series of type faces, as well as a number of experimental cuttings that have never been issued commercially.

Electra cannot be classified as either modern or old-style. It is not based on any historical model, nor does it echo a particular period or style. It avoids the extreme contrast between thick and thin elements that marks most modern faces and attempts to give a feeling of fluidity, power, and speed.

Typography and binding design by
Camilla Filancia